THE HOUSE OF NELL GWYN

The House of Nell Gwyn

THE FORTUNES OF THE BEAUCLERK FAMILY 1670–1974

Donald Adamson
&
Peter Beauclerk Dewar

WILLIAM KIMBER · LONDON

First published in 1974 by
WILLIAM KIMBER & CO., LIMITED
Godolphin House, 22a Queen Anne's Gate,
London, SW1H 9AE

Printed in Great Britain
by W & J Mackay Limited, Chatham

CONTENTS

LIST OF ILLUSTRATIONS

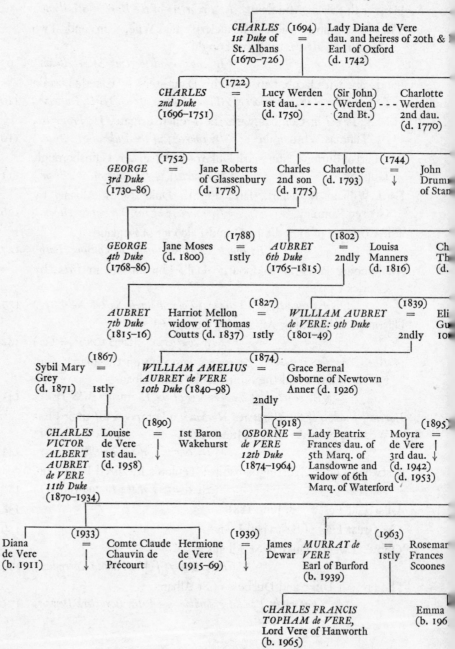

KING CHARLES II
(1625–85)

CHARLES (1694) = Lady Diana de Vere
1st Duke of   dau. and heiress of 20th &
St. Albans   Earl of Oxford
(1670–726)   (d. 1742)

(1722)
CHARLES = Lucy Werden   (Sir John) - - - (Werden)   Charlotte
2nd Duke   1st dau. - - - - (Werden)   Werden
(1696–1751)   (d. 1750)   (2nd Bt.)   2nd dau.
                                          (d. 1770)

(1752)   (1744)
GEORGE = Jane Roberts   Charles   Charlotte   = John
3rd Duke   of Glassenbury   2nd son   (d. 1793)   ↓ Drum
(1730–86)   (d. 1778)   (d. 1775)   of Stan

(1788)   (1802)
GEORGE   Jane Moses   =   AUBREY   =   Louisa   Ch
4th Duke   (d. 1800)   1stly   6th Duke   2ndly   Manners   Th
(1768–86)   (1765–1815)   (d. 1816)   (d.

(1827)   (1839)
AUBREY   Harriot Mellon   =   WILLIAM AUBREY   =   Eli
7th Duke   widow of Thomas   de VERE: 9th Duke   Gu
(1815–16)   Coutts (d. 1837)   1stly   (1801–49)   2ndly   10

(1867)   (1874)
Sybil Mary   =   WILLIAM AMELIUS   =   Grace Bernal
Grey   AUBREY de VERE   Osborne of Newtown
(d. 1871)   1stly   10th Duke (1840–98)   Anner (d. 1926)
                                2ndly

(1890)   (1918)   (1895)
CHARLES   Louise   =   1st Baron   OSBORNE   =   Lady Beatrix   Moyra   =
VICTOR   de Vere   ↓   Wakehurst   de VERE   Frances dau. of   de Vere
ALBERT   1st dau.   12th Duke   5th Marq. of   3rd dau.   ↓
AUBREY   (d. 1958)   (1874–1964)   Lansdowne and   (d. 1942)
de VERE   widow of 6th   (d. 1953)
11th Duke   Marq. of Waterford
(1870–1934)

(1933)   (1939)   (1963)
Diana   =   Comte Claude   Hermione   =   James   MURRAY de   =   Rosemar
de Vere   ↓   Chauvin de   de Vere   ↓   Dewar   VERE   1stly   Frances
(b. 1911)   Précourt   (1915–69)   Earl of Burford   Scoones
                                        (b. 1939)

CHARLES FRANCIS   Emma
TOPHAM de VERE,   (b. 196
Lord Vere of Hanworth
(b. 1965)

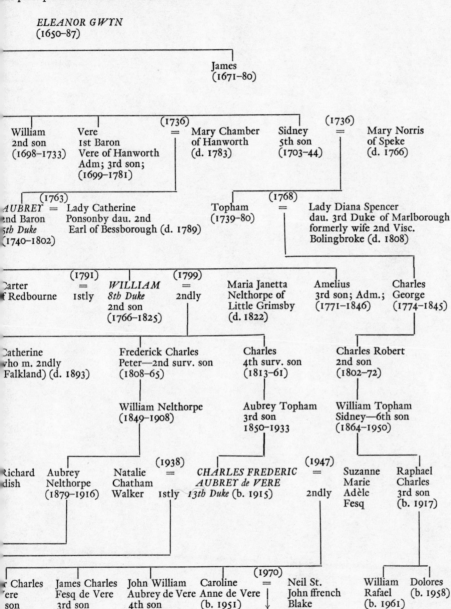

ELEANOR GWYN
(1650–87)

James
(1671–80)

William
2nd son
(1698–1733)

Vere
1st Baron
Vere of Hanworth
Adm; 3rd son;
(1699–1781)

(1736)
= Mary Chamber
of Hanworth
(d. 1783)

Sidney
5th son
(1703–44)

(1736)
= Mary Norris
of Speke
(d. 1766)

(1763)
AUBREY =
2nd Baron
5th Duke
(1740–1802)

Lady Catherine
Ponsonby dau. 2nd
Earl of Bessborough (d. 1789)

Topham
(1739–80)

(1768)
= Lady Diana Spencer
dau. 3rd Duke of Marlborough
formerly wife 2nd Visc.
Bolingbroke (d. 1808)

Carter
f Redbourne

(1791)
=
1stly

WILLIAM
8th Duke
2nd son
(1766–1825)

(1799)
=
2ndly

Maria Janetta
Nelthorpe of
Little Grimsby
(d. 1822)

Amelius
3rd son; Adm.;
(1771–1846)

Charles
George
(1774–1845)

Catherine
who m. 2ndly
Falkland) (d. 1893)

Frederick Charles
Peter—2nd surv. son
(1808–65)

Charles
4th surv. son
(1813–61)

Charles Robert
2nd son
(1802–72)

William Nelthorpe
(1849–1908)

Aubrey Topham
3rd son
1850–1933

William Topham
Sidney—6th son
(1864–1950)

Richard
dish

Aubrey
Nelthorpe
(1879–1916)

Natalie
Chatham
Walker

(1938)
=
1stly

CHARLES FREDERIC
AUBREY de VERE
13th Duke (b. 1915)

(1947)
=
2ndly

Suzanne
Marie
Adèle
Fesq

Raphael
Charles
3rd son
(b. 1917)

Charles
ere
son
1948)

James Charles
Fesq de Vere
3rd son
(b. 1949)

John William
Aubrey de Vere
4th son
(b. 1950)

Caroline
Anne de Vere
(b. 1951)

(1970)
=

Neil St.
John ffrench
Blake

William
Rafael
(b. 1961)

Dolores
(b. 1958)

de Vere

For the full pedigree of the family, see extract from 'Burke's Peerage' (pp. 218–246)

FOREWORD

When, in March 1970, Peter Dewar invited me to help him with a history of the Beauclerk family, I was delighted to do so as genealogical and historical research has always been one of my keenest interests. He is himself a cousin of the present Duke of St Albans and a descendant of the eighth Duke, and he had already been amassing material towards a history of his maternal family for seven years. A division of labour was agreed, and he undertook many of the contacts that were required with members of his family, the despatch of dozens of letters to newspapers and periodicals asking for information, the writing of hundreds of replies, and the collation of most of the findings. We shared the research into primary sources. Peter Dewar and I worked together on most of the chapters, and even when not at hand he was always available for consultation and ready with suggestions. Nevertheless, the planning and writing of the book remained my responsibility. Although he and I have discussed every word of this family history several times, I am also basically responsible for its conclusions.

Secondary sources provided less difficulty than would otherwise have been the case, in that we had had the help of the late Lord Wakehurst. In February 1969 Peter Dewar received from the former Governor of Northern Ireland the typescript of his own unpublished researches into his mother's family. They were the fruits of over thirty years of inquiry, largely carried out in the open-access Library of the House of Commons. He generously allowed us to make use of them. From them we derived a most useful impression of the available material. No Englishman of his generation delved more painstakingly into the bibliography of his family's past.

The text is, we believe, correct as at today's date. There may, however, be further developments in the Duke of St Albans's business interests between now and the date of publication.

DONALD ADAMSON
5 September 1974

L'aristocratie, en sa construction lourde, percée de rares fenêtres, laissant entrer peu de jour, montrant le même manque d'envolée, mais aussi la même puissance massive et aveuglée que l'architecture romane, enferme toute l'histoire, l'emmure, la renfrogne.

Proust: *Le Côté de Guermantes*

The aristocracy, in its heavy structure—lit by few windows, allowing little daylight inside, and showing the same lack of soaring aspiration but also the same blind, massive strength as Norman architecture—encloses the whole of history, walling it in and towering sternly over it.

ACKNOWLEDGMENTS

We are deeply grateful to Her Majesty the Queen for her gracious permission to carry out researches in the Royal Archives at Windsor Castle and for the use of both written and visual material, especially for the reproductions of the portrait of Diana, Duchess of St Albans at Hampton Court Palace and prints of Burford House and Cranbourne Lodge.

We are also deeply indebted to the Duke of St Albans for his great help, without which our task would have been infinitely greater. Not only has the head of the Beauclerk family provided much of the information contained in Chapter X, even to the extent of subjecting himself to two protracted interviews; he has also made available many of the illustrations in this volume, together with Nell Gwyn's scrapbook and other mementoes.

To the late Lord Wakehurst, K.G., the late Baroness Jane Nettelbladt-Roberts, M. Louis Robyns de Schneidauer, Mr Hugh Cavendish, Mrs Pamela Cavendish and the late Mr Richard Cavendish, Lieutenant-Colonel and Mrs John Silcock and Mr David Green we express our particular thanks for their valuable cooperation, both in the provision of unpublished typewritten material and in the imparting of personal knowledge and reminiscences. We are grateful to the Earl of Harrowby and the Trustees of the Harrowby MSS Trust for extensive use of the Ryder papers; to Lord Harrowby personally, and to his Librarians, for the active assistance they gave us at Sandon; and to the Registrar of the Queen's Archives, Miss Jane Langton (a descendant of Bennet Langton), and to her staff for similar assistance at Windsor Castle.

Of the many libraries we have laid under contribution, by far the richest vein was unearthed at Hertfordshire Record Office with its hitherto unutilized collection of over eighty letters of the second Duke of

St Albans. But an equal kindness and readiness to help was met with in the Libraries of the Universities of Nottingham and Wales, the Sheffield City Libraries with their invaluable deposit of the Wentworth Woodhouse Muniments (to which we were generously allowed access by the Earl Fitzwilliam, the Trustees of the Earl Fitzwilliam, and the City Librarian), the Archives of Childs, Coutts, Drummonds and Hoares Banks, the Archives of Barclays Bank Ltd (as representatives of Ransoms Bank), and the Record Offices of the Greater London Council, the West Yorkshire Metropolitan County Council and the counties of Berkshire, Clwyd, Dorset, Essex, Hampshire, Kent, Leicestershire, Lincolnshire, Nottinghamshire, Suffolk, Surrey and Wiltshire. The Merseyside County Museums provided detailed information on Speke Hall; and Messrs Paine & Brettell, together with Mr William Smith of the Greater London Record Office, afforded us every facility to consult and photograph the Hanworth estate map of 1738.

We thank Messrs A. D. Peters & Co. for their kind permission to reprint four lines of verse by Hilaire Belloc at the head of Chapter X.

Mr Graham Murrell has been of invaluable assistance with many of the photographs, including the cover illustration, and Mr Douglas Wilson has skilfully elucidated the Will Trust established by the tenth Duke of St Albans.

To all who have kindly allowed us the use of illustrations and to the following institutions and persons, and many others most of whom replied to our inquiries in newspapers and periodicals, there remains our final and very great debt of gratitude: to Burke's Peerage Ltd, Christie, Manson & Woods Ltd, the Crown Estate Commissioners, the Ministry of Defence, the Department of the Environment, the Foreign & Commonwealth Office, the Forestry Commission, the National Coal Board, the Österreichisches Staatsarchiv and Messrs Weatherby & Sons; and to Mr Miles Acheson, Mr Robert Adams, Mr Lewis Addison, Mr B. N. Aldridge, Mrs Cecil Baines, Mr Nowell Banister, Mrs Caroline Barron, Mr Norris Beith, Sir Frank Bowden Bt, Mr John Brooke-Little (Richmond Herald), the late Mr Robert Bury, Diana Comtesse Chauvin de Précourt, the late Mr Reginald Constable, Mr Charles Cornwall-Legh, the late Mrs Diana Daly, the Duke of Devonshire, Colonel Gordon Dewar, the late Mrs

Hermoine Dewar, Mrs Vera Fawcett, the Lord Feversham, Mr Peter Fleetwood-Hesketh, Mr Walter Goldsmith, Mrs Muriel Gordon, Mrs Clare Grant, Mr R. H. Harcourt Williams, Dr Albert Hollaender, Mrs T. H. Kent, Colonel Claude Lancaster, Colonel P. D. S. Lauder, Mr Paul Lawson, Mr Donald McDonald, Mr Robert Mackworth-Young, the Duke of Marlborough, Mr G. D. Martineau, Mr Patrick Montague-Smith, Mr Hugh Montgomery-Massingberd, Mrs Doris Langley Moore, Mr John Mountain, the late Mr Martin Newman, the Duke of Norfolk, K.G., Mrs Frances O'Donnell, Mr Robin Ollington, Mrs M. J. Owen, Mrs Eleanor Pascual, Mr John Pearce, the Duke of Portland, K.G., the Duke of Richmond and Gordon, Colonel Sir Thomas Roberts Bt, Mrs D. M. Rutt, the Marquis of Salisbury, the Hon. Lady Salmond and Mr Julian Salmond, Mr Frank Smith, the Earl Spencer, Dr Francis Steer (Maltravers Herald Extraordinary), Mr Rex Sterry, the Hon. Hedley Strutt, Mrs J. Studley, Mrs Irene Thornton, Mrs J. T. Tinniswood, Mr Peter Ustinov, Dr Peter Vernier, Dame Margaret Wakehurst and the secretary of The Club.

D.A.
P.B.D.

SOURCE MATERIAL

Space precludes us from detailing all the footnotes, which would run into many thousands. We give an exhaustive list of the sources derived from the Royal Archives at Windsor and from the Ryder Papers (Harrowby MSS) at Sandon Hall, Stafford; we also indicate some of the less obvious sources.

In time, our own documentation will be deposited in the archives of the dukes of St Albans.

Of general printed sources the more helpful have been: the *Almanach de Gotha*, *The Complete Peerage*, *Burke's Peerage*, *Burke's Extinct Peerage*, *Burke's Extinct Baronetcies*, *Burke's Landed Gentry*, *Burke's Landed Gentry of Ireland*, *Debrett's Peerage*, A. Collins's *Peerage of England*, J. E. Doyle's *Official Baronage of England*, the *Calendar of State Papers*, publications of the Historical Manuscripts Commission (principally the MSS of the Earl of Egmont, Mrs Stopford-Sackville, the Earl of Carlisle, the Marquis of Downshire and the first Earl of Charlemont), *Hansard*, *The Times*, *The Annual Register*, *The Gentleman's Magazine*, *The Marriage, Baptismal and Burial Registers of the Collegiate Church or Abbey of St Peter, Westminster* (Harleian Society X), the *Army Lists*, the *Navy Lists*, J. Haydn's *Book of Dignities*, *The Dictionary of National Biography*, the *Victoria County Histories*, D. and S. Lysons' *Magna Britannia*, J. Britton and E. W. Brayley's *Beauties of England and Wales*, *Britannia Illustrata*, J. B. Burke's *Visitation of the Seats and Arms of the Noblemen and Gentlemen of Great Britain*, *The Return of Owners of Land, 1873*, J. Bateman's *Great Landowners of Great Britain and Ireland*, N. Pevsner's *Buildings of England*, Weatherby's *Racing Calendars* and Christie's and other sale catalogues.

Amongst general manuscript sources: wills and letters of administration at the Public Record Office, parish registers, and archives of the Beauclerk family.

After each chapter are given the major works that have been consulted in the writing of that particular chapter, together with a brief selection of footnotes.

Chapter I

Nell Gwyn and her Sons

In *Absalom and Achitophel* Dryden presents Charles II under the guise of David, the father of Absalom:

> When Nature prompted, and no law denied
> Promiscuous use of concubine and bride;
> Then Israel's monarch, after Heaven's own heart,
> His vigorous warmth did variously impart
> To wives and slaves: and, wide as his command
> Scattered his Maker's image through the land.

In fact, Charles's amorous life began long before he had any real command, when he was eighteen, separated from his parents by the Civil War, and about to set sail from Holland to engage the Parliamentarian fleet; after the failure of this naval mission, his exile—and his love life—continued in Holland, the Spanish Netherlands and France. Three children, James, Charlotte and Charles, were born in 1649 and 1650, all by different mothers. Of these James, later to be created Duke of Monmouth, was always to remain his favourite son. During the nine years' exile in Paris, Cologne and Bruges after the Battle of Worcester, other affairs no doubt beguiled his enforced idleness and other illegitimate children were no doubt born to him; but of these no record remains. It was after the Restoration in May 1660 that Charles's 'scattering his Maker's image through the land' really took place, an example which set the pattern for his whole Court and was principally emulated by Buckhurst and Rochester. The 'Restoration comedies' of Etherege and Wycherley give some indication of the licentious behaviour of London in the 1660s and 1670s, reacting against the intolerance and austerity of Oliver Cromwell.

Even so, Dryden's phrase is something of an overstatement. As a very young man of nineteen or twenty Charles had certainly been fickle in his relationships with Lucy Walter, Elizabeth Killigrew, Catherine Pegge— and others. At the Restoration, however, he was exactly thirty and a little steadier with the responsibilities of kingship. Barbara Villiers was his first *maîtresse en titre*, on the model of the French kings' presiding mistresses whose semi-official status even the Royal wives had to accept. Charles had no wife when he first met and fell in love with Barbara; their intimacy began at The Hague even before the Restoration; she followed him to England, and remained his mistress—wielding great power and influence over him and the Court generally—till well into the 1670s. By her Charles had no less than five children: three sons, Charles, Henry and George, all created dukes, and two daughters, whose husbands' families were both given earldoms. George FitzRoy, the last of his sons by Barbara, was born in 1665, after which the King sought other distractions —amongst them Frances Stuart, whom Barbara herself procured for the King, preferring stupid rivals to dangerous ones.

Not all his distractions were found, however, at Court. The very fact that the theatre came into such importance at the Restoration, after its prohibition by Cromwell, led Charles to take a keen interest in it, and a still keener interest in some of its performers. Nell Gwyn was the first of his known actress-mistresses, tolerated by Barbara because she did not challenge her Court influence. Moll Davis, whom he had first seen in an ephemeral comedy *The Mad Shepherdess*, became the mother of Mary Tudor, who at the tender age of fourteen was married to Francis Radcliffe, whose father was made Earl of Derwentwater by James II.

It was not until the advent of Louise de Quéroualle, the notorious Duchess of Portsmouth, that Barbara's position as *maîtresse en titre* was seriously threatened. Louise arrived in England in the spring of 1670 as maid of honour to Charles II's sister the Duchess of Orleans, a negotiatrix of the Treaty of Dover; she was back in England again by the autumn of 1670 and his mistress a year later, becoming the mother of Charles Lennox in 1672. Louise was even more of a political animal than Barbara, having been sent over by Louis XIV as a spy and acting, even during her affair with Charles, as a double agent.

By comparison with these sirens, Charles's wife, Catherine of

Braganza, was singularly dull. It was a political marriage, one of whose chief advantages was that it brought Bombay into the British Empire. Ever since the Treaty of Windsor in 1386 Britain had been on good terms with Portugal, and Charles likewise strove to be on good terms with his wife. Catherine's barrenness made her situation still more delicate and embarrassing, but throughout she endured Charles's infidelities with meek, almost submissive tolerance; indeed, she was extremely fond of her husband, despite everything. Perhaps she realized that there was something to be said in extenuation of Charles. His long exile, in youth and early manhood, had left him with quantities of spare time and energy for which there was no profitable outlet. Besides, Charles was always punctiliously considerate towards the wife for whom he felt friendship and affection, but no passion.

Nell Gwyn stands out amongst the three great mistresses—Barbara, Louise and herself—as the only one who did not wield, and never sought, political influence. Amongst the seven or more mistresses with which Charles is credited, she was perhaps the only one to have remained utterly faithful to him, and actually to love him. It is a sad comment on the Court morals of the Restoration that both his actress-mistresses, on whom he conferred no title and little wealth, were more true to him than his high-born mistresses, Barbara and Louise, whom he created Duchesses of Cleveland and Portsmouth respectively and who were much more generously provided for. Barbara, Louise and Lucy Walter were all scheming and ambitious; Lucy Walter rapidly tired of Charles, who refused to acknowledge her daughter; she was an embarrassment both in Brussels and Scotland, and even threatened blackmail. The Duchess of Cleveland was a nymphomaniac who even during her affair with the King had Henry Jermyn, Earl of St Albans and a handsome tightrope walker, Jacob Hall, as additional lovers; Antoine Hamilton castigates 'the crudeness of her manners, her ridiculous haughtiness and her perpetual suspicions and petty passions'. As for Louise de Quéroualle, she was a beautiful intriguer worthy of Dumas or Baroness Orczy, and so accomplished in corruption that Vigny thought of writing a novel to be called *La Duchesse de Portsmouth* symbolizing the downfall of the aristocracy.

It was at The Duke's Theatre, during the winter of 1667–1668, that

Charles fell in love with Nell. He had seen her act a number of times before, but on this occasion she was not on the stage but in the next box, as the guest of a young Mr Villiers. After the play Charles insisted on inviting himself to supper with Nell and Villiers, and with him came his brother the Duke of York, who had also been at the theatre. Whilst Charles flirted with Nell, James held Villiers's attention. When the bill was presented, neither Charles nor his brother had enough ready money and the much younger man found himself paying for four, having lost Nell into the bargain.

Charles, who was irresistible to women, lost no time in declaring his infatuation, whilst Nell's comment on the evening was: 'Oddsfish! but this is the poorest company that ever I was in before at a tavern'. Charles wanted her to leave the stage immediately and place herself under his protection. As early as 11 January 1668 Pepys notes in his *Diary*: 'The King did send several times for Nelly, and she was with him'.

She was still only seventeen. Born in February 1650, probably near Covent Garden, she came of a sadly reduced family originally of Llansannor, Glamorganshire. Her grandfather, Edward Gwyn, is said to have been a Canon of Christ Church during the reign of Charles I. Her father, Thomas Gwyn, was a captain in the Royalist army who fell on hard times after the defeat of King Charles, and married much beneath himself. He is thought to have died in a debtors' gaol at Oxford. Before long Mrs Gwyn was installed in a squalid alley off Drury Lane with her two daughters Rose and Nell. In 1663 we hear of Rose being imprisoned at Newgate, again for debt. Her first husband appears to have been a highwayman.

Nell meanwhile was 'brought up in a bawdy-house to fill strong waters to the guests', but graduated from the brothel to sell oysters on the streets. No doubt on account of her beauty and gift for repartee, she was taken on as an orange-girl at The King's Theatre, where she became the mistress of the manager, Charles Hart (a great-nephew of Shakespeare). Hart, as she put it laughingly in later years, was her 'Charles I'. Realizing her potential as an actress, he urged her to train for the stage; she had deserted the orange-sellers' pit by the end of 1664. Her period of training was unusually short: she was a quick learner. By March 1665 she was playing Cydaria in Dryden's tragedy *The Indian Emperor*. After this we have no record of her performances in any play until December 1666, when she played Lady Wealthy in James Howard's *The English Monsieur* and Celia in Beaumont and Fletcher's *The Humorous Lieutenant*. In fact, we have no knowledge of her whereabouts during the Great Plague and Great Fire of London; all we know is that in 1665–1666 the theatres were shut.

The years 1667 and 1668 marked the brief climax of her acting career. Beaumont and Fletcher's *The Chances*, Dryden's *Secret Love*, James Howard's *All Mistaken, or The Mad Couple* and Beaumont and Fletcher's *A King and No King* are some of the plays in which she played leading roles in 1667. At a performance of *All Mistaken* in April of that year the poet and rake Charles Sackville, Lord Buckhurst was inflamed by her shapely thighs as she rolled from side to side of the stage in the role of Mirida. He was her 'Charles II'. In July and August 1667 Buckhurst and Nell spent several weeks in a house at Epsom, until they quarrelled and parted. (Ironically, Buckhurst was later to become her trustee.)

Her acting career, contrary to the King's wish, continued throughout 1668; her intimacy with her 'Charles III' was kept fairly quiet for two years, until in the spring of 1670 it could be concealed no longer; Dryden's *Conquest of Granada* had to be postponed owing to her pregnancy, but later in that year she honoured her theatrical engagement, and this tragedy of Dryden was almost the last play in which she ever performed. As an actress Nell was striking for her youth, good looks, impudent wit and above all her popularity with audiences. She was less endowed with acting ability in the strictly technical sense. One of her keenest admirers was Samuel Pepys, who makes many references to her in his *Diary*.

The birth of a son, Charles, on 8 May 1670 was not only the foundation of the Beauclerk family but the turning-point in her own life. She gradually withdrew from her career in the theatre, and was established by Charles. In 1671 she moved from Lincoln's Inn Fields (where her baby had been born) to 79 Pall Mall. The King's first idea was to set her up in a smaller house at the eastern end of the street, and in a leasehold house at that! Nell inisted on her own freehold: since, she argued, she had given her services free to the King, she wanted to hold her house free under the

Crown. Finally Lord Scarsdale was prevailed upon to give up his lease-hold house at the opposite end of Pall Mall, where Nell found herself next door to St James's Palace and able to talk to her lover from a terrace behind her garden wall.

On Christmas Day 1671 Nell gave birth to a second son, christened James after his father's brother. He was Charles's seventh son, and the next to the last. Now that Nell's family was complete (as it turned out), she grew more concerned about her worldly position. Her jealousy of Louise de Quéroualle increased as Charles alternated between mistresses, and indeed was expecting children by both at the same time. Louise's son, and only child by Charles, was born in July 1672. In August of that year the second of the King's sons by Barbara Villiers was made Earl of Euston; Barbara herself had been created Duchess of Cleveland in 1670, so that her eldest son was in line for a peerage as well. In 1673 Louise de Quéroualle was created Duchess of Portsmouth for life. In 1674 George FitzRoy was created Earl of Northumberland—at the age of nine! When the three-year-old son of Louise de Quéroualle was made Duke of Richmond in 1675, Nell was beside herself with rage.

'Even Barbara's brats', she complained, 'were not made dukes until they were twelve or thirteen, but this French spy's son is ennobled when little more than an infant in arms!'

Barbara's brats had in fact received their first titles, all earldoms, when aged eight or nine; by the age of twelve or thirteen her first and second sons were already dukes. As if to humiliate her still further, Charles's son by Catherine Pegge was created Earl of Plymouth in 1675. Until 1676 her two sons remained without a title, and even without a surname. Nell had never been ambitious for herself. It did not particularly irk her that she remained without a title whilst Barbara and Louise were duchesses, but her sons' future had to be provided for. Perhaps one reason for Charles's dilatoriness was her own fairly humble birth.

In spite of the rival attractions of Louise de Quéroualle, Charles and Nell spent a considerable amount of time together during the 1670s. With Barbara and Louise the King tended to remain in London, but with the much more unsophisticated and uncourtly Nell he visited, and stayed, at many mansions in the Home Counties. At Littleberries, Mill Hill, at

King's Wick, Sunninghill, at Philiberts, near Bray, and at Leyton in Essex there are records or rumours of the King and his mistress spending happy respites. Some of these places were hunting-lodges: it seems that Nell and Charles even travelled together as far as Sherwood Forest. At Bagnigge House, Bagnigge Wells, on the other hand, they were at a spa— incredibly enough, near where King's Cross Station stands today. From Gwyn House, Newmarket (possibly connected with the former Palace by an underground passage) they attended race meetings. But there are five houses particularly associated with the name of Nell Gwyn: Lauderdale House, still in Highgate; Sandford Manor, still in Fulham; a house close to Hampton Court later to be called St Albans; Salisbury Hall, near St Albans; and Tring Park, also in Hertfordshire.

The story goes that at one of these places Nell, staying with Charles, threatened to throw her elder son into a river, lake or moat. Holding him head downwards over the water, she is said to have vowed the boy's death unless he was ennobled. Whatever the truth of this tradition (and it clashes not only with Nell's kindliness but with motherhood generally), the sons were both given a surname and ennobled in 1676. The surname was that of Beauclerk, which may be a French form of 'steward' and thus a reminder of the boys' Stuart blood, or more probably a reminder of their descent from Henry I, often referred to in old documents as 'King Henry Beauclerk'. Nell's elder son was made Baron Headington and Earl of Burford whilst the younger boy, James, was in special remainder to these titles and had the 'appellation of Lord Beauclerk, with the same place and precedence as is due unto the eldest son of an earl'.

Why the reference to Oxfordshire? Two theories are current: Nell Gwyn may have been born in the county (Oxford, London and Hereford have all been suggested as her birthplace, though London is the most likely); or Charles may even in 1676 have been thinking of marrying the boy to the heiress of the Earls of Oxford. Another Burford title was, in fact, still in existence in 1676: an ancient barony by tenure, created in the fourteenth century and held by Thomas Cornewall, fourteenth Baron of Burford; being a barony by tenure, it did not entitle its holder to a seat in the House of Lords. The Cornewalls were one of the noblest of English families, with a distinguished (though allegedly illegitimate) descent from the Plantagenets; their barony did not become dormant until 1727. The parallels with both the de Vere and Beauclerk families are obvious.

As for James, the precedence he received as the eldest son of an earl is both unusual and confusing. In a comparable instance William IV allowed his younger illegitimate sons the precedence of younger sons of a marquis. Perhaps it was Charles's intention to raise James to some higher rank: he was the only son of the Merry Monarch to receive no title of his own. If Charles did intend to promote Nell's younger son to a peerage, he was prevented from doing so by the boy's untimely death in Paris in September 1680.

The arms chosen for the young peer and his brother were the Royal arms representing England, France, Scotland, and Ireland, 'with a baton sinister gules, charged with three roses argent, seeded and barbed proper', the baton sinister denoting illegitimacy. The supporters, which only the elder son was entitled to bear, were a white antelope and a white greyhound, the antelope commemorating Charles's collateral descent from Henry IV, the greyhound his direct descent from Henry VII. An optimistic motto was selected, '*Auspicium Melioris Ævi*' ('A Pledge of Better Times'), which in 1818 was to be adopted as the motto of the Order of St Michael and St George. For some of Charles Burford's successors, the motto would have been more appropriate if followed by a question mark.

As it was always the case until this century that sizable wealth should accompany hereditary titles, Charles II also provided materially for Nell and her elder son. In 1674 Nell was already receiving £4,000 p.a. out of the King's Secret Service accounts.[1] In 1676 she was granted the reversion of the Registrarship of the High Court of Chancery, a hereditament bequeathed by her to her son Charles but not actually enjoyed until 1698. It was a sinecure producing a variable income, depending on the agreements entered into by the Registrar and his deputies and on the volume of business transacted; between them they shared the fees of litigants in the Court of Chancery. The office remained with the family until it lapsed in the reign of George III.

In September 1680 came the freehold of Burford House, Windsor, a house built a few years before in part of an old garden and vineyard adjacent to the Castle. It had a staircase soon to be decorated by Verrio with stories from Ovid, for which the artist was paid £100. There was a marble hall, and a breakfast room with a 'curious clock' presented to Burford by Charles II. In an upstairs dressing-room was a chimneypiece carved by Grinling Gibbons. (Both Gibbons and Verrio had been working on commissions at the Castle). Outside were ornamental gardens, depicted in 1690 or thereabouts by Leender Knyff, and beyond them a small park. The total extent of the property is unknown, but it cannot have exceeded forty acres.

At that time the Crown was gradually, but only slowly, amassing land at Windsor; Burford House itself had only been bought a year or two earlier; Charles liked Windsor, and so sought to extend his landholding there; he did not provide any of his other sons with a property like Burford House. Welcome as this was, since a freehold property would pass to Nell's descendants (and indeed remained in the Beauclerks' ownership until 1778), it posed one big problem: demanding an income for its upkeep not provided by the property itself. Nell, it is true, had been granted £5,000 p.a. in addition to the £4,000 p.a. on the Secret Service accounts which was now primarily intended for her son's maintenance; but what of the future?

In 1681 Charles also granted her the estate of Bestwood Park, in Nottinghamshire: but it was only a lease, and the freehold was not actually conveyed to her by Charles but by his brother and successor, James II. Bestwood was the woodland retreat in Sherwood Forest where, as tradition has it, Charles and Nell sometimes sought the rare privilege of being alone. The King is said to have promised his mistress as large a tract of Sherwood Forest as she could ride round before breakfast.

In 1681 Bestwood Hall was a half-timbered hunting-lodge of thirty-eight rooms, dating back to the reign of Edward III. Though nominally part of Sherwood Forest, the estate was mostly scrubland and tillage. In John Leland's *Itinerary*, 140 years earlier, Bestwood had been described as a 'mighty great park'; but Robert Thoroton, writing four years before the granting of Nell's lease, records that the park was by then

parcelled up into little closes on one side and much of it ploughed, so

that there is scarce wood or venison which is also likely to be the fate
of the whole Forest of Sherwood.

The boundaries of the 3,723 acres were clearly defined, and had been
so since the Middle Ages: Nell's lucrative early-morning gallop is,
apparently, no more than a colourful legend. On the cultivated part of
her estate she had tenants, whose farm-rents can hardly have counter-
balanced the interest on the mortgage of £3,774 which she took out on
her Crown lease from a neighbour, Sir John Musters. Thus, the interest
on her London debts was partly funded by her Nottinghamshire estate,
which otherwise played a remarkably small part not only in her life but
in the lives of all the dukes of St Albans for the next 180 years. Admirable
as a love-nest, Bestwood would have been less satisfactory as a home,
particularly as it was already over three hundred years old. Nell's great-
grandson Topham Beauclerk was to inherit a similar house in Lancashire
in 1766, and he too neglected his.

By ducal standards, and by comparison with Charles Burford's half-
brothers, the position was still not very secure; Nell was still constantly
in debt; yet on 10 January 1684 her only surviving son was elevated to a
dukedom—the last duke to be created by Charles II. Only eight days
before the patent passed the Great Seal Henry Jermyn, Earl of St Albans
had died. He had been a close friend of Charles II, an intimate of the
King's mother Henrietta Maria, whom it was even said that he secretly
married. He also shared Barbara Villiers with Charles II. On the strength
of all these ties, except perhaps the last, his extinct title—created by
Charles himself in 1660—was recreated in Burford's favour. Other than
through their title, the dukes of St Albans have never had any close link
with Hertfordshire.

As Duke of St Albans, the boy needed further lucrative appointments.
At the time of his promotion in the peerage, his income was probably
about £1,500 p.a. whilst his mother's (when paid punctually!) was
nearing £10,000 p.a. In June 1684 he appears to have been granted the
reversion of the Chief Rangership of Enfield Chase, 'a region' (writes
Macaulay) 'twenty-five miles in circumference in which the deer wan-
dered by thousands as free as in an American forest'; but for some

reason, as yet unexplained, that reversion never took effect.

In January 1685, also in reversion, he was named Hereditary Grand Falconer of England, an office from which he drew no income until three years later. The duties of Hereditary Grand Falconer involved him in rather more detailed work than those of Registrar of the Court of Chancery were to do. Under him was a staff of one sergeant, ten falconers and twenty-two feeders. The Grand Falconer's costume was a 'coat of crimson cloth lined with blue serge and trimmed with broad gold arras lace, a pair of blue cloth breeches, a blue serge waistcoat trimmed with narrow gold arras lace and also a hat with a gold lace and gold hatband'.[2]

By 1688 the Duke was receiving from the Crown a total income of £1,372-10-0d[3] as Hereditary Grand Falconer, out of which at least £700 was spent on the duties of his office. The Grand Falconer was required to supply the King with hawking-birds for use in all the Royal forests and parks; he had charge of the birds' feeding, training and acquisition, and also of the hawking-mews at St Martin's in the Fields, though most of the detailed supervision was delegated to the sergeant.

Thomas Otway, author of *Venice Preserved*, seems to have been Lord Burford's tutor for a short spell, as was Sir Fleetwood Sheppard who also acted as Nell's steward. In 1682 the boy was sent to Paris to study French and deportment, under the care of Lord Preston, the English ambassador. He was still in France in November of the following year, living with his new tutor Jean de Gachon along the Sceaux road, a few miles out of the capital. By Easter 1684 he was home again: John Evelyn mentions having seen him attend Easter Day service at Whitehall with his father and half-brothers the Dukes of Northumberland and Richmond; the three boys preceded the King into the sanctuary as Charles II walked to make his offering at the altar. He may however have been back in England as early as January 1684, the month in which he received his dukedom. Later in the same year (23 October) Evelyn refers to St Albans and Richmond as 'both very pretty boys, [who] seem to have more wit than the rest' of Charles's progeny: all were distinctly inferior to their father in subtlety and intelligence.

The Duke attended Charles II to Portsmouth in September 1684 when the King went down to review the fleet, and in the following winter was travelling in France. His journeys were interrupted by a sudden deterioration in his father's health; with all his half-brothers except Monmouth, he was present at the King's deathbed on 6 February.

Charles's death was a more shattering blow to Nell than to St Albans. Nell was more attached to, and dependent on, her Royal lover than either of her great rivals was. And she was menacingly in debt. The King's dying words to his brother and successor, James II, were: 'Let not poor Nelly starve'.

Nell indeed received an allowance of £1,500 p.a. from James II, who also saved her from the debtors' prison (she had already been outlawed) by paying off her tradesmen's bills amounting to £729. He again came to the rescue in October 1687, not only redeeming her mortgage of £3,774 on Bestwood but also granting the freehold of that estate to herself and her descendants. She had to sell much of her plate and jewellery, including a pearl necklace with a ruby clasp which she had bought in richer days for over £4,000 from Prince Rupert's mistress, Peg Hughes. Silver valued at nearly the same amount was deposited at Childs Bank as security for an overdraft.

Like Charles II, and perhaps influenced by his example, Nell favoured Catholicism; but without becoming a convert. Rumour that she had actually turned to the other faith was strengthened when in January 1686 she went to mass with Dryden and two of his sons (Dryden had become a Catholic in the previous year): 'such purchases were no great loss to the Church', Evelyn commented acidly. The religious position of young St Albans was highly delicate. His own father had always had secret leanings towards Roman Catholicism, *his* mother's religion, and was received into the Roman Catholic church on his deathbed; Catherine of Braganza was a devout Catholic; James II practised Catholicism, paying lip-service for a while to the religion of which he was titular head. There was mounting pressure on St Albans to embrace Roman Catholicism, and on Nell Gwyn to persuade him. It was said that the young Duke was about to go to Hungary, from whence he would return a devout Catholic, and that if he did so 'the fraternity [his half-brothers] would be on the same foot or give way as to their advantageous stations'; in other words, the main inducement to St Albans was that by changing his religious allegiance he would stand to benefit financially, since he was considerably poorer than such half-brothers as Richmond and Grafton—largely because he had not had a grasping mother.

In March 1687 James II sent for Nell, telling her that St Albans

must be of the religion his father died in if she expected that he should take any care of him, and that . . . the Duke's governor or tutor, a French Protestant who has been long in England, must be removed because he was a heretic and he would place another, and has placed . . . a very fierce, active, discursive Papist who Harry Killigrew told the King would syllogize the Duke to death.

It seems that the effect of this pressure on Nell Gwyn may have been to hasten her death:

All agree [the same writer continues] that it was an inexpressible grief to her that first brought her distemper upon her, and continued upon her heart till her death that a Papist . . . was made tutor to her son, and [the French Protestant tutor] displaced.

Nell's interview with James II and her first stroke both occurred in the same week. Why should her son, rather than the others, be singled out for what must have seemed to her the rather dubious advantage of a Roman Catholic conversion? Maybe James was partly motivated by a desire to take his revenge on Nell for her earlier sympathy with Monmouth, and the part she had played as the 'Protestant whore' in opposition to Louise de Quéroualle's Catholic exercise of that profession; maybe he was actuated largely by political, or even sectarian motives. At all events, her health rapidly worsened throughout 1687, and she died aged thirty-seven towards the end of that year (14 November) at 79 Pall Mall.

She was buried at St Martin's in the Fields, her parish church. Thomas Tenison, her vicar and later to become Archbishop of Canterbury, preached the funeral sermon, taking as his text the words from St Luke: 'Joy shall be in heaven over one sinner that repenteth, more than over ninety and nine just persons, which need no repentance'.

Whether or not she repented history does not relate, and it would be churlish to presume. She certainly enjoyed her good time while it lasted, and from the very circumstances of her early childhood was well used to the ups and downs of fortune. It may not have seemed very odd to her that her mother died in a ditch, whilst her son became a duke. She was definitely the most generally popular of Charles's mistresses. Londoners, including Pepys, adored her. She had wit, sparkle and beauty; she was sincere, unpretentious and loyal. At the height of her prosperity she did not overlook others less fortunate. Owing to her influence with Charles II the Royal Hospital, Chelsea became a much larger foundation than the King had originally intended; and perhaps in urging him to increase his bounty towards disabled and elderly soldiers she was influenced by the fact that her own father and a Gwyn cousin were soldiers who had fallen on evil days. And because she herself had known debt both as a girl and in later life, she specifically asked in her will that money be provided for releasing parishioners of St Martin's in the Fields and St James's, Piccadilly from debtors' prisons. Even though she never became a Catholic, she also left £50 in her will for the benefit of Catholics in her parish.

What she had to leave she mostly bequeathed to her son, and this included not only the house in Pall Mall but also sizable debts. She died owing Childs Bank £6,900 of which £2,300 was repaid by her son and £3,791 through the sale of 14,443 oz. of silver deposited as security for a loan; but not till 20 July 1691 were her affairs finally wound up when St Albans, 'pursuant to a decree in Chancery', paid £3,355-7-6d 'in full of all accounts'. The houses and land at Windsor and Bestwood were entailed and not therefore subject to her control. At her death the Registrarship of the Court of Chancery was still only in reversion. Almost everything of value that had come from Charles had either been sold or mortgaged or was entailed.

At this time particularly, the finances of her son and heir were obscure and desperate. He was lucky enough to inherit from his mother jewels and securities valued at £7,100 which until December 1697 were deposited with Sir Francis Child. From Lord Clare (later to be created Duke of Newcastle) he must have borrowed a sum in the region of £8,000 in the early 1690s, for on 11 October 1693 we find Richard Hoare—

Nell Gwyn: from the studio of Sir Peter Lely, c. 1675.

LEFT
The First Duke of
St Albans as a Boy
in Armour:
attributed to Sir
Godfrey Kneller,
and probably
painted in 1679.

Lady Diana de
Vere, afterwards
Duchess of St
Albans: by Sir
Godfrey Kneller,
c. 1690–1691.
Her portrait hangs
in the King's First
Presence Chamber
at Hampton Court
Palace.

the founder of Hoares Bank—repaying Clare £8,859-16-0d on St Albans's
behalf; Clare, incidentally, was one of the richest of Child's customers.
To some extent, the Duke seems to have played off Childs Bank against
Hoares until, in December 1697, there came the final settlement: in
addition to the outstanding loans, Hoare advanced a further £300 to
St Albans and £175-3-0d to the Duke's agent, Pauncefote; the total now
owing to Hoares Bank was £9,600, as securities for which St Albans
deposited the jewels and securities from Childs and a further loan of
£2,500 from William Waterson and Sir Nicholas Crisp.

Until 1694, when he was forced by his creditors to sell it, St Albans
continued to live at the house in Pall Mall. Apart from Bestwood, which
was never a serious possibility, it was in fact his only residence. In
October 1686 Burford House had been leased furnished to James II's
son-in-law Prince George of Denmark, at a rent of £260 p.a. It was a
five-year lease, expiring when the Duke came of age.

He was still only seventeen at his mother's death, and his conversion
to Roman Catholicism still hung in the balance. James II and Catherine of
Braganza (living since her widowhood in Portugal) both encouraged him
with their favour. The boy's uncle must have been reasonably satisfied
with the upshot of his meeting with Nell in the previous March because
in October 1687, just a month before her death, he paid off the Bestwood
mortgage; and after her death he transferred her pension to her son.
Catherine of Braganza allowed him £2,000 p.a. out of funds she had taken
with her to Portugal. Shortly after Nell's death we hear of St Albans
travelling to Hungary, accompanied by his Catholic tutor—who in July
1688 was paid £1,100 for his services. Gachon received a further £100
in January 1689, and £73-2-6d in 1693, but by then St Albans had taken
his stand as a supporter of William of Orange against Catholicism and
the Stuarts.

In his change of political allegiance he was less of a turncoat than it
might seem. Apart from the fact that he was always fairly uninterested
in politics, he had consistently refused to change his religion—despite
the strongest pressure from the King. Besides, James II had so little
support anywhere in the country at the time of the Bloodless Revolution,
though it must have seemed hard to the exiled monarch that all his

nephews—Southampton, Grafton, Northumberland, St Albans and Richmond—disowned the Jacobite cause. In fact, only his niece's husband Lord Derwentwater remained faithful to the Stuarts, for which he paid the penalty of attainder and execution in 1716.

By a convenient stroke of fortune, St Albans was out of England at the time of the *coup d'état*, though in view of the ease with which his elder brothers switched their allegiance it would not have been difficult for him to do the same, pleading his youth. In 1687 he had been appointed Colonel of the Princess of Denmark's Regiment of Horse (now the Eighth Hussars). Colonel Langston was given charge of the regiment whilst the Duke went over to the Continent to gain experience of warfare. He entered the service of the Holy Roman Emperor, Leopold I, under the command of Prince Charles of Lorraine. It was a juncture at which the Austrians were repelling the Turks from the Danube. A bloody onslaught occurred on 20 August 1688, in which 4,000 or more Turks died whilst 2,000 men of the Imperial army were killed. The combat continued throughout the morning, Suleiman II's army were routed in the afternoon, and before dusk Belgrade was occupied by the Emperor; though Leopold's tenure of the city was destined to be brief. At the battle of Belgrade St Albans is reported by *The London Gazette* to have greatly distinguished himself. By 3 October he was at Vienna, having received a special grant of £1,500 from James II towards the expenses of the campaign. On 15 November 'The Duke of St Albans's Regiment', commanded by Langston, was one of the first to defect to William of Orange. From Belgrade St Albans brought home two Turkish children whom he had taken prisoner: these remained with him until they were grown up, when one decided to return to his homeland whilst the other remained in England and died a Poor Knight of Windsor. A portrait of the children was still hanging at Burford House in 1768.

After being nearly wiped out at Steenkirk (24 July 1692), The Duke of St Albans's Regiment was disbanded. The Duke himself left again for Flanders on 17 May 1693, to help continue William's struggle against the French. On 19 July he fought under William III at the battle of Neerwinden, another blow for the Anglo-Dutch army, defeated by the Maréchal de Luxembourg after stubborn fighting. St Albans was a great

favourite of William of Orange, and as a result of the notable part he
played in these campaigns (even though they turned out to be defeats),
he was nominated Captain of the Band of Gentlemen Pensioners in the
following November. This was the Sovereign's personal escort founded
by Henry VIII; St Albans's appointment still exists today under the more
recent name of Captain of the Gentlemen at Arms, though now it is a
political rather than a military post.

As Captain of the Band of Gentlemen Pensioners he showed great
courage in wishing to reinstate the Jacobite officers expelled in 1689 by
his predecessor Lord Lovelace; but the Privy Council vetoed this initiative, which does not seem to have put him in bad odour with William.
Even though he had just married, he returned to the Low Countries in
July 1694 as a volunteer. This was further proof, if any were needed, of
his support of William of Orange, whom he also accompanied when the
King received Peter the Great at Utrecht in September 1697 and again
when the Treaty of Rijswijk was signed later that month.

His bride was Lady Diana de Vere, to whom he seems to have been
betrothed many years before he finally married her on 17 April 1694.
Charles had been most concerned to marry all his illegitimate children
well. His daughters married landowners of substance, and he hoped that
his sons would marry heiresses. His great ambition for his sons was that
one should marry the richest heiress of the day, Lady Elizabeth Percy,
whose father had left her a vast estate in Northumberland;[4] she, however,
thought otherwise and in 1682, at the age of fifteen, married as her third
husband the Duke of Somerset. Charles was more successful in marrying
Monmouth to that great Scottish heiress, the Countess of Buccleuch,
and Grafton to Lady Isabella Bennet, who brought the FitzRoys the
Euston estate on the borders of Suffolk and Norfolk. (Curiously, Henry
FitzRoy had been created Earl of Euston ten years before his marriage
to the heiress of Euston actually took place!) Even Southampton obtained
an heiress with £30,000.

For St Albans Charles was urged by his cousin Prince Rupert to
consider the latter's natural daughter, but negotiations foundered on the
Prince's death in 1682. Lady Diana de Vere, the only surviving child of
the twentieth and last Earl of Oxford, was the heraldic heiress of the

oldest and most distinguished noble family in the land. In the imaginary figure of Lady Clara Vere de Vere Tennyson has captured something of the magic of a family who were created Earls of Oxford in 1142, who were Lords Great Chamberlain of England for close on 500 years, and one of whose members may even have written the plays of Shakespeare.

Great beauty and high lineage were Lady Diana's attributes, but wealth certainly was not. The large estates of the de Veres had been recklessly squandered by the seventeenth Earl, and though the twentieth holder of the title seems to have married a considerable heiress in his first wife Anne Bayning, little or no property came to the Beauclerks from the man whom Macaulay described as 'the noblest subject in England, and indeed as Englishmen loved to say, the noblest subject in Europe'. Even the ancestral fortress of Castle Hedingham, in Essex, had been alienated before Diana's time.

In the words used almost seventy years earlier by Lord Chief Justice Crew, sitting in judgment on the Lord Great Chamberlainship dispute: 'there must be a period and an end to all temporal things . . ., an end of names and dignities, and whatsoever is terrene; and why not of de Vere? —for where is Bohun? where is Mowbray? where is Mortimer? nay, what is more, and most of all, where is Plantagenet? They are entombed in the urns and sepulchres of mortality. And yet let the name and dignity of de Vere stand so long as it pleaseth God'.

For once a judge was affected by poetry; the earldom did not escape the 'urns and sepulchres of mortality', but the dignity of the de Veres has been commemorated by successive generations of Beauclerks who have prefixed that surname to their own, and (from the time of Lord Vere of Hanworth and the fifth Duke onwards) quartered the de Vere arms: 'quarterly gules and or, in the first quarter a mullet of five points argent'.

In the long run, St Albans's marriage turned him towards the Court and away from the army. He became a Lord of the Bedchamber in 1694 (the year in which he had to sell 79 Pall Mall); this brought him another £1,000 p.a.[5] until he relinquished the post at the accession of Queen Anne. Also in 1694, he was granted a pension of £2,000 p.a., half of which came from the 'first fruits', or first year's revenues of benefices payable to the Crown by new incumbents, £250 p.a. from tithes, and £125 p.a. from a charge on the revenues of Wales. With the reversion of the Registrarship of the Court of Chancery in 1698, he obtained a further £1,500 p.a. gross.[5] Out of the quit rents of Alexander MacDonnell, the Jacobite Earl of Antrim, he was paid a special grant of £1,643.

Politics he avoided as much as possible, though he did take his seat in the House of Lords at the age of twenty-one. But he was not averse to the brief mission of Ambassador Extraordinary to France in December 1697–January 1698, for which William III equipped him with a set of coach horses finely spotted like leopards. As events were to prove, this was the only time a Duke of St Albans ever acted as an ambassador. The object of his mission was to congratulate Louis XIV on the marriage of his grandson the Duke of Burgundy to Princess Mary Adelaide of Savoy; it was an *extraordinary* mission in that diplomatic relations had still not been restored between France and England, and highly sensitive in that it was designed to sound out French feeling towards England after nearly ten years of warfare.

Saint-Simon recalls the young Duke's arrival at Versailles.[6] William, he remarks, 'could not have chosen a more distinguished man for a simple mission; indeed, people were surprised that he had taken it on'; the aim of the 'simple mission', according to Saint-Simon, was to persuade Louis XIV to banish the Old Pretender, and the French Court were equally puzzled that such a task should have been undertaken by a man who was the Old Pretender's cousin. Saint-Évremond, writing about St Albans to Ninon de Lenclos, referred to 'a young cavalier who has the art of pleasing all our ladies' (he was twenty-seven). If the diplomatic mission was to weaken Louis XIV's support of the Old Pretender, then St Albans was clearly unsuccessful; if it was to sound out the state of French opinion, then he must presumably have sent in a favourable report to London as Lord Portland, the ambassador designate, arrived in Paris in January 1698 before St Albans left. It was a mark of William's confidence in him that he had been given this assignment at twenty-seven, but St Albans seriously compromised his mission by leaving sizable debts behind him in Paris.

A confidential report on him in 1704 by John Macky, a secret agent of the late William III, describes him as 'of a black complexion not so tall as the Duke of Northumberland, yet very like King Charles' and—more to the point—disliking business. But we hear of him voting on 17 June 1701 for the acquittal of Lord Somers, William's former chief minister who had resigned in a storm of protest over his conduct of foreign policy and who had been impeached by the House of Commons. It was a narrow division, in which St Albans found himself in the majority—whilst his father-in-law, Lord Oxford, voted on the opposite side!

In voting for the acquittal of the former leader of the Whig junta St Albans had taken a partisan line, and he was to do so again in his attitude towards the rabble-rousing Tory preacher Henry Sacheverell, who regularly denounced the Whig leader Godolphin and whose tirades, and trial in 1710, led to the fall of the Whig government. Sacheverell was condemned at his trial before the House of Lords by sixty-nine votes to fifty-two, and St Albans was amongst the sixty-nine. Whether or not he showed wisdom in helping to make a martyr of this eloquent enemy of Dissent and Whiggism is a moot point: either way it would probably have been a triumph for Sacheverell. The unquestionable point is that St Albans, a perfect embodiment of Whiggism, acted out of instinctive political solidarity—and surely without thinking the matter through. He and probably all his successors in the title (until the tenth Duke, at least) are perfect embodiments of Whiggism in that not only did they take their social status and privileges entirely for granted but on all political issues never wavered, never questioned and never achieved. Usually on the periphery of action, they maintained a keen sense of aristocratic cohesion and, for as long as Whiggism persisted, stood on an equal footing with families who—perhaps because of traditions acquired through generations of social ascent—no doubt contributed more to national life. The Tory ministry which Sacheverell made possible dismissed St Albans from the captaincy of the Band of Gentlemen Pensioners in January 1712, replacing him with the Duke of Beaufort.

It was because of his 'services' to the Whigs that in October 1703 St Albans had been granted a pension of £800 p.a., payable by the Irish Parliament. He also hoped to benefit in 1707 from the will of the eighteenth

Earl of Kildare, but much to his distress no such document could be found. By 1704 his total income, including certain other pensions, had probably risen to about £10,000 p.a.; after Catherine of Braganza's death in 1705 it dropped to around £8,000 p.a.; and Nell Gwyn had been unable to manage on £10,000 p.a. a generation previously. In 1704 he was certainly in debt to Richard Hoare, who writes on 15 February:

> I have a long time expected your Grace's settling the account. The things that I have for securities are worth more than what is owing to me, but the interest runs on daily, and will in time come to the value of them; and believing that some part of the things I have will never be of any use to your Grace, I thought it my duty to acquaint your Grace with it.

There was a wrangle lasting at least four years (1702–1706) over the £300 that Hoare had loaned to St Albans in 1697. Hoare writes plaintively in April 1706,

> I desired [Mr Pauncefote] to pay me the interest of the £300, and for answer he did assure me that he would never pay me one farthing of the interest nor principal which now comes to upwards of £70 . . .

Where the Duke banked in the last twenty years of his life is uncertain.

The latter years of the reign of Queen Anne were not the most helpful period of St Albans's life. As a Whig he found himself with no notable role to play in a Court now predominantly Tory, besides which he was not on good personal terms with the Queen. In 1714 there is a vivid sketch of his enforced but perhaps acceptable idleness, when Lady Orkney complains that the Court suffered from

> nothing but ceremony, no manner of conversation. My Lady Burlington in good earnest and imitated in perfection; the Duke of Somerset sitting at a little table by, that the ladies (and most of them his own daughters) might have room, without one bit of meat upon it till the other table had done; the Duke of St Albans

a-jesting, Lord Arran sleeping, my Lord Burlington eating with his eyes. We played after dinner, drank tea, bowed extremely and so retired'.[7]

There was also the distraction of racing. On Queen Anne's initiative a new course known as Ascot Common was opened on Cranbourne Chase in August 1711, and the Duke of St Albans's horse Doctor won the first place in the first event.

He came into his own again at the Hanoverian Accession, with Whiggish effortlessness. On 24 September 1714, within a week of George I's arrival in England, he was restored to the captaincy of the Gentlemen Pensioners. A fortnight later he was made Lord Lieutenant of Berkshire, an honour which was to descend effortlessly to two sons and a grandson. His wife, who during the Whig ascendancy in the earlier part of Anne's reign had been First Lady of the Bedchamber, now became Mistress of the Robes and Lady of the Stole, at separate salaries of £800 and £400.[5] In 1716 the Duke succeeded his late half-brother Northumberland as High Steward of Windsor, a purely ceremonial office. But he had definitely withdrawn from the modicum of political life in which he had ever engaged. In 1714 he assigned a proxy to Lord Cowper for use in the House of Lords, Cowper being Lord Chancellor. After the 1715 Rebellion he was thought of as a suitable man to present the King with a petition from the Lords on behalf of the Jacobite leaders; this he declined to do, and the task fell to another lord. All along, the dukes of St Albans were prudent in showing the strongest aversion to Jacobitism.

The stupid quarrel between George I and the Prince of Wales had its repercussions on the Duke and Duchess. At the christening of Prince George William in December 1717 the King and his son disagreed as to who should stand godfather, the King preferring the Duke of Newcastle to the Prince's choice of his uncle the Bishop of Osnabrück. In the event, the King had his way and the Prince of Wales was placed under temporary house arrest for objecting to Newcastle after the ceremony. George I expelled the young man from Court and forbade any wives of members of his own Household to occupy positions under the Prince and Princess. St Albans being Captain of the Gentlemen Pensioners, his wife gave up her posts as Mistress of the Robes and Lady of the Stole. For all such satisfactory services to the Crown he was rewarded with the Garter in March 1718.

Later, in April 1720, George I 'much importuned' his daughter-in-law to take the Duchess of St Albans back into her Household again—or so, at least, it is claimed. Princess Caroline, however, refused to have her back as Mistress of the Robes, preferring to employ the Duchess of Dorset. The King was hoist with his own petard in that, after insisting that the Duchess of St Albans should act as Prince George's godmother, he now found that his own edict regarding his son's Household prevented her from having any employment there. In September 1726 there was talk of her succeeding the Duchess of Dorset, but again it proved to be without foundation. The three years from 1714 to 1717 were the only period when a duchess of St Albans has been Mistress of the Robes.

Still retaining much of the youthful beauty depicted by Lely and Kneller, Diana lived on until 1742. At her husband's death, after a lingering illness, in May 1726, six of her twelve children were still unmarried and living at home. Having such a numerous offspring, she appears to have retained Burford House whilst the new Duke of St Albans found a home, or homes, elsewhere.

NOTES TO CHAPTER I

Archives of Childs Bank.

Archives of Hoares Bank.

J. Y. Akerman (ed.): *Moneys Received and Paid for Secret Services of Charles II and James II from 30 March 1697 to 25 December 1688* (Camden Society LII), 1851.

J. J. Cartwright (ed.): *The Wentworth Papers, 1705–1739*, 1883.

C. S. Cowper (ed.): *Diary of Mary Countess Cowper, Lady of the Bedchamber to the Princess of Wales, 1714–1720*, 1864.

P. Cunningham: *The Story of Nell Gwyn*, 1852.

A. I. Dasent: *Nell Gwynne*, 1924.

J. Evelyn: *Diary* (O.U.P. edn.), 1959.

T. E. Harwood: *Windsor Old and New*, 1929.

C. Hibbert: *The Court at Windsor. A Domestic History*, 1964.

W. H. St J. Hope: *Windsor Castle. An Architectural History*, 1913.

A. E. L. Lowe (ed.): *Black's Guide to Nottinghamshire*, 1876.

N. Luttrell: *A Brief Historical Relation of State Affairs from September 1678. to April 1714*, 1857.

S. Pepys: *Diary*, 1893–1899.

R. Thoroton: *The Antiquities of Nottinghamshire*, 1677.

---

1. Dorset RO D124/box 267.
2. Royal Archives (RA) 86672.
3. RA 57057.
4. Lord Egremont: *Wyndham and Children First*, 1968, 19.
5. RA Civil List Accounts 1747–1754.
6. Duc de Saint-Simon Vermandois: *Mémoires* (Pléiade edn), vol. I, 1953, 472.
7. D. Green: *Queen Anne*, 1970, 311–312.

CHAPTER II

'The Insupportable Labour of Doing Nothing'

Sir Leslie Stephen, asked which century he would have preferred to live in other than his own, unhesitatingly chose the eighteenth century. Many, from Lord Chesterfield at its beginning to Talleyrand at its end, experienced its *douceur de vivre*. The paintings of Watteau, Boucher and Fragonard point to every refinement of civilization—though the Hanoverian Court was rather less civilized than the French, and there was also the more disreputable side of eighteenth-century life as satirized by Hogarth. The second Duke of St Albans was not particularly rich, or particularly clever, but he like so many others enjoyed the life of an eighteenth-century nobleman to the full. There is a curious contrast between the list of his occupations as recorded in the reference books (Whig MP for Bodmin, 1718–1722, MP for Windsor from the General Election of 1722 until 1726, High Steward of Windsor, Lord Lieutenant of Berkshire, Constable and Governor of Windsor Castle, Lord Warden of the Forest, and a Lord of the Bedchamber) and the impression of busy indolence derived from the eighty-one letters he wrote between 1725 and 1750 to his friend John Clavering, and which are still preserved at the Hertfordshire Record Office. Contrary to Sir Richard Steele's phrase, St Albans found the 'labour of doing nothing' very supportable indeed!

By the very nature of his official appointments, his life was centred on Windsor although he in fact spent an incredible amount of time in moving long distances for brief visits. In this context the letters to John Clavering are most revealing, because no trace of his endless journeying from place to place would otherwise be apparent. On 6 July 1732, for instance, he writes: 'I have been upon the road almost ever since' 25 June: first at Cassiobury, as a guest of Lord Essex; then at his own house at Crawley, near Winchester; then at Little Somborne three miles away;

then back at Windsor: 'tomorrow', he adds, 'designing to go to Kensington'. Again in September 1743 he writes that shortly

> we set out for Bath . . . and shall return to Windsor to the Mayor's Feast. I shall then stay three or four days between this place [Cranbourne Lodge, outside Windsor] and Windsor and then go to Euston [near Thetford], but that I reckon will depend upon what account the Duke of Grafton has of the King's coming.

Such journeys often necessitated overnight travel. 'I . . . dined with my Lord Vere in town and came back at night [to Windsor]', he notes in June 1732; in the same letter he remarks that the Duke and Duchess of Devonshire have just set off overnight from London to Chatsworth. Otherwise, if it was a fairly long journey, the traveller had to set out at first light; and there was always the danger, even if it was a short stretch of three miles, of losing one's way and being overturned—as happened to his friend Jack Spencer between Somborne and Crawley, the roads being so bad.

The Duke was brought up at Windsor, and educated at nearby Eton (from 1706 to 1707, aged ten and eleven) and subsequently at home; in 1714 he was at New College, Oxford and in 1716–1717 on the Grand Tour, accompanied by another close friend Lord Nassau Paulet. There are references to his being at Turin in October 1716 and at Rome in June of the following year. Paulet, in fact, was not only a close friend but a sort of cousin, being the son of the second Duke of Bolton by his third wife, Monmouth's illegitimate daughter; thus, the Duchess of Bolton was first cousin to St Albans. Needless to say, the young men's movements on the Continent were closely followed by Jacobite leaders such as Mar. St Albans, however, was to prove even more inexorable towards 'the King over the water' than his father had been.

His wife, Lucy Werden, came from the vicinity of Windsor. Her father Sir John sprang from a Cheshire family of self-made capitalists who had amassed their fortune as brewers and barons of the Exchequer at Chester after playing a somewhat equivocal part in the Civil War. Before living in Cheshire they had been established at Leyland in Lancashire, where Sir John still had an estate; an Orskell Werden was flourishing near Preston in 1530. Half of the Cheshire property was at Cholmon-deston, close to Nantwich; the remainder nearer Chester or in the county town itself. There were freeholds in the Strand, farms in York-shire, the Leigham Court estate at Streatham in Surrey, and farms and tithes in Berkshire at East Challow and Cholsey. Still in Berkshire, but within easier reach of Windsor and London, Sir John Werden had a house at Holyport, six miles from Windsor; this may only have been a rented house—perhaps, ironically enough, the mansion of Philiberts where Charles II had sometimes gone into amorous retreat with Nell!

St Albans married Lucy, then sixteen years of age, on 13 December 1722 at St Michael's, Bray, the parish church of Holyport. His brother Lord William Beauclerk married Lucy's younger half-sister Charlotte on the same day. Where the young Burfords lived after their marriage is not known: his father presumably kept the London house, now in Old Bond Street; and Burford House did not become his home, though nominally his, even after his succession to the dukedom. He was nego-tiating to rent a house from a Mrs Aldsworth when in July 1726 Sir John Werden came to the rescue, offering to share both Holyport and his keep-like Elizabethan manor-house at Burton, near Tarvin, with the young couple. Dame Judith Werden, Sir John's second wife, had died in the same week as the young Duke's father, and Sir John no doubt felt it would help both his elder daughter and himself if they were to share houses. 'He [is] to pay us so much a year and to have no further trouble', St Albans explained to Clavering. Lord and Lady William also came to live at Holyport in August 1726. But the Duke's stay both there and at Burton was unexpectedly short, and the same may be assumed of the William Beauclerks.

The problem was that Sir John Werden was contemplating a third marriage, which would seriously jeopardize the inheritance prospects of the Duke and his brother, whose wives were the sole surviving children of Sir John's first and second marriages. In August 1728 St Albans writes to Clavering:

Sir John Werden assures me he is not married nor has he any thoughts of marrying, for I was afraid the other day it was over.

He asked Billy if my sister [Lady William Beauclerk] could not see her in friendship, if such a thing was to be.

The problem whether to marry or not to marry may have continued for as long as two years, no doubt heightened by discreet pressure from both daughters—whose great expectations would have been smashed by the birth of a brother. By 14 November 1730 Werden's third marriage was an accomplished fact; his bride, a London merchant's daughter with a considerable dowry. St Albans confided to Clavering on 24 November:

I was very much surprised to hear of Sir John's being married for I really did believe him a man of honour. He wrote to me ten days ago to notify it but had not the impudence to mention his drab. I have not answered his letter, neither do I propose it; a civil letter I could not write and upon my brother William's account I would not write any other, so I think 'tis better left alone.

And the Duke stuck to his word, much to Sir John Werden's annoyance at finding his letter unanswered. St Albans repeated his position to Clavering on 17 December 1730:

By what you mention I find Sir John is angry at my not having answered his letter. I should have done it if my brother had been out of the case.

The reference to Werden's 'drab' implies that he had been carrying on an affair before his third marriage, an indulgence which greatly angered the Duke regardless of the fact that the 'drab' satisfied Sir John's needs of the flesh whilst leaving the inheritance prospects intact. As it was, there was now the possibility of a son being born to his father-in-law, with the consequent loss of four or five valuable properties—not to mention the as yet completely undeveloped Adelphi site.

The Duke might have done better to remain under his father-in-law's roof, thus making Sir John's marriage more difficult to bring about. Instead, by June 1728 he had moved to a rented house at Frogmore (only a short distance from Windsor Castle and Burford House); and so began the succession of rented and grace-and-favour properties which included a rented house at Tidworth on the borders of Hampshire and Wiltshire,

Crawley Court between Winchester and Andover, and Cranbourne Lodge in Windsor Forest. There was never any question of Bestwood, which the Duke refers to in September 1726 as 'a cursed drinking-place', adding that his estate was hopelessly mismanaged. Just as St Albans moved from Holyport into rented properties to keep clear of Sir John Werden, so in November 1728 Lord William's problem was solved with his appointment as Vice-Chamberlain of the Queen's Household, a post which carried a salary of £500 p.a.[1] together with a house in the Castle.

Sir John Werden did not have a son, or indeed any children, by his third wife, who died leaving her husband £30,000 in March 1733 after three years of marriage. 'He does not deserve so many pence' was his son-in-law's crushing comment to Clavering in the December. Undeterred by all these setbacks, Sir John proceeded to marry for a fourth time, in March 1734. The Beauclerks' consternation can be imagined, except that by then they had probably written him off as a law unto himself. He still failed to produce a son, though after a long interval of seven years another daughter arrived to threaten the plentiful inheritance for which her half-sisters had hoped. The second and last baronet outlived his St Albans daughter and son-in-law, and also Lord William Beauclerk, dying in 1758 in his seventy-fifth year. (Contrary to what is often written, even in eighteenth-century peerages, Lady William did not die in 1745 but on 3 July 1770.)

Tidworth was, and is, a fine Palladian house, square and elegant with handsome pedimented windows and an elaborate garden ornate with statuary. It belonged to an eccentric family, the Smiths, who achieved prominence when John Smith became Chancellor of the Exchequer in 1699 and afterwards (in 1705) Speaker of the House of Commons. On his death in 1723, his three sons inherited Tidworth in turn. It was from the eldest, Thomas, that St Albans took on the house, but no sooner had he done so than his landlord died. He writes on 18 August 1728 to Clavering:

I . . . lately have been in a great fuss about poor Tom Smith's death, there being no lease signed and having to do with so odd a fellow as the Colonel is. . . . He was taken ill at cards with the King on the

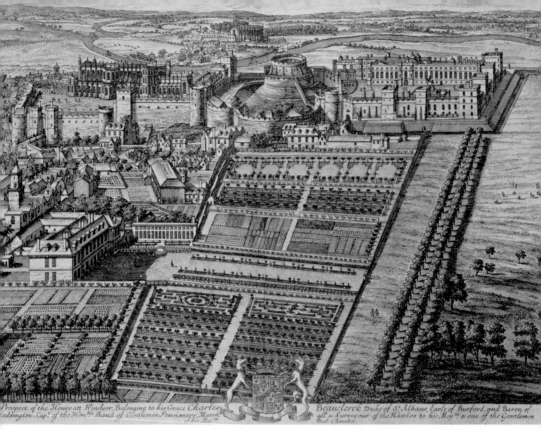

Burford House, Windsor: drawn by Leender Knyff, and engraved by Jan Kip, c. 1690.

The Twentieth and Last Earl of Oxford and his Wife: by Sir Peter Lely, c. 1673.
They were the parents of Diana, Duchess of St Albans.

The Second Duke of St Albans bearing the Queen's Crown at the Coronation of King George II, 11 October 1727: engraved by Thomas Medland after the painting by Thomas Stothard.

Tuesday night, went to town on the Wednesday and died on the Saturday' [3 August 1728].

St Albans asked his friend John Cope, later the General Cope defeated at Prestonpans, to speak to the next brother, Colonel Smith, in an attempt to regularize the lease; with Tom Smith it had only been an agreement by word of mouth. The Colonel honoured the oral promise, but would not lay out a farthing more on maintenance.

Of all the houses he occupied, St Albans seems to have enjoyed Tidworth the most. His near neighbours and friends were the Duke of Queensberry (whose wife was Gray's patroness) and Henry Hoare, grandson of the Richard Hoare with whom his father had banked, who had a house at Quarley—seven miles from the Smiths'—in addition to Stourhead. When the Queensberrys were at Amesbury Abbey, only about eight miles distant, St Albans would pay them a visit. One such visit is reported to Clavering in November 1728:

> Her Grace so extremely civil as I never saw anything like it. We left them at breakfast at half an hour past one, and Bludworth not then come down. I suppose his hair not quite set in order.

But the great advantages of Tidworth were its solitude and excellent hunting. As befitted a man who was soon to become Lord Warden of the Forest, St Albans was a passionately addicted huntsman. On one occasion (5 November 1728) Colonel Smith even went hunting with his tenant but did not stay at the house he himself owned, preferring a neighbour's hospitality. But though the Colonel was ready to honour his brother's promise, he would only do so for the period of time Tom Smith had specified.

By 1730, if not earlier, the Duke had removed himself to Crawley Court. This house, together with its home farm, was sublet to him by Anthony Henley, the rakish young Member of Parliament for Southampton who came into savage conflict with his constituents over the Excise Bill. Henley had the estate on a long lease from the Bishop of Winchester, whose successors owned it until 1869; but he was heavily in debt and could not afford to live there. Though rented, Crawley was often described in reference books as St Albans's 'seat'. The house, less than a

hundred years old, was 'a structure of brick, faced with stone, containing
several fine rooms'; the village was delightful, with a fourteenth-century
church near the park wall, and a street lined with thatched Tudor
cottages most of which were destroyed in the fire of 1738.

But Crawley was still not as agreeable as Tidworth. St Albans felt
obliged to dine out at least once or twice a week and so 'run the risk of
one's neck coming home'. Crawley Down was treacherous until the
mid-nineteenth century. In the parish churchyard there is still the stump
of a cross erected on the Andover road by an archdeacon who, after once
losing his way on a winter's evening in 1831, always hung a lantern on it
when he passed by at night.

Even after the suicide of Colonel Smith on 5 December 1731 the
'prodigious pleasant' Tidworth remained unattainable. His next and
youngest brother, a Captain Smith, was more eccentric still. A week
after the suicide St Albans writes to Clavering that much as he would
have liked to lease Tidworth again, 'the Captain is so strange a creature
that I am afraid 'tis to no purpose to think of it'. He had also had to
abandon the idea of taking over Abbotstone, a hunting-lodge belonging
to Nassau Paulet's half-brother the Duke of Bolton, near Old Alresford on
the other side of Winchester. In 1719 this had been described as:

> A large, noble brick house edged with stone built for the Duke of
> Bolton for a convenient hawking-seat of which sport he was a great
> admirer, in allusion whereof he caused two vast large hawks to be
> fixed on top of the two banqueting houses just before entering into
> the house.

Queen Anne had been entertained there. By 1731, however, it had
become a ruin and the Duke had to admit, sadly, that he 'never saw a
place so out of repair. One side of the house is sunk a foot, that without a
good deal of money laid out it would be impossible to live there, and that
neither of us could afford to lay out'. Sir John Werden was still very much
alive! Abbotstone was allowed to remain in a crumbling condition and
by 1769 it had become derelict, when its materials went into the rebuilding of Old Alresford Church.

Unable to afford Abbotstone and failing to lease Tidworth again,

St Albans continued in his occupancy of Crawley (hunting across the downs, and becoming more and more friendly with 'Bad' Jack Spencer and his brother Lord Sunderland, whose houses were at Rookley and Somborne nearby) until by 1734 his thoughts were increasingly turning to Cranbourne. No letter from Crawley can be dated with certainty after 2 September 1734.

Cranbourne was the grace-and-favour house granted to him in his capacity as Lord Warden of the Forest at Windsor, to which he had been appointed on 26 May 1730. On the very same day he was made Constable and Governor of Windsor Castle: the offices were seldom jointly held, and it was a mark of George II's favour that he forced Lord Carlisle to resign the governance of the Castle to the Duke. St Albans, in fact, was a great favourite with the King, who in 1728 gave him permission to build a door into the Home Park from Burford House; Lord Egremont records that once in January 1730 the King snubbed all the other lords at Court, speaking only to the Duke of St Albans. Queen Caroline's decision to make Windsor her principal summer residence dates from about the same year and it is not surprising that the King should have asked St Albans to supervise the building arrangements, the renovation and the furnishing. Perhaps it was in this connection that we find St Albans writing to the Duchess of Portland:

> When your goods are removed out of the Tower, ... you will order the keys to be delivered to my servants here, whom I shall order to take care of the apartments. I hope I shall be satisfied ... as your Ladyship makes so little use of them'.[2]

The Duke seems to have made greater use of his own apartments in the Round Tower; he had no need to rely on Burford House as a Windsor residence, and indeed until 1742 his mother presumably lived at Burford.

Cranbourne Lodge was a mere five miles out of Windsor. Anne Hyde, the first wife of James II, was born at the original house in 1637, and according to Pepys, James and his brother Charles II had once been 'hopelessly drunk there after hunting'. Prince Rupert actually lived there for a while. In 1711 it was rebuilt around the old tower dating back to early Tudor or even earlier times—a tower which is still standing today, although the rest of the house was demolished on William IV's orders about 1830. Soon after its rebuilding in 1711 Celia Fiennes described the Lodge as a fine square house, with fourteen windows along the front and extensive gardens. Not long after 1711 the first Duke of St Albans had lived there for a time. In 1722 John, Duke of Marlborough died there. The fact that Cranbourne did not always go with the Lord Wardenship may explain why St Albans only received it in 1733. By then it was in a dilapidated condition: yet another indication, like Abbotstone, of how rapidly houses were sometimes allowed to deteriorate in the eighteenth century.

> I shall desire, [writes the Duke in May 1734], to have this repaired and not pulled down. The gardens are in a very ruinous condition. I don't propose keeping them as they were kept but I hope to have them in a little better order in time.

This suggests that prior to 1733 the Lodge may have stood empty. Work on the house and gardens continued for two and a half years, though by September 1735 there had been 'such an alteration as you would scarcely know it'. By that time the Duke was in the habit of going down for a few days to supervise the workmen. The terrace was expected to be finished before Christmas 1735; he was making a haha in August 1736. In a delightful comment on the usefulness of the work on which so many had laboured for so long, he observes to Clavering in June 1740: 'I come here pretty constantly and dine two or three times a week. It is a little variety, and indeed I can't help thinking the place pretty enough'. Cranbourne Lodge was little more than a gigantic summerhouse.

What were the duties which earned him such an expensive toy? In Cranbourne Chase, and over a large terrain extending from Sunninghill to Finchampstead and from Sandhurst to Old Windsor, he and a chief secretary Philip Rendick supervised over thirty rangers, keepers, bailiffs, underkeepers, gamekeepers, vermin-killers etc. whose task it was to maintain the Royal parks and forest, provide hay for the deer, police the hunting and shooting, and mark the deer, cows and hogs.[3] For St Albans himself it was not an onerous responsibility. There is no reference either to these duties or to his supervision of the castle repairs in his extensive correspondence with John Clavering. Later in his life, his duties as Lord Warden involved him with George II's son the Duke of Cumberland in the remodelling of the new Ascot racecourse, where the first meeting was held in June 1751, a month before his death.

But the biggest way in which the duties of Lord Warden impinged on his personal life was in his quarrel with Sarah, Duchess of Marlborough. He had control of Windsor Forest and outlying parks; the 'Old Fury', as he liked to describe his opponent, was Ranger of Windsor Great Park and claimed jurisdiction over both that and the Home Park. To get from the Round Tower of Windsor Castle to Cranbourne Lodge, it was easiest for the Duke to pass across his own garden, through the gate granted him in 1728, and down the Long Walk; thence into the Great Park. Years before he had been allowed to walk in the Home Park by the great Duke of Marlborough, and the quarrel had first flared up when Lord Burford (as he then was) called Sarah 'without the least provocation of any kind . . . such names . . . as I never yet saw written', and tried 'to break my servant's head and to send him home all bloody and his clothes torn off his back'.

The grant he received from Queen Caroline was 'to go through the [Home] Park with mortices' (20 September 1735), and from George II 'to pass through the said park on horseback or in a chaise with one horse' (21 May 1736), but according to Sarah he far exceeded the privileges allowed him. Not only did he have duplicate keys cut, handing them out to his friends and giving them to his staff so that they could let cattle in to graze; the height of iniquity came when he actually had the temerity to drive through the Home Park in a coach and four. Not even Prince Rupert, when he was Constable and Governor, had presumed to do such a thing—even though he too held Cranbourne Lodge. In those days the Home Park was laid out like a formal garden with parterres, but if the Duke of St Albans was allowed to have his way he 'would bring that most beautiful park into the same condition as Hyde Park is by allowing a road out of Grosvenor Square'!

Sarah ordered her keepers to stop him if he was seen riding through in a coach, or on horseback in the company of other people; in March 1739 the locks on gates leading into the Home Park were changed and St

Albans was only provided with a new key on the strict understanding that he would have no further copies made. She had prevailed in the Home Park, for the time being, though not even she could countermand St Albans's special privilege of riding through 'on horseback or in a chaise with one horse'; in the Great Park, on the other hand, her orders were absolute: on no account must that 'man of so very little consequence', that 'insolent idiot' be allowed in. As to the gates leading from the Great Park to Cranbourne Lodge, they were chained up; 'but to be sure such a mad fool as he is will break them down again; and I believe there is nothing to be done but to go to law with him. . . . He has no more right to come into that park, otherwise than I allow it, than he has to make a door in my garden to go to Whitehall through St James's Park'.

The Marlboroughs do not come well out of this dispute, particularly as Sarah had opened the Great Park to a previous occupant of Cranbourne, Lord Ranelagh, 'whom I allowed to have everything, because he was my friend'. It is hard to recognize Clavering's friendly correspondent in the man whom Marlborough, her grandson, calls 'silly and impertinent' and on whom she showers abuse: 'I am contented and glad', she writes in 1738, 'to have nothing more to do with his Grace, who has many contradictions in him, a great deal of pride and dirty meanness, for which there is no excuse but ignorance and folly'. Though St Albans may at times have given way to a violent temper, there is little or no trace of violent resentment in the Clavering letters. He does, however, indulge in a few stories at Sarah's expense. He remarks in July 1732:

> She has actually burnt her will. The courage of the Old Fury at above seventy, for it will take up some time to make another. The young Duchess [her daughter] is for having her proved lunatic and locked up. She was always of opinion she was mad but was now convinced. About fifty years ago she did much a thing; a fine picture the Duke had of the Duchess of Cleveland upon some fit of jealousy she cut out the face of it, and at another time because the Duke was fond of her head of hair she cut it quite off.

The dispute was more embarrassing in that St Albans was friendly with Jack Spencer, one of Sarah's grandsons. It was finally stilled when Sarah died at the advanced age of eighty-four in October 1744.

From the harassments of supervising the building at Windsor, renovating Cranbourne Lodge and quarrelling with Sarah, Charlton—near Goodwood in Sussex—made a pleasant interlude. Hunting in the early eighteenth century was a more genial and leisurely occupation than at any time before or since. Not only did great magnates, such as the Duke of Beaufort and Lord Tankerville, have their own private hunts, maintained without subscription; noblemen and gentlemen came from all over the country to stay at the hunt's headquarters, where the richer members built themselves small lodges or hunting-boxes whilst the remainder slept at inns or with the tenantry. But, as in a club, meals were taken together and banqueting halls specially built for the purpose. On the Duke of Bolton's estate at Abbotstone there were actually two banqueting halls; at Charlton one large hall was built, in which on one unique occasion seven crowned heads ate with the party.

Charlton was only three miles from Goodwood House, yet the Duke of Richmond built himself a fine lodge, Fox Hall, which still stands today. Even a hunting-box had to be designed in miniature Palladian style, with one well-proportioned bedroom on the first floor (complete with wind-clock, oil paintings and marble mantelpiece) whilst the ground floor no doubt served the purpose of a club or inn parlour during the day. The Dukes of Devonshire and St Albans also built their own hunting-lodges, and—*sic transit gloria mundi*—some remains of the latter are still in use as a sheep-pen. St Albans came regularly to Charlton between 1734 and 1746, usually in November and even (in 1735) staying there till about Christmas. In 1739 and 1746 he was still at Charlton on 25 February. Amongst the friends he enjoyed meeting there were Clavering's nephew Lord Cowper, and Lords Harcourt, Lincoln, Hartington and Dalkeith (a great-grandson of Monmouth). In 1740 he also leased a house and stables at Findon, twenty-three miles from Charlton, but did not use them himself, lending them instead to Harcourt. There was usually a drift away from Sussex as the opera season began.

Charlton was not to have a long history of privileged ease. With Richmond's death in 1750 the hunt lost both its master and its animating spirit. His son, the third Duke, moved the pack from Charlton to Goodwood; the hunt became less of a national centre, the domed banqueting hall was pulled down in 1758, and the hounds were eventually destroyed by rabies. Fox Hall remained unoccupied for nearly a hundred years, though it has since been converted into a private house.

Building a hunting-lodge of his own at Charlton, and leasing a house and stables at Findon which he did not personally need, St Albans seems at this time to have been more affluent than in any other phase of his life. A quite different man from the one who had regretfully abandoned the idea of acquiring Abbotstone in 1731, he actually moved on a par with Richmond, whose family's recently purchased Goodwood was destined in the much longer term to completely outshine Bestwood. At Hoares Bank, where he opened an account on 7 January 1740 with a note for £4,800, he was very amply in credit during the short period he remained their customer: £14,327-10-9d was paid in between 7 January 1740 and 11 February of the same year, with withdrawals between 10 January and 10 March 1740 amounting to over £9,767; but the account was virtually closed by April 1741.

There is some evidence for supposing that St Albans had been involved as a shareholder in the South Sea Bubble disaster, in view of his frequent references to it in the Clavering correspondence. If so, he was (like so many of his contemporaries) as unskilled in finance as in politics. As a politician he was completely out of his depth, a fact he was only too ready to admit to John Clavering. Wisely, he seldom spoke in Parliament, and unwisely voted sometimes for and sometimes against the Government in a discussion of the South Sea Company in 1733; hesitancy which earned him the biting opprobrium of Lord Hervey: 'one of the weakest men either of the legitimate or spurious brood of the Stuarts'. But there was one political fact he was always aware of, that he must emphasize his loyalty to the Hanoverians, disowning the Jacobites entirely and even, if necessary, disparaging the Scots.

At the outbreak of the 1745 Rebellion even he had to bestir himself. Until then he had played no more of a military than a political role. He had not in fact served in the army at all, which made his appointment as a Knight of the Bath in 1725 a little curious—except that George I revived this military order for his favourites. As strongly as he could, this favourite now rallied support for the Crown. Though worried by the turn of events, he refused to remain uncommitted. Eight days after the Young Pretender was proclaimed at Perth, he wrote to Clavering of the 'low Scotch cunning' of the turncoats and looked forward to the Dutch regiments' arrival at Gravesend, and 'then some of the neutral princes in Scotland will declare for us'. Lord George Murray, William Murray and Lords Nairne and Ogilvy had already joined the Pretender.

Two days later (14 September 1745) St Albans was hoping for reinforcements from Maria Theresa in return for British support of her in the War of the Austrian Succession. 'Come in she must, I think, as we pay', he argued, referring to the subsidies by which Britain had been helping her to resist Prussia; furthermore, it had been agreed on 4 June 1745 that 7,100 infantrymen and 900 hussars from Maria Theresa's army should be placed under the Duke of Cumberland's command till 31 May 1746 and that, of these, six infantry battalions, five companies of grenadiers and six squadrons of hussars were to be immediately transferred to the British pay-roll. These soldiers presumably crossed the Channel, helping to relieve St Albans's anxiety.

By 19 September 1745 Prince Charles had been proclaimed at Edinburgh, but for St Albans (his second cousin!) there was a crumb of comfort. The rebels were apparently short of money and arms.

> I hear they are quarrelling and plundering, but it is thought they
> will go to Glasgow which is a rich place for a town in Scotland. I
> hope they will spare the Marquis of Tweeddale's house. . . .

Far from sparing the house of Jack Spencer's brother-in-law, the Young Pretender actually used it as his headquarters, and to make matters worse inflicted a crushing defeat on Cope at Prestonpans. As the rebels' strength grew into October, the Duke became more scathing towards the Scots, and more active in resistance. In conversation with the Murrays on 22 October, 'I could not help laying into the Scotch, for they have now proved themselves what I always thought they were'. He even agreed with Nassau Paulet's brother-in-law Lord Leicester 'that the Union is dissolved, and that if we get the better they ought to be looked upon as a conquered nation'.

Even after Culloden (16 April 1746) there were renewed fears. With the Young Pretender's escape from Scotland in the following September, a further invasion seemed possible, indeed likely. And, minus the Dutch and Hessians, next time Britain might be less prepared. It is curious to find St Albans writing to Clavering in 1747: 'you know the last [project] eighteen months ago was only a pretence of' the Jacobites;

> I wish we were as well provided now with troops, and as we are not am a good deal more uneasy now than I was then, not that I thought the last a joke ...

The events of September 1745, far from being a joke, had made him unusually single-minded and energetic. Hearing from the Southern Secretary, Newcastle, that 'treasonable practices were carrying on at Reading', he had acted in his capacity as Lord Lieutenant of Berkshire, summoning the deputy lieutenants and magistrates to a hastily convened meeting in the county town on 12 October, but without finding proof of any conspiracy. A further meeting was arranged for 2 November 1745, 'when I shall propose an association and subscription as has been done in other counties'.

Otherwise, he was perfectly happy to perform his Court duties, with the more ceremonial—and less arduous—functions of Lord Warden of the Forest for good measure. At the coronation of George II he bore the Queen's Crown, whilst the Duke of Dorset bore the King's. In April 1736 he attended the Prince of Wales's wedding to Princess Augusta of Saxe-Gotha, dressed in a suit of gold brocade that had cost over £300.[4] In 1738 he was appointed a Lord of the Bedchamber, at a salary of £1,000 p.a.[5] The Clavering letters occasionally mention his turns of duty at Kensington, exchanging stints with Lord Fauconberg who 'is obliged to go into Yorkshire', or being relieved by the Duke of Manchester who travels to London specially for that purpose, after which 'I shall set out for Cranbourne'. Until one realizes how closely he was involved with the Court as Constable of Windsor Castle, Lord Warden of the Forest and as a man anxious to affirm his allegiance to the House of Hanover, it is astonishing—almost incredible—how keenly concerned he was with the King's movements. From Windsor he writes on 15 September 1732:

'As soon as the wind comes east, I will come [to London] to be there against His Majesty's arrival'. And again in 1736: 'They say the King will be over by the middle of October, but that you know must depend upon the wind'.

George II always liked to be in England for the official Birthday (30 October), but dreaded the crossing from Helvoetsluys to Margate; meanwhile, in England his courtiers listened for news of the Royal Yacht. Occasionally, the King arrived earlier than expected. In 1747 St Albans asks Clavering if he might use his room in Kensington Palace to change in, after the journey from Cranbourne; 'not thinking the King's coming so soon my house is painting'.

Even his country-house visits were regulated by the King's arrival. In 1743 a journey to Euston would have been prevented if the King had arrived early. When Queen Charlotte seemed to be recovering from the uterine hernia which shortly afterwards led to her death, he wrote from Charlton (fifty-eight miles from London): 'I propose now coming for a day to congratulate'. He may have been right in the early years of the reign to paint himself as 'a very bad courtier', going 'but seldom to Kensington, and in the summer never to town but when obliged', but he certainly became more assiduous on his appointment as a Lord of the Bedchamber. 'Tomorrow', he writes in August 1747, 'I shall go to Swinley to meet the Royal Family hunting'; probably it was such duties that pleased him most of all, combining his attendance as a courtier with his undoubted love of the countryside and forests. In 1741 such assiduity gained him a place in the Order of the Garter.

All in all, it was an agreeable existence. The Windsor Forest which appealed to Alexander Pope exerted no less a charm on him; and the New Forest was more spectacular still. His Court and social connections gave him a vivid prospect of life in the metropolis, of Lord Burlington preparing a splendid entertainment at Chiswick in 1732 and of Sir Robert Walpole preparing another almost in rivalry; the Prime Minister 'has furnished Chelsea and brought his fine pictures there. His dessert [service] cost, they say, £700'; at Hampton Court in 1728 St Albans 'saw Their Majesties dine in public'. His long succession of country-house visits, and stays in his own houses, were mingled with hunting and shooting whenever possible. He was always rather bored with the newfangled custom of going to Bath to take the waters but was delighted by his visits to the Duke of Bolton at Hooke Court, Dorset; the Duke of Kingston's house at West Dean, near Salisbury; Wilton; Cassiobury; Hackwood; Somborne; Stowe; Langley; Euston; and many other estates.

> I never saw anything more agreeable than my Lord Cobham's [Stowe]: the house not a bad one, the gardens charming, and woods that he is laying into his park with ridings through them that are very fine.

Hunting-lodges such as his own at Charlton and the Duke of Richmond's Boldre Wood, near Lymington, gave him the agreeable variety of a country-house visit together with a sense of the magic of a forest in autumn. During a London winter there was the more refined magic of Handel and Senesino. And there were always letters to write, in which the Duke cultivated his gift of crisp irony—not only on the subject of Sir John Werden, but (for instance) on Windsor Corporation:

> My friends in the Corporation dine with me. We shall be about twenty. I am sure you envy me.

Sometimes we can picture the quill pen moving across the paper, so sharp is the sense of immediacy. 'I am not yet dressed', he scribbles to Clavering on a Sunday morning in December 1733.

> The clock has struck eleven and I expect to hear the bell for church every minute that I can say no more at present.

NOTES TO CHAPTER II

Archives of Hoares Bank.
Archives of Drummonds Bank.
Hertfordshire RO: letters of 2nd Duke of St Albans and Lord William Beauclerk to John Clavering (Panshanger Collection).
Letters in the Spencer archives (Althorp).
G. E. Cokayne: *Complete Baronetage*, 1900–1909.
W. H. St J. Hope: *op. cit.*
H. Hughes: *Cheshire and its Welsh Border*, 1966.
Earl of March (later 8th Duke of Richmond): *Records of the Old Charlton Hunt*, 1910.
Earl of March: *A Duke and his Friends*, 1911.
G. Ormerod: *The History of the County Palatine and City of Chester*, 1882.
F. W. Pledge: *Crawley. Glimpses into the Past of a Hampshire Parish*, 1907.
J. E. Sheppard: *Memorials of St James's Palace*, 1894.
T. Wotton: *The English Baronetage*, 1741.

---

1. RA 54007.
2. Portland Papers (Nottingham University) PWE 2.
3. RA CP70/119.
4. *Gentleman's Magazine*, April 1736, 230.
5. See Chapter 1, note 5.

CHAPTER III

Milord Saint-Alban

Little is known of the early life of the second Duke's only son and heir George, whose boyhood and adolescence are as obscure as his later escapades were notorious. He was born on 25 June 1730, probably at Crawley, and educated at Eton from 1742 to 1748. Whilst still at school he is said to have produced an illegitimate son, who died at Brussels in 1758. The second Duke writes to John Clavering on 6 August 1747 that Lord Burford 'is at home upon account of the election': Burford's uncle, Lord George Beauclerk, was re-elected as MP for Windsor on 13 August 1747 and altogether held the seat for twenty-three years in the Whig interest. What contribution the young man could make to Lord George's re-election is uncertain. Judging from his adult life, it would not have been a positive or practical one except that the Hogarthian scenes of debauchery associated with election campaigns in the mid-eighteenth century must have been to his taste. He succeeded to the dukedom on 27 July 1751, on the death of his father, and thus was in a position to launch into politics on his own account, being just of age.

From his father he inherited not only the dukedom but an expectation of the continuance of public offices. Two days after the second Duke's death he was elected High Steward of Windsor (being sworn in three weeks later, on 22 August). In August 1751 George II appointed him a Lord of the Bedchamber, which meant £1,000 p.a. in additional income[1]. And in December of the same year he was installed as Lord Lieutenant of Berkshire, the third generation of his family to occupy that office.

With the second Duke's death, however, two offices of profit and honour passed from the family. The young heir was not continued as Lord Warden of the Forest, the King's son and the victor of Culloden, William Duke of Cumberland, having the preference; and with the Lord

Wardenship of the Forest went Cranbourne Lodge. Nor did the young St Albans become Constable and Governor of Windsor Castle, an appointment which was conferred instead on the fourth Earl of Cardigan (later first Duke of Montagu). And with the office of Constable and Governor of Windsor Castle went the rooms in the Round Tower occupied by his father; St Albans, of course, still retained Burford House, which was a freehold. The fact that he did not obtain the Court appointments specifically connected with Windsor must probably be put down to his extreme youth in September 1751 (Cardigan was thirty-nine and Cumberland thirty): he had discredited himself, and was living out of the country, by the time he might have expected to succeed to them.

Of the three offices in which George Duke of St Albans succeeded his father, the Lordship of the Bedchamber—with its general but fairly light Court duties—must have been by far the most gratifying. Its £1,000 p.a. was desperately needed. Even at this early stage in the family's history, its fortunes in relation to families of comparable status were decidedly precarious. Despite the second Duke's sybaritic existence, renting the lovely Georgian Tidworth, building himself a hunting-lodge at Charlton, entertaining Jack Spencer at Crawley, he had done nothing to augment the family's finances in the short term. Indeed, he had tended to dilapidate them. He had married an heiress, but neither he nor his wife outlived her father, the redoubtable Sir John. And so it was necessary for the young St Albans to look round for an heiress himself: an heiress with one inestimable advantage over his own mother in that the fortune to which she was heir was already hers. By 1752 he was already in debt to the tune of £9,000.

Not that this was the only step he might have taken to restore the family's crumbling position. The Registrarship of the Court of Chancery granted to Nell Gwyn, the first Duke and his son had been surrendered by the second Duke on 24 January 1726, about four months before he came into the title. It was regranted to him for his own life in 1727, but without the addition of further lives—if only because at that time he had no son. Now that the son he lacked in 1727 had actually succeeded to the dukedom, it only needed a convincing application to the King for the grant of at least one further life to secure the £1,000 p.a. which went to dukes of St Albans out of the fees of the Court of Chancery: this £1,000 p.a.—sometimes a little more, sometimes a little less—would have been a welcome addition to the meagre £3,000 p.a. to which the third Duke of St Albans was entitled from his Bestwood rents, emoluments as Lord of the Bedchamber, net salary as Hereditary Grand Falconer and pension from the tax on logwood.

But the young man did not bestir himself on the subject, either now or later, and when in 1764 efforts were being successfully made to add his life to the patent of Hereditary Registrar of the High Court of Chancery it was his uncle, Lord Vere of Hanworth, who took up the matter with the then Prime Minister, George Grenville. Obviously the twenty-two-year-old duke must have found the quest of a rich heiress much more to his taste, but by an abler man the two objectives could have been pursued together.

Jane Roberts, of Glassenbury Park near Cranbrook in Kent, was the younger and only surviving daughter of Sir Walter Roberts, sixth baronet, who had died in 1745 when she was fourteen years old. Sir Walter had also had a son and heir, Thomas Roberts, but he—conveniently for the Duke of St Albans—had died in November 1727 aged four months. A portrait by Nathaniel Hone, which is still at Glassenbury, shows Jane and her elder sister Elizabeth, who died aged fourteen in February 1743. Surprisingly perhaps, the Roberts family were of Scottish, not Welsh, extraction; they had long been settled in Kent. Their property stretched from Cranbrook to Brenchley, including land in Goudhurst and Hunton: in the latter village they had another fine house, Gennings, which was the house Jane always preferred. In Surrey, forty miles nearer London, were the manors of Streatham and Peckham. In Leicestershire the Robertses held the manors of Wigston Magna, Frisby and Galby.

The mansion at Glassenbury was approached by a bridge over a moat; a forecourt separated the moat from the front of the house, but the sides and back of the building plunged sheer into the water. An oak tree said to have been mentioned in the Domesday Book stood not far from the forecourt, and on the terrace beside the moat—at the top of the bowling green—was a Chinese temple. A lime avenue led down to the lake.

As a girl, under her father's tutelage, she was brought up at Glassen-

Jane, Duchess of St Albans: attributed to Thomas Hudson, c. 1753.

Mademoiselle La P___e.　　　　　*The D. of S. A.*

The Third Duke of St Albans and his Mistress, Marie Petit: engravings published in *The Oxford Magazine* in November 1773. The miniaturist is unknown.
A miniature of the third Duke by Gervase Spencer, dated 1754, was sold at Christie's (lot 134) on 20 February 1973.

Cranbourne Lodge, Windsor in the time of the Second Duke: engraved by Samuel Hollyers after the drawing by Henry Perr.
The house in the middle ground has been demolished, and only the Tower remains.

bury. After his death it seems that she lived mostly with her guardians, since the estate accounts show that from 1747 a certain Thomas Greenhill tenanted the farmland at Hunton and occupied the house and grounds of Gennings whilst Glassenbury stood empty. Her guardians, Lord Romney and Sir Philip Boteler, both had houses in Kent: the former lived at the Mote, Maidstone and at Cuxton; the latter at Barham Court, Teston—quite close to Gennings. It was at Barham Court that St Albans gained the affection of Jane Roberts, now aged twenty or twenty-one. He flattered her, writes John Aikin in his *History of the Environs of London*,[2]

> That she should have the most superb equipage of any lady in England; forgetting the promise she made to Sir Philip and Lady Boteler not to listen to his addresses, they having humanely cautioned her against his attack by showing the profligacy of his character, Miss Roberts became a duchess, and the most unhappy of women—she soon gave place to the lowest female in her house. Some little time before her death, a gentleman hearing her Grace mention her sister, observed that her dying young was a fortunate event; she replied, 'By no means, Sir: if she had lived I should not have been an object to gratify avarice, nor a dupe to grandeur'.

Her much-needed dowry of £125,000 'procured her the splendid misery' (in Aikin's phrase) of being married to St Albans at St George's, Hanover Square on 23 October 1752. The bridegroom's uncle Lord James Beauclerk, Bishop of Hereford, performed the ceremony.

The marriage settlement, dated 21 October 1752,[3] had as its trustees the Duke of Dorset (a neighbour from Knole), Thomas Lambard (of North Ash Manor), Sir Philip Boteler, Lord Romney, Lord Vere of Hanworth and Lord Henry Beauclerk (uncles of the bridegroom), Lord Folkestone and Gabriel Hanger. Just prior to her marriage Jane had presumably been living at the house of Gabriel Hanger, who was her father's first cousin, as his accounts for her board and maintenance until 19 October 1752 still exist. Between Sir Walter Roberts's death and Jane's marriage seven years afterwards Hanger drew allowances for her upkeep amounting to about £3,750 in all, so that she must also have spent a fair amount of her time at Hanger's house at Driffield in Gloucestershire, in addition to her stays with Lord Romney and Sir Philip Boteler.

In the marriage settlement it was agreed that, in consideration of a sum of £400 p.a. to be paid to Jane in four equal instalments, St Albans should have the right to draw 'the whole rents, issues and profits of the ... manors and premises'; if she were to predecease him, the usufruct would remain his for life; if there were to be sons of the marriage, the estates would descend in fee simple to the eldest son and so on by primogeniture through the male lines of their issue; failing male descendants of the Duke and Duchess of St Albans, Glassenbury, Gennings and the other estates would pass 'in tail male with remainder' to 'the heirs male of Jane Roberts by any husband she might marry after George Duke of St Albans's death'; failing which the property was to be equally divided between any daughters of Jane Roberts and George Duke of St Albans; and there were stringent safeguards against the felling of any timber on the estates 'without the consent of the said Jane Roberts, his intended wife, testified in writing'.

An estate so effortlessly captured and so efficiently placed under the Beauclerks' control and ultimate ownership must, in 1752, have seemed the salvation of a duke who owed Drummonds Bank £5,000 on two separate mortgages and a further £4,000 to creditors in Brussels. There was also the possibility of a sizable inheritance from Sir John Werden, providing he did not marry yet again and produce a son, and this inheritance came a step nearer with the death of the Duke's mother, a co-heiress of Sir John Werden, in November 1752.

Even today Georgian Glassenbury could still have been the principal seat of the St Albans family, just as Euston Hall became the principal seat of the Graftons through marriage with an heiress or Chelsea came largely to the then impoverished Cadogans through marriage with a daughter of Sir Hans Sloane. This would have happened if George and Jane had had male issue descending to the present day. But the marriage quickly proved a disaster. St Albans is said to have been cruel and unfeeling towards his wife; they parted, childless, within two and a half years.

On 15 April 1755 the separation was agreed: St Albans made his wife two annual payments, the £400 p.a. originally set aside for her as pin-money together with an additional £1,600 p.a.,[4] but retained the free-hold of the Leicestershire estates which had become his absolute property when he married. Jane chose to live at Gennings with a dear companion, Fanny Davies, whilst Glassenbury stood empty.

Whatever the allegations of cruelty and insensitivity made against St Albans—and it is frankly impossible to place the onus for the break-down of his marriage—it is a fact that the separation was a tragedy from the family's point of view. Both perhaps had married too young, and she perhaps—orphaned from her mother at thirteen, from her father at four-teen, and having previously lost a sister whom she knew and loved, and a brother she never knew—needed a specially affectionate and consider-ate husband. Both too, perhaps, had come into their great stations in life at too early an age. As it was, St Albans still derived a great financial comfort, if no other, from his unfortunate and unhappy marriage, for by the terms of the marriage and separation settlements the revenues of the Roberts estates were his for life providing he continued to pay her £2,000 p.a. and allowed her to reside at Gennings.

Like stars shooting at different tangents and destined only to meet briefly and sadly again, St Albans and Jane Roberts now proceeded to lead lives as various as their habits were incompatible. As she continued in a long diminuendo amongst the orchards of Kent, with the occasional visit to her house in St James's Place, he launched—however reluctantly—into a glittering crescendo of feats of incompetence quite unparalleled in the lives of any other dukes in the eighteenth century, and involving mistresses, elopements, debts, bankruptcy, fleeing from creditors, self-imposed exile, imprisonment, and the procreation of illegitimate children.

Twice, we are told, he had to flee abroad to avoid creditors. In 1755–1756 we find him, then aged twenty-five or twenty-six, eloping to Paris with Molly, a Windsor dairymaid. By her he produced a son, George, who died in the following year. Like a man who only finds his youth in middle age, he then undertook a Grand Tour, travelling with Lord Archer's son, Andrew, to Geneva. This autonomous Calvinist republic seems a strange place for a man as fiery and dissipated as St Albans to go to, for it was in that very year that d'Alembert attacked the city for refusing even to possess a theatre. The fifth Earl of Gainsborough, however, was to die there on his travels, aged eighteen, in 1759, and Gibbon visited Geneva and lived at Lausanne in 1763.

The Paris of Mme de Pompadour, Sophie Arnould and Marie Fel was a far more attractive haunt to a man of his leanings; and in a city that contained everything, even the society of Diderot and Mme du Deffand, Montesquieu and Mme Geoffrin, we find him mixing with opera singers who rapidly divested him of his money, plunging him into such dire straits that he was rumoured to have shot himself on his way to Italy; but, according to a family tradition, Sophie Arnould herself was one of the opera singers in St Albans's circle: she is even said to have been his mistress, but this would have been at the very beginning of her career (which was in 1757), the Duke was certainly her inferior both in intelligence and wit, and in *Arnoldiana*—the book of her published witticisms—there is no mention of him by name.

His 'great fondness for the fair sex' is in fact the main theme of *Memoirs of the Duke of St Albans*, a satirical sketch of this rake's progress published in a newspaper in November 1773. This passion, besides perhaps causing him to undervalue Sophie Arnould, involved him in many escapades and misfortunes. Hotfoot to Venice, he indulged in 'salacious' debauchery, and damaged his health. Brussels was the next capital to which he turned: whether for recuperation or for further indulgence, the *Memoirs* do not relate. But, at any rate, within a short time of his arrival in the Austrian Netherlands he had formed a liaison with a spurious *marquise*, and friendships with all kinds of confidence tricksters including cardsharpers and an intriguer masquerading as an army captain. At one game of piquet he lost 1,000 ducats (the rough equivalent, in modern terms, of £1,000), then borrowed another 2,000 ducats, and in a single evening is said to have lost over 10,000. The outcome of his gambling sprees was that he was arrested for debt, but allowed out on parole in Brussels.

Brussels was a great attraction to English and other foreign nobility in the mid-eighteenth century. The sixth Earl of Kellie, for instance, lived in Brussels for some time and died there in 1781. In the year of Lord Kellie's death Aubrey Beauclerk, later to become fifth Duke of St Albans, was also visiting there. And as many of the nobility, both native and foreign, were in the habit of running up huge debts, St Albans felt himself entirely at home. It was also a city of exceptional beauty, of which the Comte de Ségur has left a description surprisingly at variance with the present face of the Belgian capital.

Brussels was, he writes, 'one of the finest, largest and best situated cities not only in Brabant but in the whole of Europe'. Its old quarters preserved 'an aspect so singularly picturesque with their sloping and tortuous streets, the fine *hôtels* of darkened stone sculptured in the Spanish fashion, and the magnificence of the Place de l'Hôtel de Ville'. The Parc de Bruxelles, much more spacious than nowadays, was filled with rare trees and fragrant flowers. The Forêt de Soignes, a mile or two to the south-east, provided great numbers of stags and roe deer for the incessant hunting-parties. A century before St Albans's time, Jean Puget de la Serre had actually called it a Paradise on earth. It was a Paradise which welcomed the sensuous delights of the flesh, so far as this nobleman was concerned, and where shame was comparatively unknown. In December 1756 a daughter Anne-Amélie was born to him, apparently the result of an earlier frolic in Brussels, before the revels in Paris and Venice; a bastard son followed hard on her tracks in September 1757; twin daughters Mariette-Victoire-Rose and Marie-Agnès arrived in December 1758. Of the son Horace Walpole acidly remarks in a letter to Sir Horace Mann, dated 9 February 1758:

> The simple Duke of St Albans who is retired to Brussels for debt, has made a most sumptuous funeral in public for a dab of five months old that he had by his cook-maid.

The Château d'Indevelde, at Eppegem, was the simple Duke's home in 1758.

Oddly enough, this mansion—otherwise known as Het Cattenhuys—had been the temporary headquarters of William of Orange after his defeat at Neerwinden in 1693; St Albans's grandfather must have known it well. The missives that poured from Indevelde in this St Albans's time gave Cobenzl, Prime Minister of the Austrian Netherlands, many headaches and no doubt some wry amusement. Believing that bandits lay in wait for him in the grounds of his château, he wrote asking Cobenzl to call in the mounted constabulary. On another occasion he might well have fallen foul of the law himself. Colliding with a carriage on his way home one evening, he and the servants on the carriage began lashing at one another with their whips. Afterwards he vainly urged Cobenzl to have the insolent lackeys imprisoned. Cobenzl suspected him of lashing out first.

The cause of St Albans's brief reappearance in England in 1759 was probably the man who had given his family more worry than any other person during the last thirty years, Sir John Werden. Aged seventy-four, Sir John had finally consented to die on 15 February 1758, at Holyport.[5] The land in Cheshire, Lancashire, Yorkshire, Berkshire, Surrey and London passed to the descendants of his daughter Lady William except that the third Duke benefited from a charge on the Werden estates and, in particular, from a life-interest in Durham Yard, a property between the Strand and the river Thames once owned by the Pembrokes, bought for Sir John Werden in 1716, and amazingly described in 1768 as 'an unprofitable heap of ruin'! _The Scots Magazine_ records that by the death of Sir John Werden 'a large estate comes to his grandson the Duke of St Albans', but this report may have been based on rumour and to some extent exaggerated. The 'unprofitable heap of ruin' in the Strand was not exploited until 1769.

It is a striking fact that in the will of Sir John Werden dated 31 July 1754 all the Cheshire estates are bequeathed to his wife Susanna during her lifetime and then to another Susanna, their daughter and only child. The will even refers in specific terms to Sir John's property within the city of Chester itself, his house and garden in Forest Street and fields on either side of the Dee. Yet Lady William's son Charles refers in his will, drawn up on 9 May 1775, eleven years before Dame Susanna's death, to property within the city of Chester, and it is certain that he—not Dame Susanna's daughter—inherited the Cheshire estates of Cholmondeston, Burton, Leighton, Worleston and Bruen Stapleford totalling around 3,600 acres. The presumption is, therefore, that Sir John Werden disposed of his Cheshire estates to Lady William Beauclerk's family in the four years between the date of his will and the date of his death. As for his daughter Susanna, later to become the wife of Edward Bayntun, one can only assume that in the closing years of Sir John's life she—like her mother—incurred his gravest displeasure. All the Werden estates passed to the Beauclerks; the Bayntuns apparently received no land whatsoever; and Dame Susanna Werden's letters of administration (27 February 1787) show that she died worth less than £300.

By May 1760 St Albans was back in Brussels, now accompanied by his wife, with whom he had arrived at some form of reconciliation whilst in England. Their home was at the Château de Fontange,[6] at Saint-Gilles just south-west of Brussels, for which he signed a nine-years lease at a rental of 504 florins a year. Meanwhile, he was running into difficulties with his duties as Lord Lieutenant of Berkshire. During the short respite from profligacy, in England in 1759, he had provided 560 men, in eight companies, to police Marlborough, Hungerford and Devizes when there were fears of a French invasion. Then, fading from his native scene and unable through absence abroad to take the oath of allegiance and supremacy at George III's accession, he ceased to be Lord Lieutenant of Berkshire and was replaced in the following year by his uncle Lord Vere of Hanworth; likewise, his uncle Lord James Beauclerk, Bishop of Hereford, temporarily replaced him as Registrar of the Court of Chancery.

In 1760 Lord Vere also seems to have acted on his nephew's behalf as High Steward of Windsor, in delivering to George II the 'humble address of the Mayor, Recorder, Aldermen, Bailiffs, Burgesses and Commonalty of the Borough'. It is a sign of the prestige and established authority of the high aristocracy in 1761 that St Albans's dispossession of the office of Lord Lieutenant of Berkshire was only on a provisonal basis.

Jane Roberts did not remain in Brussels for long, and this was the end their reconciliation. She refused to vie with the Duke's mistress Marie Petit for her husband's favours. Marie had lived with St Albans before his return to England in 1759, and was the mother of several of his children. But he was harsh and violent towards her—as perhaps to his own wife—and in 1762 she fled from him, fearing for her life and not even waiting for him to get her diamonds out of pawn. True to the form of rejected lovers, St Albans complained to Cobenzl that she had run off with jewels belonging to him. Then, somehow, came a healing of the breach and in 1763 St Albans was overtaken by the Brussels police trying to escape with Marie to England. Thrown into a debtors' gaol, the Duke was apparently only released when an estate had been sold (we do not know which, if any). On 29 March 1763, as we learn from a letter of the Duchess to her agent, he was 'still in confinement' in Brussels. Yet before the end of the following month St Albans had arrived in England with his mistress.

Contrary to the provisions of the marriage settlement, he was trying in 1763 to have timber felled at Glassenbury—his share of the Roberts estates for his lifetime. Despite all the melancholy and anxiety of her seclusion at Gennings the Duchess had begun to think constructively about her will. She had no children; and the most important provision in the marriage settlement, from her present point of view, was that in the absence of children she was free to dispose of Gennings and Glassen-bury, after her husband's death, as she chose. Having come to the con-clusion that at all costs *he* must not obtain outright ownership of her estates, she was already making discreet inquiries in 1763 regarding a junior branch of the Roberts family long settled at Boarzell in Sussex. The dandy George Hanger, son of her cousin Gabriel Hanger (recently created Lord Coleraine), also expected to become Jane's heir. So did another Roberts cousin, less distant than the Boarzell line, whose family were seated at Brightfieldstown in county Cork. But there was just a little doubt whether the Irish Robertses were actually related to Jane, as it was not conclusively proven that their founder, Thomas Roberts, was the younger son of the first Glassenbury baronet. She was to ponder for many years before eventually making up her mind.

St Albans was now in England 'in a private capacity'; though people knew who he was, and why he was there, there was never even the shred of a possibility that he would be reinstated as Lord Lieutenant of Berk-shire. It is an unusual, almost a unique, case in the history of the aris-tocracy in eighteenth-century England. His presence, though known to officialdom, was unofficial and undignified, an interval between two 'official' periods as Lord Lieutenant and flawed pillar of the Establish-ment. Returning to the Austrian Netherlands, he lived again at the Château de Fontange which, although a moated house, was too small for the increasing lavishness of his style of life. His debts, financial subterfuges and sexual excesses led the Archbishop of Malines to insist on his departure from Brussels and its vicinity. He retreated to Dinant, thinking that there he would be beyond the Archbishop's reach, but even at Dinant his goods were distrained upon and sold.

Similar disasters and humiliations were occurring, more or less simultaneously, on the other side of the Channel. The Act of Parliament passed in 1767 'for vesting part of the estates of George, Duke of St Albans in Trustees for raising money to pay debts: and for other purposes therein mentioned' instilled some sense of urgency in the Duke, whose trustees turned that 'unprofitable heap of ruin', Durham Yard, to good account in 1768 by leasing it to the Scottish architects Robert, James, John and William Adam for ninety-nine years at an annual ground rent of £1,200.

Here the four brothers proceeded to embank the Thames, against much opposition, and to build both the row of houses named after themselves as Adelphi Terrace and whole groups of houses in the area which became known as the Adelphi. The present site value of the Adelphi runs into many millions, yet until St Albans's parlous finances compelled a development of Durham Yard there were no houses on the site, only ruined buildings and two business premises. Having paid off some of his debts through the lease of Durham Yard, St Albans was able to return to England in a public capacity! He was in Windsor by 4 September 1769, just in time to be re-elected High Steward of Windsor. The Corporation of the borough had threatened on 5 September 1768 to elect a new High Steward unless he was back within twelve months.

Burford House, which he now reoccupied, had been described room by room in a book published in the previous year (1768).[7] In the Marble Hall were fruit pieces by Jakob Bogdany. Portraits of Charles I and Henrietta Maria (the latter by Van Dyck) hung in the Breakfast Room, together with paintings attributed to Rubens and Bassano. In the Duchess's Dressing-Room (ironically named!) were portraits of Nell Gwyn and Lady Diana de Vere, two of the founders of the Beauclerk dynasty; also a Lely portrait of Mary, Countess of Exeter. The Duke's Dressing-Room boasted two Canalettos, an 'Entrance into Rome' and 'The Castel Sant'Angelo', together with Dutch genre and marine paintings presumably by such masters as Ostade and Vandevelde. Both these dressing-rooms seem to have been on the ground floor.

The house had two dining-rooms, an intimate dining-room for the immediate family and close friends, and a 'Public Dining-Room' suitable for life on the grand scale, and displaying three *vedute* of Venice and an 'Interior of the Pantheon'. Adjacent to the Public Dining-Room was a Picture Gallery, with three birdpieces by Bogdany and an '*Ecce Homo*', 'Ascension', 'Virgin and Child' and other paintings in the Italian grand manner. The Public Dining-Room led out into the Great Drawing-Room, with its tapestries of 'Nebuchadnezzar' and 'Joseph Interpreting Pharaoh's Dream', and a painting of the two Turkish boys taken prisoner at the Battle of Belgrade. Spitalfields tapestries hung in the Duke and Duchess's Bedchamber, another optimistically named room; there were also four flower-paintings by Jean-Baptiste Monnoyer. Elsewhere a whole room was devoted to eight flowerpieces by Monnoyer, each of which had cost 100 guineas.

In addition to religious, genre, marine and flower paintings, a quantity of family portraits were scattered throughout the house: portraits of Charles I, his Wife and Two Sons; of Charles II in Garter Robes, William III and Prince Rupert; the Dukes of Monmouth, Northumberland, Grafton and Richmond (the other illegitimate sons of Charles II); Aubrey, Earl of Oxford; a Kneller portrait of the Duke of St Albans in Armour; and Diana, Duchess of St Albans, also by Kneller.

Of all these paintings, most have disappeared without trace, but the Kneller portrait of Diana Duchess of St Albans is in the possession of the present Duke whilst the portrait of the first Duke of St Albans in Armour belongs to Mrs Vera Greig.

An unusual collection of clocks—including one which went for a whole year without needing to be wound up, and which indicated the name of the month and day of the week—completed the décor of this somewhat cold, museum-like, largely unoccupied house whose 'elegant gardens' extended to the Home Park.

In England during the 1770s St Albans enjoyed a renewal of favour, and (from Durham Yard) an increase of income. He presumably lived at Burford House again, after a decade of comparative neglect of the house in the 1760s. On 11 July 1771 he was reinstated as Lord Lieutenant of

Berkshire, an office which he was now to occupy—through many further vicissitudes—until his death. A fortnight later he carried the Sword of State at the installation of the Prince of Wales and others as Knights of the Garter. And in the same year, but not (it would seem) from his own purse, he distributed £400 in coals, candles and bread to the poor of Windsor, Eton and Slough. This was, as it were, the belated honeymoon period of the Duke of St Albans with Windsor, but as with his other honeymoon it did not result in a lasting union.

Although retaining the Lord Lieutenancy of Berkshire during the fourteen years from 1771 until his death, he did not retain his Windsor freehold. George III, with his numerous family of seven sons and five daughters in 1778 (three more were to come), had for some years been eager to buy Burford House. In October 1777 he wrote to his Prime Minister, North:

I am desired by the Queen that when on Tuesday you decline in my name the borrowing his [St Albans's] house you will add the Queen's offer of purchasing his house, stables and gardens for £4,000,

an offer which the Duke accepted. *The Reading Mercury* of 2 February 1778 records the sale:

Orders have been given for the house at Windsor, lately the property of the Duke of St Albans, to be immediately fitted up in an elegant manner and the necessary alterations to be made.

Apparently, it was to become the home of the King's eldest son, the Prince of Wales (later George IV), and two of his younger sons Frederick and Edward. *The Reading Mercury* adds, in its edition of 25 May, that Burford House 'is altering and repairing for the residence of the Prince of Wales and his brother, the proprietor of Cliveden [the fifth Earl of Inchiquin] having refused to sell that seat'; the Prince had lived at Cliveden in the fourth Earl's time, and Lord Inchiquin at Taplow. The gardens of Burford House were combined with those of the Queen's House, and Queen Charlotte writes to her son William on 9 July 1779: 'the Duke of St Albans's house will be finished by the beginning of autumn'.[8] Its new name was Lower Lodge. The house still stands in the

Windsor Castle complex and has now been converted into servants' flats.

To make up for St Albans's loss of Burford House, George III considered granting Cranbourne Lodge to him and his successors in the title; but nothing came of this, although a pension of £909 p.a. did pass the Great Seal, 'payable quarterly for and during the joint lives of His Majesty and His Grace'.[9] The Duke was in the extremely rare, if not unique, position of being Lord Lieutenant of a county in which he had no residence.

Despite his ownership of Wigston, Frisby and Galby, his interest in Durham Yard and his claims on the Roberts rent-rolls, he was evidently in serious financial trouble; and his difficulties were fairly general knowledge. In 1771 the Duke of Portland approached him with an offer to buy Bestwood: an offer which would have been insulting and presumptuous (Bestwood being the main freehold landholding of the family), had not St Albans been in such a dire predicament. St Albans refused his offer, writing on 3 December 1771[10] that he had no intention of selling Bestwood to anybody but would inform him if he ever changed his mind. Thus, within a decade both freehold estates of the dukes of St Albans nearly passed out of their ownership.

At a time when the more enlightened mid-eighteenth century landlords were introducing more advanced agricultural techniques, Bestwood had been neglected. Writing in 1784, François de La Rochefoucauld comments that in England:

> most of the gentlemen who live on their estates for eight months of the year have some portion of land under their own care, sufficient to ... guard them against disaster in the event of losses being incurred as the result of bad farming.

Such was not the practice followed by St Albans, who—like his father and grandfather before him—did not choose to spend even one month of the year on his own estate. Though his presence at Bestwood would probably not have helped matters, the Nottinghamshire landholding certainly did not prosper in his absence. A Norfolk farmer, Mr Barton, became tenant of the park in 1775 on a twenty-one-year lease at a rental of £504 p.a.

No doubt, profiting from the examples of Townshend and Coke, Barton may have had more skill in the science of farming than in business, but the fact is that he lost £10,000 and went bankrupt before the turn of the century.

Neglecting Bestwood and being about to sell Burford House, St Albans contemplated living at Glassenbury as early as 1777. It was a refuge, if not for the family in perpetuity then at least for him during his lifetime; for by the terms of his marriage and separation settlements he was entitled to the use and rents of Glassenbury providing he paid his wife £2,000 p.a. and did not fell timber without her consent. In November 1778, about a year after selling Burford House to the Royal Family, he had six cases of goods transferred from Windsor to Glassenbury where he seems to have lived until 1780, when he moved back again to Brussels. Amongst the things he transferred to Kent in 1778 were beds, mattresses, Wilton carpets, lamps, blue and white linen chair covers, and many pictures: 'William III', 'Prince Rupert', 'Nell Gwyn and her Children', 'Charles II', 'The Duke of Monmouth', 'The Duke of Richmond', 'Aubrey, Earl of Oxford', 'The Interior of the Pantheon', etc.—most, if not all, of which are mentioned in the 1768 description. In the estate papers at Glassenbury is a list, dated 8 July 1780, of pictures to be packed up and shipped across to the Duke of St Albans, who by now was in the Low Countries, and these again include 'Charles II in his Robes', 'The Interior of the Pantheon' and an interesting addition: 'The Duke of St Albans and Sister when Children', not mentioned either in 1768 or 1778, and presumably of the third Duke of St Albans and his sister Lady Diana (Barrington); this painting is so far untraceable. Throughout 1780 St Albans was trying to gather together his various possessions scattered between Glassenbury and Gennings.

The fact that he actually had possessions at Gennings was due to the death of his wife, Jane, on 16 December 1778 and to the provisions of their marriage settlement whereby he inherited her personal effects. To George Hanger's disappointment, Jane Roberts had decided not to leave him Glassenbury. Hanger writes in his *Life, Adventures and Opinions*:

The Duchess of St Albans . . . had made a will in my favour, that was witnessed by my mother, is which she made me heir to her whole property, to a very considerable amount. Within the last twelve months of her death, a Mr Roberts came over from Ireland. She had never seen him before, or ever heard of him. He, however, proved, to her Grace's satisfaction, that he was related to her; so that she reversed her intentions, made a new will, and left everything to him.

The tone of resentful disappointment is unmistakable, even to the extent of leading Hanger into inaccuracies: the will excluding him was not made, as he claims, within six months of her death but on 24 July 1776; and she had invited the Irish Robertses to meet her, and had known them for more than a year. In her will she bequeathed the freehold of Gennings to her devoted companion, Fanny Davies, whilst the rich prize of the Glassenbury freehold went to the second son of Mr Thomas Roberts, who as head of the Brightfieldstown family claimed to be a descendant of the first baronet of Glassenbury and even aspired to describe himself as Sir Thomas Roberts.

On behalf of his son, Sir Thomas Roberts was anxious to take possession of Glassenbury. He feared the counterclaim of the Robertses of Boarzell, with their great advantage over him that they were so much nearer Glassenbury in the event of the wretched life-tenant's death; but through the Glassenbury agent, Thomas Redford, he kept himself well informed of the Duke's movements and state of health, and was ready to act when the moment arose. He even attempted to buy St Albans's life interest, writing to Redford in 1783:

As I have determined on going to Kent, I hope the Duke of St Albans would have no objection to selling me the house and demesne of Glassenbury. I therefore beg (if you think proper) to make a proposal immediately for me for it.

To Redford, however, it was an 'improper' request:

The Duke of St Albans [he replied] has hitherto refused to let Glassenbury House, though several good offers have been made —as His Grace is very fond of it, and I believe has not yet given over the notion of making it his future residence, and at his desire the house, garden, etc., is kept in proper order to receive him at any time.

Two years later, in October 1785, Roberts made a second attempt to forestall his Boarzell rivals, only to receive the discomfiting reply from Redford that the Duke, though in Brussels, considered Glassenbury as his very last line of resort: if all else failed, if credit dried up and ducats were exhausted, he would still have Glassenbury as a safe haven in which to end his days. 'If His Grace converted all or much of his estate into ready money he [the Duke's man of business] was fearful of the consequences', Redford cautiously hinted.[4] For £1,500 St Albans had already disposed of his life-interest in Gennings to Fanny Davies, and she in her turn disposed of the freehold of Gennings to Lady Twysden.

Meanwhile, heedless of the expectations and anxieties he was arousing both in England and Ireland, the Lord Lieutenant of Berkshire carried on his reckless folly and extravagance in Brussels where he now lived at the Château de Molenbeek just on the outskirts of the city. Parts of this château can still be seen in Brussels today, now engulfed in the sprawling northern suburbs. The tower, cellars and underground passages survive, although the Duke's actual house was burned down in 1886. In its place are the newer buildings of an Ursuline convent and a flourishing girls' school with a thousand pupils. In St Albans's time a large pond containing an island was a natural feature of the park; there was a farmhouse within the grounds; and proud chestnut trees bordered the park walls.

But all this was insufficient extravagance for the proud Duke. He decided on a palatial residence a little further north of the city, at Laeken itself. Laeken had become a favourite haunt of the nobility ever since Maria Theresa's daughter and son-in-law Albert Duke of Saxe-Teschen and the Archduchess Maria Christina had made it their home. St Albans, who in 1779 had managed to persuade the Regents to recognize his titles and precedence, hoped to outdo them in the splendour of his surroundings. On 9 September 1783 he purchased a Castel van Platz, or Ter-Plast, for 24,500 florins—and then proceeded to demolish it. During the next two and a half years a new Ter-Plast emerged from the rubble of the old:

at the time of his death only the floors were lacking. The man who handled these matters for him was his legal administrator Simon Fromont, who had just recently become his son-in-law.

In October 1784 St Albans was making a pleasure garden. From Glassenbury he demanded shrubs, greenhouse plants, cherry trees, pinks and cauliflowers,[11] and even linen in December 1785.[12] Yet in that selfsame month *Milord Saint-Alban*[13] was renting a box at the Théâtre de la Monnaie close to that occupied by the Regents! It is perhaps an indication of his painfully distressing lack of credit in Brussels that he even has to write to Redford in February 1785 for beer,[14] and in April for hams,[4] to be sent over from Kent.

It is also odd that a man who throughout his life had been so wickedly unconstructive should, at the end, set to work constructing a building; but, characteristically of him, it was a building that was never quite completed. Sold at his death, it was fairly soon demolished and so became the rubble on which a newer, more modest house stands. Whilst waiting for Ter-Plast to be finally ready, he appears to have lived in Brussels itself, in the Rue Ducale close to the Park; and there, on 1 February 1786, he died.

In his will drawn up on 13 September 1785 he bequeathed annuities of £100 and £50 to Simon and Anne-Amélie Fromont for their joint lives, and a flat sum of £200 to Rose, his unmarried daughter. The Leicester-shire properties of Wigston Magna, Galby and Frisby together with all the residue of his estate on either side of the Channel passed to Charles George Beauclerk, his godson and the son of his cousin Topham, subject to the Fromonts' life-interest. Wigston was still in the possession of Charles Beauclerk's son Aubrey in 1846, though by then Frisby had been sold. There are still descendants of the third Duke of St Albans alive today, including Princesse Raoul de Broglie.

His body was embalmed for the long journey to what was for him the most unfitting of resting-places: Westminster Abbey. To the collegiate church which Beaumont has celebrated as

> A world of pomp and state,
> Buried in dust, once dead by fate,

Diana Lady Bolinbroke, afterwards Lady Diana Beauclerk by Sir Joshua Reynolds, 1765.

Topham Beauclerk: a pastel by Francis Cotes, 1756.

Burton Hall, Tarvin,
Cheshire.
A seat of the fourth Duke
of St Albans.

View of Windsor Castle
from the South-East:
engraved by John
Boydell, 1783.
Burford House can be
seen in the background
to the left. George III
and his family are
standing on the terrace,
with the Queen's Palace
at the centre of the scene.

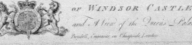

SOUTH EAST VIEW of WINDSOR CASTLE.
With the Royal Family on the Terrace, and A View of the Queens Palace.

the mortal remains were conveyed of a man who, in the year prior to his death, had already been celebrated in a *Narrative of the Conduct of that Illustrious Peer the Duke of St Albans*.

They were conveyed, according to the unwittingly ironical account of a contemporary newspaper:

> in funeral pomp, to Westminster Abbey, attended respectfully by the chief officers under his Grace, as Lord Lieutenant of co. Berks, and the other officers under him, in his several high departments. The procession arrived at the West door, about twelve o'clock, where it was met by the Bishop of Rochester, Dean of Westminster, and other officers of the church, who preceded it to Henry the Seventh's Chapel; where, in consequence of an order from the Lord Chamberlain of his Majesty's Household, it was interred in the Ormonde Vault, the ceremony being performed by the Bishop. His Grace's remains are not far distant from his ancestors, King Charles the Second, and the former Duke of St Albans. The hearse and pall were decorated with escutcheons of his Grace's arms, and other pageants suitable to his rank. The coffin was of crimson velvet, enriched with ducal coronets, with a plate engraved, affixed to it, announcing his several titles. The attention paid by the Bishop, on this occasion, was becoming and highly respectful.

No stranger looking in on that ceremony would have guessed that its solemn triumphalism disguised the bitter failures of the sale of Burford House, the neglect of Bestwood, the pitiful hanging-on to Glassenbury with the two rival branches of the Roberts family waiting to step in when he was dead, and the hopeless, abortive confusion of all the Brussels escapades culminating in the unfinished folly at Laeken and the auction of his picture gallery, clocks, furniture, silverware, jewellery, porcelain and linen at Brussels in June 1786.

NOTES TO CHAPTER III

An unpublished typewritten history of the Roberts family (based on Glassenbury estate records).

Baptism, marriage and burial registers of the Église Notre-Dame du Finistère, Brussels.

J. H. Moses: 'Elections and Electioneering in the Constituencies of Nottinghamshire, 1702–1832' (Nottingham Ph.D. 1965).

Catalogue des tableaux qui se trouvent à la mortuaire du feu Duc de Saint-Albans, et dont la vente se fera publiquement à Bruxelles . . . à l'hôtel de ce seigneur . . . le 12 juin 1786 et les jours suivants.

H. H. Bolitho and D. Peel: *The Drummonds of Charing Cross*, 1967.

J. D. Chambers: *Nottinghamshire in the Eighteenth Century: a Study of Life and Labour under the Squirearchy*, 1932.

J. D. Chambers and G. E. Mingay: *The Agricultural Revolution, 1750–1880*, 1966.

J. T. Godfrey: *The History of the Parish and Priory of Lenton, in the County of Nottingham*, 1884.

E. Hasted: *The History and Topographical Survey of the County of Kent*, 1797–1901.

C.-M.-J. Hennequin de Villermont: *La Cour de Vienne et Bruxelles au XVIIIe siècle. Le Comte de Cobenzl, ministre plénipotentiaire aux Pays-Bas*, 1926.

J. Langton (ed.): *The Second Hall Book of the Borough of New Windsor, 1726–1783*, 1973.

R. R. Sedgwick: *History of the House of Commons, 1715–1754*, 1970.

W. J. Smith (ed.): *The Grenville Papers*, 1852.

H. Walpole: *Correspondence*, 1937–1973.

H. Walpole: *Journal of the Reign of King George the Third*, 1859.

————————

1. See Chapter I, note 5.
2. J. Aikin: *History of the Environs of London*, 1811, vol. II, 292–293.

3. Kent RO U55–T651.
4. Estate papers, Glassenbury.
5. *Gentleman's Magazine*, February 1758, 94.
6. A. Wauters: *Histoire des Environs de Bruxelles*, 1855, vol. III, 558.
7. *Windsor and its Environs*, 1768, 74–77.
8. RA Add. 21/1/3.
9. *Reading Mercury*, 23 November 1778.
10. Portland Papers (Nottingham University) PWF 330.
11. Kent RO U410–C4/2.
12. Kent RO U410–C4/4.
13. J. Isnardon: *Le Théâtre de la Monnaie depuis sa fondation jusqu'à nos jours*, 1890, 66.
14. Kent RO U410–C4/3.

CHAPTER IV

Topham Beauclerk

In the familiar pattern, Topham Beauclerk was a quite different type of man from his father, Lord Sidney. The fifth son of the first Duke of St Albans was the most notorious fortune-hunter of his time: 'worthless Sidney', in the words of Sir Charles Hanbury Williams;[1] 'Nell Gwyn in person with the sex altered, [who] occasions such fracas amongst the ladies of gallantry that it passes belief' (mockingly summed up by Lady Mary Wortley Montagu). In her old age Lady Betty Germaine was almost persuaded to marry him, but bought him off with £1,000.[2] Aged twenty-seven, he persuaded the Windsor Member of Parliament, Richard Topham, to bequeath him his estates at Windsor and Clewer Brocas. Aged thirty-four, he narrowly failed to score the same triumph with Sir Thomas Reeve, the Chief Justice of the Common Pleas. His greatest triumph, however, was to secure the hand and fortune of a Lancashire heiress, Mary Norris; but it was a triumph which had its duller side, as Mary was thirty-six years old and (according to Samuel Johnson) had 'no notion of a joke . . . and . . . a mighty unpliable under-standing'. He combined the third Duke's instincts for debauchery with the calculations of a politician: as lordling politician he was, sitting for Windsor for ten years until his death and rising to be a Privy Councillor and Vice-Chamberlain of the Household.

Topham, who inherited Clewer from him when he was not quite five years of age, never entered Parliament, had the greatest contempt for politicians, married a brilliant artistic wife but a woman with no fortune, and had the civilized sophisticated tastes of a man of the En-lightenment. Differing from his mother almost as much as from his father, his understanding was mighty pliable, indeed mercurial; differing from his cousin the third Duke, he sought out the *philosophes* in Paris rather than the actresses and opera-singers; he longed to meet Rousseau. He was a dazzling conversationalist, a discerning book-collector, a founder member of The Club, a friend of Johnson; and so close a friend of Johnson that the latter confessed: 'I would walk to the extent of the diameter of the earth to save Beauclerk'.

It was through Bennet Langton, an Oxford friend, that Topham met the celebrated Doctor in 1757, in the year of his matriculation at Trinity, when the young man was aged seventeen. What was the link which bound the two men together, one an adolescent, the other approaching fifty? 'What a coalition', Garrick remarked of 'the moral, pious Johnson and the gay, dissipated Beauclerk' being companions. But Johnson, said his biographer Boswell, 'delighted in the good qualities of Beauclerk, and hoped to correct the evil'. Johnson, who outlived Beauclerk, commented on his deceased friend: 'Beauclerk's talents were those which he had felt himself more disposed to envy, than those of any whom he had known'.

Clearly, the God-fearing and fairly straitlaced Doctor must have found much to reprove in Beauclerk's conduct; but Topham's youth tended to exonerate him, besides which there was a latent streak of sensuality in Johnson's make-up: 'if I had no duties, and no reference to futurity', he confessed to Boswell, 'I would spend my life in driving briskly in a postchaise with a pretty woman'.

Not the least of Topham's successes was to cause Johnson occasionally to forget that he had duties and a reference to futurity. Once, at about three o'clock in the morning, for instance, Johnson was knocked up at his chambers in the Temple by Beauclerk and Langton.

'What, is it you, you dogs!' he began gruffly, but quickly relented: 'I'll have a frisk with you'; and all three, despite the disparity in age, frisked together around Covent Garden, stopped at a tavern where they drank a mixture of wine, oranges and sugar which Johnson had always liked, then rowed to Billingsgate; Beauclerk and Johnson were so pleased with their amusement that they continued their dissipations for the rest of the day.

Both men were inspired talkers, though talkers of a different kind: Beauclerk more fascinating than Johnson, but Johnson more incisive and dogmatic. Both men had the instincts of a dilettante, but Beauclerk could fulfil his, through affluence (even before his mother's death, he was paying £6,000 or £7,000 a year into his account at Hoares Bank), whereas poverty compelled Johnson to discipline his genius: 'no man but a blockhead', Johnson pontificated, 'ever wrote, except for money'. And Topham did not write, except for the endless stream of letters in which— like Lady Mary Wortley Montagu, Horace Walpole, Voltaire and other figures of the eighteenth century—he regularly indulged.

Both men were book-collectors. The sale catalogue of Dr Johnson's library boasts nearly 700 books: rare editions of Lucian, Cicero, Macrobius, Galen and Philo, an even rarer volume by Boethius, but above all, many dictionaries and concordances together with a First Folio edition of Shakespeare.

Topham, thanks to his private means and tendency to extravagance, was able to amass a finer library still. It was, indeed, one of the finest libraries belonging to any eighteenth-century bibliophile. It comprised, in the words of the sale catalogue published in 1781: 'upwards of thirty thousand volumes, in most languages, and upon almost every branch of science and polite literature': almost 1,500 books by classical authors, including many published in the sixteenth century and some incunabula; works on mathematics and physics, including astronomy and mechanics; a large section on botany, zoology, geology, mineralogy, crystallography and metallurgy; a still more important collection of travel books, dealing amongst other countries with Spain, Portugal, France, Switzerland, Italy, the Netherlands, Germany, Siberia, Tartary, Turkey, Greece, the Levant, Asia Minor, Palestine, Arabia, Persia, China, Japan, Africa and America; grammars and dictionaries of various languages, including a 1565 edition of Scaliger's Latin grammar and books on Hebrew, Arabic, Persian, Turkish, Danish and Swedish; Roger de Piles, Félibien, Bellori, Descamps, Du Bos and Batteux on aesthetics; many books on the philosophy of history (though not Vico) and world history, including the history and topography of the British Isles; works of the deists and atheists of the seventeenth and eighteenth centuries, such as the notorious *Traité des Trois Imposteurs* and the major writings of Voltaire, D'Holbach, Shaftesbury, Toland, Tindal, Collins and Bolingbroke; studies of Provençal poetry; the original 1567 edition of Surrey's sonnets, a first edition of _Comus_, Middleton's _A Game at Chess_, a 1550 edition of _Piers Plowman_, Lydgate's translation of Boccaccio; the plays of Garnier, Montchrestien, Jodelle and Larivey, the _Roman de la Rose_, a first edition of Rousseau's _La Nouvelle Héloïse_, Mme de La Fayette's _Zaïde_, and works by Crébillon, Marot, Brantôme, Bouhours and Mellin de Saint-Gelais.

It was not only the library of a bibliophile but a working library as well; and this, too, was a point of similarity with Johnson's. Stories are told of the assiduity and enthusiasm with which Topham used to track down his quarry. Malone writes to Lord Charlemont that, on the first day of an important sale, his servant would be at the bookseller's by six or seven o'clock in the morning,

> and runs away with everything rare; this is not, I imagine, the least inconvenience either to him or his valet de chambre, for I believe that is his usual time of coming home and going to bed— so that his servant has no other trouble except lying down half an hour later than ordinary.

Not that he tried to cheat people, however: having bought Samuel Clarke's folio edition of Caesar's _Commentaries_ for four guineas from the mother of its deceased owner, he checked its proper value with an antiquarian bookseller and, finding that the true price was seventeen guineas, more than made up the difference.

To house his immense quantity of books he had a special library built behind his home in Great Russell Street, a building which Horace Walpole said reached halfway to Highgate and quite 'put the Museum's nose out of joint'; it cost £2,000, and was designed by Robert Adam. The books themselves had to be mortgaged to Topham's brother-in-law the Duke of Marlborough for £5,000, and at the forty-nine days' auction in 1781 fetched a total of £5,011 which just paid off the mortgage. There is a nice appositeness in the friendship of a man who claimed he only ever wrote books for money and a man who spent all the ready money he had, and more besides, on books.

Above all, Topham and Johnson were men of the Enlightenment. Both believed in the primordial importance of reason in human affairs and both, though Johnson tended in the direction of Paley and Topham in that of Voltaire, believed in the supremacy of the natural over the super-natural. Johnson was a man of practicality and pragmatism, as witness his celebrated rebuttal of Berkeley's idealism; Topham, elected a Fellow of the Royal Society in 1770, had an empirical mind and a passionate fondness for scientific experiments. Even as a young man he entertained Johnson to 'experiments in natural philosophy' when the latter was staying with him at Windsor. During their tour of Scotland in 1773 Johnson and Boswell decided that, if ever The Club were to set up as a College at St Andrews, Topham should teach natural philosophy.[3] But Topham's pragmatism was combined with a refinement that Johnson lacked. It was partly an intellectual refinement, partly social but most of all a refinement of sensibility. He was the reverse of insular, cultivated the society of the Prince de Conti and the latter's mistress Mme de Boufflers in Paris, sought out Rousseau in England. He was sensitive to currents of thought and feeling which left Johnson unmoved.

The Club, of which Johnson and Sir Joshua Reynolds were co-founders, provided Topham and Johnson with a regular meeting-ground in London for most of the sixteen years between 1764 and 1780. Beauclerk was one of the nine original members and amongst the remainder were Bennet Langton, Edmund Burke and Oliver Goldsmith. Garrick, Adam Smith, Fox and Gibbon were soon recruited to its ranks. Until 1783 they used the Turk's Head Coffee House in Gerrard Street, Soho as their head-quarters, meeting at seven, having supper together and talking on late into the night; for, in the words of Dr Thomas Percy, author of *Reliques of Ancient English Poetry* and another later recruit to The Club: its members, 'it was intended, should be men of such talents that if only two of them should meet for the evening they should be able to entertain each other'.

For an unknown reason, but certainly not because he was 'unclub-bable', Topham withdrew from The Club a year or two after its inception; such an uncharacteristic act may well have been due to the antagonism which is said to have sprung up in The Club at one time between Johnson and Burke. Soon, however, he was wishing to be reinstated, and his reintroduction and Percy's introduction both took place on 15 February 1768. Sir John Hawkins, branded by Johnson as unclubbable, had resigned; amity reigned; and Topham was more instrumental than anyone in securing Boswell's election in 1773. Boswell recalls dining at Beauclerk's house with Johnson, Reynolds and others just before his election came up before The Club. He writes in his *Life of Johnson*:

> The gentlemen went away and I was left at Beauclerk's till the fate of my election should be announced to me. I sat in a state of anxiety which even the charming conversation of Lady Di Beauclerk could not entirely dissipate. In a short time I received the agreeable intelligence that I was chosen.

Johnson had been his proposer, Beauclerk his seconder but the more 'zealous' of the two supporters, and between them they had sponsored a most valuable acquisition if only because in Boswell they had found a man to record some of the Doctor's *obiter dicta* at The Club. The practice of publicizing conversations at The Club, or details of its composition, is one which members have frowned on now for over two centuries; the only recent transgressor, and one far more severely censured than Boswell, was Sir Mountstuart Grant Duff.

It is thanks to Boswell and Bennet Langton that we know Johnson's remark to a fellow member of The Club concerning Beauclerk's death: that he admired 'the wonderful ease with which he uttered what was highly excellent'; a tavern group believed to be by Samuel Percy shows Beauclerk, Boswell, Johnson, Reynolds, Gainsborough, Fox, Thomas Warton and Joseph Nollekens engaged in the conversation of which Beauclerk was master.

It was London which made such conversation possible; to Johnson, in his famous phrase, 'when a man is tired of London, he is tired of life; for there is in London all that life can afford': and Topham agreed. The irony was that, following the death of his mother Lady Sidney Beauclerk in 1766, he possessed one of the architecturally finest timber-framed manor houses in England, and perhaps the most beautiful of all to look at: Speke Hall, near Liverpool. Moreover, until that year there had been the Court and country attractions of Windsor, of which (excluding the Parks) he owned almost half, and more than George III—with, in addition, a mansion at Clewer Brocas and land at Burnham and Sunninghill.

In 1766 the Windsor property was sold to Sir Edward Walpole, no doubt because if Topham was to live anywhere in the country at all he planned to live at Speke. But London, and the weekly meetings of The Club at the Turk's Head, maintained their spell, for Topham still saw members of The Club individually even when he had withdrawn from membership, and although it is true that he was living at Speke for some part of the year around 1766 the fact is that the Lancashire manor house engaged his attention and interest less and less.

The Rousseau whom he admired, and was so eager to meet at Ashbourne when travelling in December 1766 from Speke to London,[4] did not fill him with a love of rustic simplicity; and, a generation in advance of Scott, he could not respond to the attractions of a medieval hall. Speke under his aegis fell gradually into disrepair. There is a record, in a letter to Lord Charlemont, of Topham being about to stay in Lancashire in July 1774, but certainly in the last few years of his life the house was let off as tenements. It was occupied by farmers and others; in the Great Hall the wainscoting and large carved panels were defaced and broken up; and the inlaid oak floor of the Great Parlour was used as firewood, and its tapestries as horsecloths. Yet it had been his mother's wish that he should make Speke his principal home, just as she had hoped—equally vainly—that he would assume the surname of Norris, in lieu of Beauclerk, after her death.

To Topham rustic simplicity was at its best when viewed through the enchanting but artificial medium of his wife's paintings. Lady Diana Beauclerk, whom he married in 1768, had formerly been the wife of Lord Bolingbroke (and niece-in-law of the philosopher-statesman); she was a daughter of the Duke of Marlborough who, with his grandmother Sarah, had crossed swords with the second Duke of St Albans over the right to enter Windsor Home Park. The separation from her first husband, effected by Act of Parliament in 1768, was due to her desertion; Bolingbroke, writes Lady Sarah Lennox,

> is much the same as mad when he is drunk, and that he is generally. Lady B.'s reason for parting is that she cannot live with him with safety to her health.

She was already the mistress of Topham Beauclerk, married him within two days of the divorce, and had even borne him two daughters eighteen months previously. 'The woman's a whore, and there's an end on't', was Johnson's outspoken reaction, though he was full of indulgence for similar foibles in Topham: 'who thinks the worse of Beauclerk for it?' he asked, on learning that Topham had seduced Bolingbroke's wife. Horace Walpole, on the other hand, did not like Topham, but deeply admired Lady Di. Gibbon wrote to Mme de Boufflers that she was 'handsome and agreeable and ingenious far beyond the ordinary rate'. And both Walpole and Reynolds praised her drawings and paintings.

> Has any painter ever executed a scene, a character of Shakespeare, that approached to the prototype so near as Shakespeare himself attained to nature?

Walpole argued in his preface to the fourth and final volume of *Anecdotes of Painting*.

> Yet is there a pencil in a living hand as capable of pronouncing the passions as our unequalled poet; a pencil not only inspired by his insight into nature, but by the graces and taste of Grecian artists. ... Whoever has seen the drawings, and bas-reliefs, designed and executed by Lady Diana Beauclerc, is sensible that these imperfect encomiums are far short of the excellence of her works.[5]

In a special room, the 'Beauclerc Closet', at Strawberry Hill he hung seven of her drawings against India blue damask: scenes, from his recent tragedy *The Mysterious Mother*, that 'would be fully worthy of the best of Shakespeare's plays—such drawings that Salvator Rosa and Guido could not surpass their expression and beauty', combining (as he confesses in another letter) 'Guido's grace, Albano's children, Poussin's expression, Salvator's boldness in landscape and Andrea Sacchi's simplicity of composition'. To yet another correspondent, Lady Ossory, Walpole confesses that

> If the subject were a quarter as good as the drawings, [they] would make me a greater genius than Shakespeare, as she is superior to

Guido and Salvator Rosa. Such figures! such dignity! such simplicity! Then there is a cedar hanging over the castle, that is more
romantic than when it grew on Lebanon.

These seven illustrations of scenes from *The Mysterious Mother* have
long since disappeared (they were last heard of in the ownership of Lord
Portarlington), yet total neglect of Lady Diana Beauclerk's work is as
false as Walpole's praise was unduly lavish. Nothing in her work has the
poetry which Reynolds instilled into his portrait of her, but her art is a
delightful expression of Rococo sensibility in which can just be discerned
the beginnings of pre-Romanticism. Her sketches and drawings abound
in *putti*, winged cherubs, cupids sporting, cupids with doves, nymphs,
fauns, peasants in pastoral scenes, Bacchuses and Bacchanals. There are
resemblances with Fragonard, especially in composition, but her style is
distinct from that of the Rococo artists of France, Fragonard, Boucher,
Pater, and from the earlier, more wistful Watteau. She is an eclectic
artist, but strongly individual: neo-Classical in inspiration in the
renowned Wedgwood Plaques, similar to Mme Vigée-Lebrun in her
portrait of her daughters Mary and Elizabeth, strangely Greuze-like in
some of her portraits of children. She is individual because unmistakably
naïve. Even in the sculptural neo-Classicism of the Wedgwood Plaques
there is exuberant levity in the fauns. The young ladies in her work
display the exuberance of her personal life in a more rustic setting than is
to be found in Fragonard. It is partly in these settings, partly in the facial
expressions of figures at close range that is to be found the true evidence
of her sensibility: the faces of her children, the overarching boughs of the
trees, the stippled leaves suggest a response to nature and human
nature as personal as that of Constable, whose friend in her old age she
became.

It was perhaps her misfortune to be the superior of both her husbands
in feeling and purposefulness; and yet with Topham she was happy. He,
compared with his father Lord Sidney, was an aimless dilettante, with
some of his father's moral weaknesses but none of his material successes.
He was unfaithful to his wife, cruel and unfeeling towards his children;
by the age of thirty-five, his dissipations had permanently undermined

his health: he died aged forty. Unlike his father, however, he suffered from what he freely admitted to be 'insuperable idleness'. 'There is nothing in this world', he writes to Lord Charlemont, 'I so entirely hate, as business of any kind'. Bennet Langton lamented to Boswell that if only their friend's talents could have been disciplined and organized, he could have become an illustrious figure. He talked but could not act, and even Johnson envied the dominating power of his conversation. His indolence and lack of self-discipline extended even to personal hygiene.

He was, writes Lady Louisa Stuart, '*cynique* in his personal habits beyond what one would have thought possible in anyone but a beggar or a gipsy'; and she goes on to describe a Christmas visit which Topham and his wife paid to the Marlboroughs at Blenheim, when other guests became infected with lice and the origin of the trouble was eventually traced to Topham: 'why!' he exclaimed disarmingly, 'I have enough to stock a parish!' No wonder that there was always a certain coolness between Topham and his brother-in-law the fourth Duke of Marlborough. Johnson, in his sagacity, perceived this without ever meeting the Duke. Asked whether Topham could obtain someone an introduction to Blenheim, he replied: 'I doubt whether our friend be on such a footing with the duke as to carry anybody there, and I would not give him the uneasiness of seeing that I knew he was not, or even of being himself reminded of it'.

Indolence, dissipation and self-neglect were compounded with a growing moroseness. 'Your philanthropy', he observes to Charlemont in July 1773, 'engages you to think well of the greatest part of mankind; but every year, every hour adds to my misanthropy'; and he would quote lines from Pope's *Essay on Man*:

> Life can little more supply
> Than just to look about us and to die.

So negative a final view of life is sad in a man who, after all, lived for an ideal. Unlike his father's dissipation, his dissoluteness was redeemed by the qualities of sanity, tolerance and a certain receptiveness to ideas and feelings, qualities which are the finest products of eighteenth-century civilization. He delighted in the minds of others: this was the joy of belonging to The Club. He was gregarious and urbane. He shunned extremes. He hated the excesses and fanaticism of religion. Like many greater eighteenth-century figures, he was conservative in his views as to the possibilities of social reform; and he distrusted politicians. Just as to Samuel Johnson 'politics [were] now nothing more than means of rising in the world', so to Beauclerk 'the leading men in both the countries [Britain and Ireland] at present are, I believe, the most corrupt, abandoned people in the nation'. What basically mattered was not the reform of the framework of society, with all that that implied in terms of the greatest happiness of the greatest number, but the civilization of clubbable men within the existing framework.

It was an ideal meant for, and perhaps only desired by, the happy few; yet it was a conservative, realistic ideal which allowed for the imperfections of human nature. And it was an ideal with which Johnson agreed. Whatever his reservations as to Topham's conduct, the appeal of his friend's personality was irresistible. Whatever his doubts as to Topham's religious position, he had to respect the sense and sensibility, the poise and mellowness of his worldly outlook. 'Thy body is all vice', he scolded him admiringly, 'and thy mind all virtue'.

NOTES TO CHAPTER IV

Archives of Hoares Bank.

A Catalogue of the Large and Valuable Library of the late Hon. Topham Beauclerk, 1781.

J. Boswell: *Life of Johnson* (O.U.P. edn), 1953.

Lady M. Coke: *Letters and Journals*, 1889–1896.

B. C. Erskine: *Lady Diana Beauclerk, her Life and Work*, 1903.

T. E. Harwood: *op. cit.*

T. Heywood (ed.): *The Norris Papers* (Chetham Society IX), 1846.

W. S. Lewis (ed.): *Notes by Lady Louisa Stuart on 'George Selwyn and his Contemporaries' by John Heneage Jesse*, 1928.

H. Walpole: *Correspondence*, 1937–1973.

H. Walpole: *Journal of the Reign of King George the Third*, 1859.

Lady M. Wortley Montagu: *Complete Letters*, 1965–1967.

------

1. C. H. Williams: *Works*, 1822, vol. I, 46.
2. R. R. Sedgwick: *op. cit.*, 449.
3. J. Boswell: *Journal of a Tour to the Hebrides*, 1785, 114.
4. J.-J. Rousseau: *Correspondance Générale*, vol. XVI, 1931, 162–163.
5. H. Walpole (ed.): *Anecdotes of Painting in England* (by G. Vertue), vol. IV, 1771, viii.

CHAPTER V

The Scramble for an Inheritance

By the standards of his predecessors, the fourth Duke of St Albans had a vast inheritance of freehold land. Little is known of this young man, who was twenty-seven on succeeding to the dukedom in February 1786 and who died just over a year later, unmarried, after a lingering illness. He was the grandson of Lord William Beauclerk, whose wife Charlotte was a daughter of Sir John Werden, and he was the heir and only surviving child of Colonel Charles Beauclerk, lieutenant-colonel in the 3rd Foot Guards and Governor of Pendennis Castle in Cornwall. His father probably took over Burton, Cholmondeston, Leighton and the other estates in Cheshire, Lancashire, Yorkshire and Berkshire on Lady William's death in 1770, and his mother was probably a girl from the Welsh border. But the future Duke's mother had died two years before Lady William.

On the Colonel's death in 1775 George Beauclerk (the future fourth Duke), then aged sixteen, was an orphan; Henry and Robert Drummond, the bankers and friends of his late father, became his guardians. He joined the Army in his father's regiment, served in the American War of Independence from April 1777, was promoted captain in 1778 at the age of nineteen, and returned to England in 1780 for his 'private affairs'.[1] These 'private affairs' obviously related to the Werden estates; he had just come of age, and the trust managed by the Drummonds had lapsed. In the month following his succession to the dukedom he took his seat in the House of Lords, but never spoke, and it is not absolutely certain that he was a Whig. In the same month, March 1786, he was promoted lieutenant-colonel, and so died at the same rank and in the same regiment as his father. His death occurred in Grosvenor Square, but it is not even certain that this was his home. No portrait of him remains, and none perhaps was ever painted. The year from February 1786 to February 1787 is a mysterious, inconclusive interlude in the dukedom's history.

By 1786 Burford House had been sold; Bestwood at this time was never occupied by the family, and the land and house were leased to farmers; the life-interest in Glassenbury had expired; subject to the Fromonts' life-interest, Wigston Magna, Frisby and Galby in Leicestershire had passed to Topham's son; Durham Yard in the Strand, though now owned by him outright, had been let by the third Duke's trustees for ninety-nine years from 1768; but against this there were the estates that were now united with the dukedom after descending through Sir John Werden's second daughter and her son. Although Burton Hall and Leigham Court were no Chatsworth or Welbeck and the fourth Duke's property fell far short of the Devonshires' and Portlands', the total extent of his land was about 10,000 acres and his rent-roll around £6,000 p.a. Including his emoluments as Hereditary Grand Falconer (c. £600 p.a.) and Registrar of the Court of Chancery (c. £1,000 p.a.) and his pension from the tax on logwood (£1,000 p.a.), his net income in modern terms must have been roughly equivalent to £80,000 a year. Of the 10,000 acres about two thirds came from the Werdens, thus counterbalancing the income from the first Duke's appointments and sinecures—for the fact is that the first Duke's income after 1705 was almost as large as the fourth Duke's eighty years later.

Now, however, instead of pensions dependent on royal whims or charges on the Irish Parliament there were ground rents from sixty houses on land leased in Durham Yard, 1,070 acres at East Challow and Cholsey, a Tudor mansion just seven miles out of Chester, and 3,700 acres of farmland scattered across the Cheshire plain: it was an inheritance with distinct promise, a seemingly certain 'pledge of better times', if its owner's health had held out and he had married and set up a dynasty of dukes of St Albans established in Cheshire, Surrey and Nottinghamshire.

The will of the fourth Duke of St Albans[2] could not affect Bestwood, the firm base of the family settled on them by Charles II through Nell Gwyn. This passed to his successor in the title. The estate at Leigham Court was sold in 1789 to the Lord Chancellor, Lord Thurlow, to pay off debts of £8,000. A life-interest in the Adelphi development at Durham Yard and in the Cheshire, Berkshire, Lancashire and Yorkshire estates was bequeathed to his father's elder sister Charlotte, the widow of perhaps the richest banker in his day: John Drummond. The will stipulated that after her death all the Werden property was to descend to her elder son George, and St Albans expressed the hope,

> in case of failure of issue of his body lawfully begotten or to be begotten, that in any disposition he may think proper to make of such of the said estates as shall have been in [the Werden] family such disposition be made with all due attention to that circumstance.

It was right that there should be this division of the family estates, as Charlotte and George Drummond were descendants of Sir John Werden whereas the fifth Duke of St Albans was not.

An irony of the Beauclerk history is that before 1799 part of the Adelphi was to be leased to another eminent banker, Thomas Coutts, whose widow less than thirty years later became Duchess of St Albans. A further irony is that, although the Drummonds retained possession of the Adelphi until the 1930s, the Cheshire and indeed all other Werden properties were sold by Charlotte's grandson George Harley Drummond to whom they had passed directly on Charlotte's death in 1793 and who was just as much of a rake as *Milord Saint-Alban*. Even before he became a rake, ninety acres at Eaton had been sold off about 1804 to Lord Grosvenor for £5,500. In 1817 Worleston wiped out some of his debts, Leighton served the same purpose in 1823, Cholmondeston suffered a similar fate about 1830, and all the Cheshire lands had been frittered away by Drummond's death in 1855.

But the Drummonds retained, at least until 1973, a more treasured memento than the Cheshire farms: that of the various Stuart and Beauclerk portraits and miniatures bought at the third Duke of Albans's sale at Brussels in 1786. These included Gervase Spencer's miniatures of the third Duke and Jane Roberts, initialed and dated 1754; a portrait of Queen Henrietta Maria, of the school of Van Dyck; two portraits of Nell Gwyn, one attributed to Lely and one a studio work; 'Diana, Countess of Oxford', by Lely himself; Kneller's portrait of the Twentieth and Last Earl of Oxford; a painting of Ladies Diana and Mary de Vere, attributed to Dahl; a portrait of the two sons of Nell Gwyn, attributed to Netscher; and one of the younger of these two sons, Lord James Beauclerk, from the school of Kneller. Besides which an English silver pair-cased verge clock-watch, traditionally a gift from Charles II to Nell Gwyn, was also bought by the Drummonds from the Brussels sale. The portrait of Lord James Beauclerk attributed to Kneller's studio now belongs to the Duke of St Albans.

So impenetrable is the mystery surrounding the fourth Duke that it is not certain how many of the entailed heirlooms of the family were transmitted safe and sound to him from the wreckage of the third Duke's finances, nor what picture-heirlooms (if any) passed from him to the fifth Duke. His successor in the dukedom may even have been a bidder at the Brussels auction, though there is no firm proof of this presumption. What *is* beyond doubt is that the fifth Duke owned, and handed on to his descendants, a number of family portraits that have the status of heirlooms; and also, that besides housing a collection of family pictures the fifth Duke of St Albans went on to become an art-collector of a more serious kind.

Though only inheriting Bestwood from his cousin (together with minor heirlooms and a very uncertain quantity of paintings), the fifth Duke of St Albans—or Lord Vere of Hanworth, as he then was—could not have been unduly dismayed at the difficulties he faced in maintaining a ducal position. His seat in Middlesex was Hanworth Palace, only a mile or two distant from Hampton Court; his London house was in Mansfield Street. The title of Lord Vere of Hanworth came to him in 1781 from his father, to whom it was a reward for services to the Navy only surpassed in the second quarter of the eighteenth century by Anson's; in 1783, Hanworth came to him from his mother, born Mary Chamber, in whose family the estate and Tudor mansion had been since 1670. The former palace of Anne Boleyn and also of Katharine Parr, on whom it had been settled by Henry VIII in 1544, was extensively improved by Sir Francis Cottington in the reign of Charles I; Cottington had made a walled garden, an open gallery and 'dainty walks', but the house had been transformed by the Chambers, who incidentally employed Kneller to paint a ceiling. 'The park of 108 acres', we read in a near-contemporary account, 'still contains much fine timber, chiefly oak and elm, and is intercepted by the King's river cut by Wolsey for the supply of Hampton Court'.

The Chambers were sugar-planters in Jamaica, where Mary's grand-father had married a Portuguese half-caste at Fort St George. Mary and her sister Anne were substantial heiresses; they had no brother. Their mother was a sister of James, Earl of Berkeley, who until his death in August 1736 was Vice-Admiral of Great Britain, and (more importantly) of Lady Betty Germaine, the childless widow of Sir John Germaine. This notorious man had obtained the estate of Drayton in Northamptonshire from his first wife Mary, formerly Duchess of Norfolk. Drayton had originally belonged to the Duchess's father Lord Peterborough, who had inherited it by marriage from the de Veres, and Germaine had to endure many lawsuits both from Norfolk, seeking a divorce and naming him as the seducer, and from the third Earl of Peterborough, seeking unsuccess-fully to recover Drayton from his cousin's husband. Lady Betty played a considerable part in arranging the marriage of Vere Beauclerk and Mary Chamber, which took place on 13 April 1736 at St James's, Piccadilly.

As early as 20 February 1734, writing to the first Duke of Dorset, she was in favour of their marriage.

> He certainly is a pretty sort of man [she remarked to Lord Vere]; the whole world gives him a great character. I am very fond of him, I do think he will make her prodigious happy. I suppose he likes her extremely, or he is the best of actors. . . . I never yet saw any man that I liked so well for her, and I verily believe she never saw a man she liked so well for herself.

In that year she gave her niece £10,000, noting in another letter to the Duke of Dorset that the girl's father Thomas Chamber had refused to do likewise: 'there was no moving the old villain'. It is said that, thanks to Dorset, Vere was able to pursue his courtship of Mary Chamber at Knole. With his passion for fortune-hunting, Lord Sidney Beauclerk—who equalled Sir John Germaine in profligacy and had even proposed to Lady Betty himself!—considered that his brother was throwing himself away, and seems to have tried to persuade him against the match. But he was not throwing himself away, as became abundantly evident when Thomas Chamber died in January 1736, bequeathing to Mary the 738 acres of the Hanworth estate (increased to 849 by 1748). Swift congratulated Vere Beauclerk on obtaining a bride with a dowry of £40,000.

In the year following Mary's marriage, her sister married Pitt's brother-in-law Lord Temple, bringing him £50,000. Lady Betty Germaine was to leave Mary Beauclerk more money at her death in 1769, but her principal heir—at Drayton—was Lord George Sackville, the ill-fated military commander who subsequently became Irish Secretary and was the father of the fifth and last Duke of Dorset.

Vere Beauclerk's naval career ceased in the year before he was raised to the barony of Vere of Hanworth. It had spanned twenty-eight years; he had fought under Sir Charles Wager at Cadiz; and he had served in the Mediterranean. Except for an interval of two years, he had been a Lord of the Admiralty from 1738 to 1749; before his flag-rank promotions he was slightly senior to Anson (they were gazetted Rear-Admirals in 1744 on the same day, but Beauclerk was six years ahead of Anson as a Lord of the Admiralty); they were appointed Admirals of the Blue Squadron together on 12 May 1748; Anson, in 1748, had received a peerage before him, yet even before Anson's ennoblement Beauclerk had written in 1746 to the Prime Minister's brother, the Duke of Newcastle:

> My only view and desire ... is to be moved from the House of Commons into the other house. ... I have served the Crown three and thirty years, have been above twenty in Parliament, and I don't know that in all that time I ever asked or desired what impartial people have thought unreasonable.

The appointment of Lord Sandwich as First Lord of the Admiralty in February 1748 was a further blow, for though Beauclerk had no claims to this post on grounds of seniority, Sandwich had far less naval experience and had been brought in as Second Lord from the outside; only the Duke of Newcastle dissuaded him from resigning from the service there and then. In 1749 Anson's promotion over his head as Vice-Admiral of Great Britain seemed to him the final insult. He wrote bitterly to Newcastle:

As His Majesty has thought proper to give a junior officer a superior commission over my head I therefore request your Grace to obtain his leave for my quitting it, I mean both at the Admiralty and as a flag officer.

The reference, in 1746, to having served the Crown for more than twenty years in Parliament is to the fact that he had replaced his eldest brother as member for Windsor on the latter's succession to the dukedom in 1726. Until the 1760s Windsor, like New Windsor, was a pocket borough of the Beauclerks—though it was not always well managed. On the second Duke's resignation of Windsor, his next available brother had taken his place: Lord William Beauclerk already having a seat in the House of Commons as member for Chichester.

Somewhat grudgingly perhaps, the barony rewarding his naval achievements was conferred on him through the Pelhams in March 1750, eight months after his resignation from the Navy; and with that barony came another resignation, as member of Parliament for Plymouth, to which he had transferred from Windsor in 1741. A sign of his enthusiasm to migrate to the upper House was that he took his seat there within two days. The zenith of his career (if such it was; and, reviewing Anson's career and European celebrity, he may well have had doubts) was followed by a sedate thirty-one years as family elder statesman. He interceded on his rakish nephew's behalf to get the Registrarship of the Court of Chancery extended; he interceded with Grenville in a vain attempt to get his brother James, Bishop of Hereford translated to the see of London[3]; he acted on the third Duke's behalf as Lord Lieutenant of Berkshire from 1760 to 1771.

At Lady Betty Germaine's death in 1769, her favourite niece Lady Vere received a legacy of £20,000 as well as a quarter share in stocks worth £120,000. Lord Vere also received a quarter of the £120,000, and Lord George Sackville the remaining half. Even the Veres' children were each bequeathed a diamond. 'I have abundant reason to be thankful and satisfied', was Lord Vere's conclusion to his brother-in-law, Temple. Lady Mary Coke, however, expresses disappointment that Drayton, with its 4,000 acres, was left to Lord George Sackville rather than Vere's son and heir Aubrey. She wrote to her sister Lady Greenwich:

> I can't say her will is exactly what I wished or expected, but I cannot
> make any reflection on the memory of so excellent a woman.

Lord and Lady Vere, on the other hand, had never expected that they or their children would inherit the Northamptonshire estate, not only because it was apparently Sir John Germaine's wish (in 1718) that Drayton should descend to the then two-year-old George Sackville but also because the boy's father and brother, successive Dukes of Dorset, had obtained an increasing ascendant over Lady Betty, who lived with them at Knole. Curiously enough, her will stipulated that Lord George Sackville was to forfeit Drayton if he became Duke of Dorset, or died without sons; and Vere's son Aubrey and his children were to enjoy the reversion. Lord George missed the dukedom by fourteen years but his son inherited it, thus combining Drayton and the peerage.

Politics were the main concern of Aubrey Beauclerk's public life until inheriting the Vere barony and Hanworth estate within the space of fifteen months (1781–1783); and even they were not of crucial concern. The chief interest, in fact, lies in the manner of his election to the House of Commons. At first, in May 1761, he was to stand at Windsor with the support of his father and his cousin, the third Duke; his opponents had the support of the King's uncle, the Duke of Cumberland, to whom the St Albans interest had virtually passed by 1754. In return for Beauclerk's agreement to stand down at Windsor, the Duke of Grafton promised him the borough of Thetford. Horace Walpole's friend Conway, who had also been member for Thetford before vacating the seat to Lord Henry Beauclerk, successfully negotiated with the future Prime Minister. 'We are more successful, Madam, than I could flatter myself we should be . . .', writes Walpole to Lady Suffolk.

> It will be expected, I believe, that Lord Vere should resign Windsor
> in a handsome manner to the Duke of Cumberland. It must be your
> Ladyship's part to prepare this—which, I hope, will be the means
> of putting an end to those unhappy differences.

It is obvious that during the third Duke's absence abroad Lord Vere controlled what remained of the St Albanses' interest in Windsor.

Through his marriage to Lady Catherine Ponsonby on 4 May 1763 he acquired splendid connections rather than a fortune. Her father, the second Earl of Bessborough, was a noted art-collector who had held public office as joint Postmaster General; her mother, a goddaughter of George II, was a daughter of the third Duke of Devonshire; her sister was to marry the fourth Earl Fitzwilliam. It was a marriage which could have provided him with a fine entrée into political life on the grand scale, especially as Catherine's cousin by marriage was the Prime Minister Duke of Portland and Catherine and Aubrey used to be his guests at Welbeck. The Beauclerks had never been closer to the heart of Whig power.

But Aubrey Beauclerk preferred domesticity, and politics at a more local level, during the thirteen years he was in the Commons (such as defending a bill 'for the better paving, cleansing, lighting and watching the streets, lanes and alleys within the town of Windsor'), and not even politics at a local level in the years after he became Duke. Most of all he enjoyed field sports: getting the consent of the Duke of Portland to shoot on his farm at Dunwood, near Romsey; buying a pack of hounds, about which he asked Portland's advice in 1773; fishing on the Duke of Norfolk's estate at Ewood, near Dorking;[4] and owning a small racing-stable from 1784 to 1790.

With his father-in-law Lord Bessborough he shared a passion for art-collecting. His pictures, drawings, marbles, bas-reliefs, bronzes and ivories were, in the words of his 1798 sale catalogue, largely 'collected during a long residence at Rome, and other parts of the Continent': he was, in fact, often abroad in the 1770s and until his inheritance of his father's title in 1781, and it was these visits to the Continent which gave him his taste for the fine arts. Lady Mary Lowther remarks in a letter to Lady Mary Coke, on 4 June 1778, that 'Mr Beauclerk, Lady Catherine and Mr Brand were gone together abroad, being so in debt they found it troublesome staying at home' (Thomas Brand, of The Hoo, Welwyn, Hertfordshire was so close a family friend that it may have been on his account that rumours built up which Lady Catherine's father did his best to dispel). Aubrey and his wife were also abroad in August 1781, but returning home through Brussels, and Lady Mary Coke suspected that their homecoming 'was a sudden resolution, for I heard they had no intention of going back while Lord Vere lived'. In 1779 we hear of a bas-relief of 'Castor and Alcyone', by Thomas Banks, being raffled by Lady Catherine Beauclerk in Rome,[5] and it was probably in Italy in 1781 that the rather stiff, stilted family portrait of Aubrey, his wife, their eldest son and two of their daughters was painted by the ageing Pietro Longhi. And no sooner had the future Duke returned to England in 1781 than Reynolds painted his portrait (for £36-15-0d!); Romney, not long afterwards, painted separate portraits of himself and Lady Catherine.

The picture of the fifth Duke which George Romney has left us matches his description by the Rev. William Cole:[6] he is a country squire rather than a ducal magnate—ruddy-complexioned like a farmer, with metal-buttoned waistcoat, green shooting-jacket and gun, obviously in a rude state of health but rather unimaginative in appearance, standing solidly, ruminatively and even a little red-nosed against a wooded background. Nor is the portrait by Longhi more flattering, for there he is shown as stolid, puffy and obese. To all appearances he is the type of man who loves his children deeply but undemonstratively, will never set the Thames—or the Tiber—on fire, will not even be a pillar of the community in the fullest sense but to whose care and attention many a confidential matter can be entrusted, a healing, prospering influence ensuring that things go quietly and uneventfully forward.

Even when there were suspicions of an affair between his wife and Thomas Brand, he was conciliatory, almost complacent, in his way of handling the matter. 'You can't imagine how much that foolish affair concerning my daughter has affected me . . .', Lord Bessborough writes despairingly to his other daughter Lady Fitzwilliam.

> I knew last year it would be taken notice of in some of the papers, and I gave her, as you know, a hint of it, but Mr Beauclerk did not think proper to attend to it. . . . He says indeed he wishes he could stop their mouths, but as that cannot be he has recommended to her to go on just as she always has done.

Aubrey gives every indication of having been as indulgent, and even permissive, towards his wife as her cousin the fifth Duke of Devonshire was self-indulgent in the celebrated *ménage à trois* consisting of himself, his wife and another woman.

How different all this seems from Lady Mary Coke's much earlier opinion of Lady Catherine: 'she is one of the few young people who has not a fault in her behaviour'! The fault may have been more apparent than real—'nothing but a little indiscretion', in Lord Bessborough's words—yet it gave rise to scandalous talk. To her father's dismay, and no doubt her husband's, there was even a 'paragraph in one of the papers, reflecting on her conduct'. Nevertheless her death, of cancer in 1789 at the bitterly early age of forty-seven, was a grievous and irreparable blow to the fifth Duke. Although bereaved before fifty, he did not remarry. His eldest daughter Catherine managed his house and did not take a husband until six months after his death.

As a trustee for his brother-in-law Lord Fitzwilliam, his business hours as a widower were occasionally filled with transactions for land in Northamptonshire, Nottinghamshire, Yorkshire, Huntingdonshire and Lincolnshire. Gradually he found himself going more and more regularly to Weymouth, which with the frequent visits of George III, his brother the Duke of Gloucester and the Court had usurped something of the popularity of Bath and Tunbridge Wells. In July 1790, a year after his wife's death and a year after George III's visits to Weymouth began, he was given permission 'to erect a seat on the esplanade opposite his house, and make steps to the sand there'. This house was probably what is now known as 12 Clarence Buildings; the adjacent small street, formerly Petticoat Lane, was renamed St Albans Street in his honour.

Mr Barton, who in 1775 had taken the farm of Bestwood Park on a twenty-one-year lease from the third Duke, died in the early 1790s but the lease was retained by his family. Robert Lowe, writing a report on Nottinghamshire agriculture in 1794, notes that the park was then sublet into eight farms. In 1796 the fifth Duke secured a new tenant, William Ellis, at £1,500 p.a., almost three times the former rent. Ellis was fortunate to benefit from his predecessor's initial work. Whether through good luck or his own skill and labour, or both, he was successful to the extent of making a profit on his farming of £3,000 p.a. The only sad, and too businesslike, aspect of the fifth Duke's management of Bestwood is that around 1796 Barton's widow was left to face an expensive action brought by the landlord for dilapidations. Yet the poor, recently bankrupted dependants of the dead man presumably had nowhere in the world to go, as they were still living at the Old Hall in 1798 despite William Ellis's tenancy. Ellis appears to have been resident at Bestwood Hall by 1813.

The same slight abrasiveness is to be found in the running of the Hanworth estate. The fifth Duke greatly incensed Horace Walpole who, writing to Miss Mary Berry on 8 June 1791, laments the felling of 'all the brave old trees at Hanworth'. What had once been a beautiful park of oaks, ashes and chestnuts was 'consequently reduced . . . to what it issued from,—Hounslow Heath'. The Hanworth property did not stretch as far as the river, and the Duke had had to rent a meadow across which to embark the timber. This had blocked one of Walpole's views on to the Thames, and though not blocking the Miss Berrys' view it was something of an eyesore as the timberyard lay beneath their window. It was intensely annoying to have so enterprising a neighbour, but with considerable prescience Walpole foresaw 'one street from London to Brentford, ay and from London to every village ten miles round'—so that with luck the timber would quickly be used up, 'so impetuous is the rage for building'.

The destruction of Hanworth Palace by fire on 26 March 1797 was perhaps the greatest of events in St Albans's uneventful life and certainly an even more sensational event than the creation of a timberyard by the river Thames. The house was almost totally burned down, and so was the ancient parish church which stood beside it. Nowadays only a few vestiges of the Palace remain, by the vague outline of the former moat. Apart from the Kneller ceiling, no valuable work of art was lost as there were no Beauclerk pictures in the house at the time of the fire except a few portraits which were copies. With his interest in art-collecting, St Albans had wished to centralize all his paintings, and these were assembled at his house in Mansfield Street where he mostly lived.

He seems to have spent little time at Hanworth after his wife's death, and in 1793 the house with twenty acres had actually been leased to a tenant, Edward Russell Howe; another tenant leased the lodge, parkland, wood and 'pieces of water' extending in all to 142 acres. To compensate for the temporary relinquishment of Hanworth, and as an occasional retreat from London, he himself had a smaller house, Hampton Deep, only four miles away—purchased after the drawing-up of his will (22 June 1795).

Meanwhile Hanworth had to be rebuilt, and the rebuilding was rapid. A site was chosen on higher ground, half a mile distant from the original. Work began in 1798, and was completed by 1802. The church too was rebuilt, under the supervision of the Duke's chaplain the Rev. James Burgess, but this was a later assignment—in the time of the sixth Duke—for which funds began to be raised in 1808, and which was finished by 1812. The present parish church of Hanworth is not even the one built in the early nineteenth century, but a newer one dating from 1865.

It was in order to raise funds for the new Hanworth House (the rebuilt mansion has never been known as a Palace) that the fifth Duke auctioned a large part of his art-collection on 8 and 9 June 1798. Not all the paintings, marbles and bronzes had been acquired by him personally: indeed, the finest of the twenty-four pictures, Claude's 'Jacob with Laban and his Daughters', was bought in 1739 from the sale of the Earl of Halifax, presumably by Lord Vere Beauclerk; yet this gallery of works of art—and especially statuary—establishes St Albans as one of the more important dilettanti of his time. The antique sculptures (including an 'Apollo' formerly in the collection of his father-in-law the second Earl of Bessborough at Ingress Abbey, Greenhithe, a 'Marcus Aurelius' found near the ancient aqueduct of Centocelle, vases of marble, alabaster and porphyry, a marble 'Diana Triformis', and an antique bronze of Anchises and Æneas) were the finest feature of what must have been a very extensive gallery in Mansfield Street; but besides the Claude, which fetched £220-10-0d and is now in the Dulwich College Picture Gallery,[7] there were also apparently a Poussin and a Rembrandt. The Poussin, 'A Bacchante crossing a River', was sold for £73-10-0d and Rembrandt's 'Matron Giving Advice to her Daughter' for no less than £315. Neither of these has so far been traced. Horst Gerson's revised and complete edition of the paintings of Rembrandt gives no clue to the elusive masterpiece; and it is a fact that Rembrandt rarely painted group portraits, and only once (to our knowledge) a painting of a mother and daughter.

Oddly enough, within three years (5, 6, 7 February 1801) we find St Albans at Christie's bidding at the rather belated auction of his father-in-law, Lord Bessborough, who had died in 1793. He came away with forty-two lots—and many more than that number of items—after spending a total of £2,109-15-6d. This stolid, phlegmatic man, with his fox-hunting and country pursuits, had in the very evening of his life been transformed into a passionate collector, yet one not so sure of his own judgement as to resist the temptation of buying so largely from his father-in-law. He paid £409-10-0 for a 'Landscape with Cattle' by Aelbert Cuyp, £304 for a Claude 'Seaport on the Coast of Italy' and £231 for a 'Madonna and Child' said to be by Raphael and formerly in the collection of the second Earl Waldegrave to whom it had been given by Stanislas Leszczyński. His other expenses included £157-10-0d for a painting of 'Pharaoh's Baker and Butler in Prison' by Ribera; £67-4-0d for 'Venus Dormant with Cupids', by Poussin; £43-1-0d for a Sassoferrato Madonna; £64-1-0d for an Annibale Carracci, 'Venus and Young Satyrs'; and £99-15-0d for another alleged Raphael, 'St John in the Desert', which was one of twelve Raphaels in the gallery of Philippe Égalité, Duke of Orleans, and had been acquired by the third Earl of Bessborough in London in 1798.

At St Albans's death on 9 February 1802 at least eleven of the twenty-nine paintings bought at the Bessborough sale were sold at a second St Albans auction on the instructions of the fifth Duke's sole executrix Lady Catherine Beauclerk (soon to marry that most enterprising of rectors of Hanworth, Mr Burgess); she had been left the residue of her father's estate, and a ledger entry of her account with Ransoms Bank shows that Christies paid her £1,000 on 5 April 1802. Amongst the eleven paintings were Hondecoeter's 'Live Poultry', Liotard's pastel of 'A Young Lady and Gouvernante at Breakfast' and Raphael's 'Madonna and Child'. The Bessborough paintings had not been a sound investment. The sums Lady Catherine drew in 1802 were often much less than those her father had paid for the same works of art a year previously: £38-17-0d instead of £89-5-0d for the Liotard; £21 instead of £43-1-0d for the Hondecoeter; £131-5-0d instead of £231 for the Raphael.

In a seemingly tireless interchange of family treasures, statues of Flora and Hecate were bought by the third Earl of Bessborough, the fifth Duke's brother-in-law. St Albans's 'porphyry vase and cover by Silvio of Veletri' may have been the vase purchased by Sir John Soane, who also bought a cinerary urn to add to his famous room with its shelvesful of urns of the dead at Pitzhanger Manor, Ealing. These objects from the later St Albans auction are now in Sir John Soane's Museum. In June and July 1802 the sixth Duke of St Albans took out two bonds totalling £41,000 from the banker Robert Drummond, and it seems therefore that in addition to the costs of rebuilding Hanworth House he had to pay for his father's lavishness—and moments of recklessness—as a connoisseur.

Of the four sons of the fifth Duke, two became sailors, one a parson and the eldest a soldier. Lord Burford was granted a commission in the 1st Foot Guards in 1781, promoted captain in the 45th Foot in 1783, transferred in the same year to the 34th Foot, and successively promoted major and lieutenant-colonel in 1789. In 1787 he was serving in Canada, and writes to the Duke of Portland on 8 August 1794 of 'fifteen years' service, four of which in America'. In this letter he vainly asked to be appointed A.D.C. to George III, and in the following month insisted on obtaining special leave from his regiment, which was about to be posted from Ireland to the West Indies. He even threatened to resign his commission if his request for special leave were not granted, but his threat would not have terrified the War Office as his service career was entirely without distinction. His moment of greatest achievement came in 1787 when, during a voyage from Quebec to England in the *Lord Shelburne*, the ship was struck by a gale lasting five days and was in danger of foundering; the lives of 150 souls were at risk, and the boats had room for only eighty-one; on orders from his commanding officer, Burford seized a brig that had come to assist the sinking ship, threw its cargo overboard, and so saved the lives of all the passengers aboard the *Lord Shelburne*.

To his brother Amelius such episodes were almost commonplace. Aboard H.M.S. *Dryad* in June 1796, with 251 men under his command, he captured the French frigate *La Proserpine*, with its larger complement of 348 men. This engagement off the coast of Ireland is said to have been close and spirited, and lasted a mere three-quarters of an hour. Thirty

The First Lord Vere of Hanworth: by Thomas Hudson, c. 1749.
Admiral Lord Vere was the father of the fifth Duke.

Hanworth Palace, Middlesex: a coloured drawing on an estate map of August 1738.
This map, of demesnes in Hanworth, Feltham, Heston and elsewhere, was executed two
years after Lord Vere Beauclerk came into the estate. Hanworth Palace was destroyed by
fire on 26 March 1797.

The Honourable Aubrey
Beauclerk, his Wife, Son
and Two Daughters:
attributed to Pietro
Longhi, and painted
c. 1781.

Aubrey Beauclerk soon
afterwards became second
Lord Vere of Hanworth,
and later fifth Duke of St.
Albans. The son was to
become the sixth Duke,
and the two daughters
are Caroline and
Georgiana. The portrait
may well have been
painted during one of the
Duke's stays in Italy.

French sailors were killed, against two of his own, and forty-five wounded against seven. It is the action commemorated by Thomas Whitcombe in two fine seascapes which still belong to the dukes of St Albans. He was present at the blockade of Toulon in 1794, at the blockade of Brest in 1803, and in 1809 superintended the debarkation of Lord Chatham's army in the ill-fated Walcheren expedition. He rose to be Admiral of the White and principal naval A.D.C. to William IV and Queen Victoria.

In all but the eldest son and heir, such patterns of strenuous activity are the norm for the fifth Duke's sons. Even the youngest, Lord Frederick, combined his cure of souls as Vicar of the Hertfordshire parishes of Kimpton, Redbourn and St Michael's, St Albans with outstanding prowess on the cricket-field (as Vicar of Kimpton his patron was Lord Dacre, son of the Thomas Brand who had been his parents' friend; as occupant of Kimpton Hall he was Dacre's tenant). Long before Charles Kingsley had ever heard of the phrase, he embodied the sternly Victorian ideal of 'muscular Christianity'—passionately addicted to all field sports and riding to hounds until a green old age. He was President of the M.C.C., and an earlier incarnation of W. G. Grace. He was the best all-round gentleman player in England for many years, and in matches of every importance his word was law. In his pulpit at St Albans he fixed a saddle on which he sat as he delivered his sermons; the feel of the saddle gave him confidence. He made eight centuries at Lord's between 1796 and 1809, and he raced and rode horses under pseudonyms (such as 'Mr Brand'!) so as not to offend the Bishop of Rochester.

Such energy and resourcefulness were not the provinces of the sixth Duke. His political career as member for Kingston-upon-Hull from 1790 to 1796 was no more distinguished than his career in the Army. He failed in his attempt in 1806 to revive the pension of £1,000 p.a. granted to his ancestor by Queen Anne, which had lapsed in 1803; he failed in 1810 to revive the Chancery Registrarship, which the Lord Chancellor insisted to the Home Secretary could not be regranted 'for two or more lives—for an estate of inheritance';[8] and yet he had voted in Parliament for the abolition of all sinecures. He took his seat in the House of Lords on 20 November 1802 but did not speak on any important issue.

His first marriage was to an heiress, Jane Moses of Kingston-upon-

Hull, daughter of a rich Jewish merchant with Norwegian trade connections. She did not live to become Duchess of St Albans, dying as Countess of Burford at St Paul's Waldenbury (a house close to Kimpton an Welwyn) in 1800, 'an eminent instance of the riches of divine grace, and an exemplary pattern of everything excellent and praiseworthy in the Christian character'. At the tender age of ten her only child and heiress, Lady Mary Beauclerk, came into an estate valued at £100,000. It is doubtful whether Lady Mary could be termed an exemplary pattern of Christian conduct. She was only sixteen, George Elers writes,[9] when she used to walk with Lieutenant Saunders, of the Derby Regiment of Militia, in the park at Helmingham where she was then living as the guest of Lord Dysart.

> [She] gave him every encouragement. But wishing to know as much of him as she could, she employed her maid, who got hold of a very material part of his history: that he was already married and had two children. . . . She afterwards, in 1811, ran away with Lord Deerhurst. All the world knows how badly this match turned out, and Lord Deerhurst has no one to thank but himself.

Deerhurst, heir to the earldom of Coventry, was a widower of twenty-seven when he married her in Scotland. Soon after 1815 she separated from her husband, and lived in Italy with her daughter Augusta—later the wife of the Henry Fox (eventually fourth and last Lord Holland) who knew the ninth Duke of St Albans and his duchess. The Foxes were an unconventional couple, and Augusta scandalized Roman society by riding astride. The Countess of Coventry allowed her daughter £1,000 p.a. after marriage; and, at her death in Naples in 1845, Lord and Lady Holland inherited pictures, jewels, furniture and works of art but only £3,500 in cash. Elers's reference to Helmingham indicates that Lady Mary was staying with her stepmother's uncle at the time when she knew Saunders.

This stepmother, Louisa Duchess of St Albans, married the sixth Duke six months after his succession. She was the fourth daughter of Lady Louisa Manners, later Countess of Dysart in her own right. In Lady Harriet Cavendish's view, she was a 'very great beauty'; the diarist and landscape-artist Joseph Farington, seeing her bust being sculpted by Nollekens, 'admired the beauty and expression of the countenance of the Duchess. He [Nollekens] said she is extremely good-natured'. To Lady Harriet Cavendish 'the Duke [was] the most hideous, disagreeable little animal I ever met with'; and, reading between the lines, it is possible to sympathize with her point of view.

His death, of apoplexy aged forty-nine, gave the succession to his only child by Louisa, a son Aubrey aged four months. Within a few days of the death a sensation had occurred not only in the Beauclerk family but in the Duchess's household in Stratford Place, Marylebone. Whether for fair reason or foul, and however solid or flimsy their suspicions, Lords Amelius and William believed that the infant Duke might not have been their brother's son. If the baby was illegitimate, Lord William would succeed his deceased brother. 'You are perhaps aware', wrote Amelius to his uncle Lord Fitzwilliam, 'that the general opinion of the world is that the child . . . is not my brother's, but by a person of the name of Sinclair', and William in a further letter to Lord Fitzwilliam noted that Sinclair was the Duchess's 'reputed lover'. Although (for instance) almost twice as long a period had gone by between the marriage of Anne of Austria and the birth of Louis XIV, the fact that the baby Duke of St Albans was born over twelve years after his accepted father's marriage lent weight to the suspicion. William and Amelius were incensed by 'reports most injurious to [their] brother's widow'.

This 'person of the name of Sinclair' seems almost certainly to have been the future Sir George Sinclair, second baronet, ancestor of Lord Thurso. In August 1815 this man became twenty-five.

Now there arose a further complication. The new Duke might not be their brother's son, but he was an ailing, puny infant not expected to live long. But what if the Duchess became pregnant again? The first Lord Amelius knew of the gathering storm was when the Duchess's house-keeper arrived breathlessly at his house in Tenterden Street on the morning of 16 August 1815. The previous evening, whilst the late Duke's body was still in the house, Sinclair had called to see Louisa at half past eleven. They were together in a small first-floor room until three in the morning, when a footman let Sinclair out of the house.

Having checked this account with Louisa's other servants, Lord Amelius—perhaps exceeding his authority—left instructions that on no account should any visitors be admitted to the Duchess's house apart from the immediate family. His next tactic was to protest about her 'impropriety' to her brother John Manners, but Manners refused to be drawn in and Amelius was still wondering what to do next when that evening the housekeeper returned with the devastating news that Sinclair was with Louisa again. Anxious to obey Lord Amelius, the servants had refused to admit Sinclair, whereupon Louisa had sent them all out of the house until midnight.

Amelius again hurried to Marylebone. There is something odd, and even a little officious, about the conduct of a man who had seen life in the Navy and who was even to produce a bastard of his own—born to him at the unseemly age of sixty-five. On his second visit to the Duchess's house he met Louisa herself and also her sister Laura Dalrymple. Laura appeared, descending the stairs with Sinclair. 'I accosted her', Lord Amelius wrote to Fitzwilliam, 'and asked her who her friend was, on which she immediately without giving me an answer ran upstairs to the Duchess'. Though it was turned eleven o'clock, Sinclair insisted that he had come 'on business' to the Duchess; but Amelius insisted on confronting her with this tale. She hustled papers under her seat as they entered, offering to show them to him the next morning at ten. This compromise did nothing to appease her brother-in-law: 'no, Madam', he answered, 'your conduct is of such a mysterious nature, and of so little delicacy to my brother's memory, I shall never enter your house again'. Louisa dismissed most of her servants the next day and gave strict orders that Lords Amelius and William should not be admitted. Amelius took care to obtain an affidavit from the housekeeper; he was convinced that Louisa was 'acting the part of hypocrite in a Most Diabolical Manner'!

The next stage in the family drama was reached on 23 August, when Louisa announced to her physician Sir William Knighton that she had become pregnant again. The sixth Duke had now been dead eleven days, and Knighton refused to believe her. The prospect of a posthumous heir gravely damaged Lord William's personal hopes of succession, and also the family's honour in that it was soon established to the brothers' complete satisfaction that a posthumous child could not possibly be the late Duke's. Amelius questioned Louisa's 'own maid and her housekeeper' about her periods, and they 'both solemnly declared . . . that she had had her regular *menses* the day after [the sixth Duke's] death'.

On 26 August, exactly a fortnight after the Duke's death, Lord William himself spoke to Sinclair, reminding him that '[his] stake was a great one'. The whole family, William warned, felt 'jealous of his mysterious visits to the Duchess, whom we looked upon as a very strange woman. He acknowledged that he thought so also, and he gave . . . his word of honour that he would not visit her for a month'. Sinclair even volunteered to leave London for Scotland, and in any case Louisa was strictly watched.

Lord Fitzwilliam, however, went a stage further than his nephews in suggesting that the seventh Duke may not even have been his *mother's* child. By August 1815 it was impossible to dispute the baby's paternity, since the late Duke had always accepted him as his son; but even after the boy's succession it was possible to dispute the identity of his mother. With this in view, Lords William and Amelius investigated every aspect of the seventh Duke's entry into the world, only too well aware of 'the mysterious manner in which it was brought into the world, and which will for ever carry a doubt in many persons' minds and for ever leave a stigma on the proceedings of the parents'.

The family doctor, the monthly nurse, the wetnurse, the wetnurse's son, a Mrs Dunbar and various maids were all questioned by the diligent Amelius; the maids, it appeared, had been sworn to secrecy about the Duchess's pregnancy in 1814 and about the loose-fitting clothes she wore to disguise it. There was even some fear that Louisa might have exchanged her baby for the wetnurse's; but all these doubts were dispelled to the uncles' satisfaction although there remained the possibility—such was her reputation—that even at this late stage she might try to exchange the sickly Duke for a sturdier child of the people.

The infant Duke was not born at the time (18 July 1814) when his father's will had been drawn up. Hence the absence of any specific mention of the boy. This will bequeathed all freehold and copyhold lands in Hanworth, Feltham, Heston and Isleworth to Louisa for life, with remainder as she should appoint: a remarkably loose provision. Clearly, the Hanworth estate was not entailed on the sixth Duke's immediate successors in the dukedom, born or unborn. Such *entailed* property as there was went, of course, to the seventh Duke: the Bestwood estate, the family's settled pictures and plate, and £40,000 in the stocks—together with the emoluments of the Hereditary Grand Falconership. Lord Amelius estimated the income from the entailed property, including the Grand Falconership, at around £3,000 p.a. net.

Morally, at least, the seventh Duke was as entitled to Hanworth as any of his immediate ancestors. Lord William resented the alienation of the estate. The family would not accept the will without a struggle. William wrote to Fitzwilliam that 'the original part of the Duke's will is . . . missing, and no one can have it but her'. Despite threats of legal proceedings, however, they failed to regain Hanworth from Louisa. On 28 November 1815 she herself made a will. Presumably angry at the Beauclerks' treatment of herself, she left all her possessions to her sister Laura Dalrymple for life with remainder as *she* should appoint. In default of such appointment, Hanworth and the other estates in that district were to go to her infant son, the seventh Duke. Failing his issue, Hanworth and the property in Feltham, Heston and Isleworth were to become her sister's absolutely. Mrs Dalrymple had reaped a rich reward, including many Beauclerk heirlooms, in return for her devoted friendship with the Duchess.

On 19 February 1816 Louisa died, aged thirty-eight. The final bizarre aspect of the story is that she died only three hours after her son. Both appear to have died of a 'hectic disease, which no medical skill could subdue', and the double death gave rise to much public comment. Bestwood, where the family had never chosen to live, was all that was salvaged from the wreckage of the Beauclerks' hopes, as Hanworth—on which tens of thousands of pounds had just recently been spent, and for which the great Claude had been sold—slipped effortlessly away into the hands of Mrs Laura Dalrymple.

Amongst the many Beauclerk heirlooms she inherited were family pictures which she distributed amongst her own relatives. Perhaps the majority of these were given to her nephew Wilbraham Tollemache, whose widow bequeathed them in 1883 to her cousin Sir Thomas Munro Bt of Lindertis; one of the Beauclerk heirlooms bequeathed to Sir Thomas Munro was a Bible once owned by Nell Gwyn. To her companion Jane Beauchamp Laura Dalrymple left £20,000 at her death in 1834, and Jane Beauchamp in her turn left this money to Arthur, the son of her brother John; he was the grandfather of Katherine Mansfield, and though the line of inheritance from the Chambers of Jamaica to the Beauchamps who settled in New Zealand may at first seem jagged and arbitrary, it is not without a strange romantic logic.

As for the crux of Laura Dalrymple's will, Hanworth passed to her brother Charles Tollemache's younger daughter Lady Ailesbury with the provision that her own mother Louisa Countess of Dysart should enjoy it for life. On Lady Dysart's death in 1840 the Marchioness of Ailesbury sold it to the Perkins family, who still held 463 acres around Hanworth in 1873. This was the acreage to which Hanworth had been roughly reduced by the Beauclerks themselves, who in 1811 sold a great part of it—including the actual park—for £56,175 to pay off the mortgage of £41,000 advanced by Robert Drummond. James Ramsey Cuthbert, who leased the park and lodge, had become nominal owner of Hanworth in September 1810, thus releasing from the marriage settlement what remained of the original 849 acres of Hanworth after 1811. In 1816 this remainder of Hanworth was valued at £100,000.

The Beauclerks' proneness to financial disaster has been the dominant theme of this chapter as first the Werden estates were lost to the Drummonds on the fourth Duke's death, then Hanworth (won by Lord Vere) razed to the ground by fire, then rebuilt at harsh sacrifice only to be entirely lost within fifteen years through the Most Diabolical activities of a *femme fatale*!

majority of these were given to her nephew Wilbraham Tollemache, whose widow bequeathed them in 1883 to her cousin Sir Thomas Munro Bt of Lindertis; one of the Beauclerk heirlooms bequeathed to Sir Thomas Munro was a Bible once owned by Nell Gwyn. To her companion Jane Beauchamp Laura Dalrymple left £20,000 at her death in 1834, and Jane Beauchamp in her turn left this money to Arthur, the son of her brother John; he was the grandfather of Katherine Mansfield, and though the line of inheritance from the Chambers of Jamaica to the Beauchamps who settled in New Zealand may at first seem jagged and arbitrary, it is not without a strange romantic logic.

As for the crux of Laura Dalrymple's will, Hanworth passed to her brother Charles Tollemache's younger daughter Lady Ailesbury with the provision that her own mother Louisa Countess of Dysart should enjoy it for life. On Lady Dysart's death in 1840 the Marchioness of Ailesbury sold it to the Perkins family, who still held 463 acres around Hanworth in 1873. This was the acreage to which Hanworth had been roughly reduced by the Beauclerks themselves, who in 1811 sold a great part of it—including the actual park—for £56,175 to pay off the mortgage of £41,000 advanced by Robert Drummond. James Ramsey Cuthbert, who leased the park and lodge, had become nominal owner of Hanworth in September 1810, thus releasing from the marriage settlement what remained of the original 849 acres of Hanworth after 1811. In 1816 this remainder of Hanworth was valued at £100,000.

The Beauclerks' proneness to financial disaster has been the dominant theme of this chapter as first the Werden estates were lost to the Drummonds on the fourth Duke's death, then Hanworth (won by Lord Vere) razed to the ground by fire, then rebuilt at harsh sacrifice only to be entirely lost within fifteen years through the Most Diabolical activities of a *femme fatale*!

NOTES TO CHAPTER V

Archives of Drummonds Bank.

Wills of Sir John Werden, Colonel Charles Beauclerk, 4th and 6th Dukes of St Albans, Louisa Duchess of St Albans and Lady Laura Tollemache.

Hanworth deposit: Greater London RO.

Wentworth Woodhouse Muniments in the Sheffield City Libraries.

Capital Original Pictures and Drawings, Valuable Antique Marbles, Bronzes, etc., H. Phillips, 67 New Bond Street, 8, 9, 11 June 1798.

A Catalogue of the Well Known, Valuable and Truly Capital Collection of Pictures ... formed by the late Earl of Bessborough, Christie, Pall Mall, 5, 6, 7 February 1801.

A Catalogue of a Capital and Valuable Collection of Italian, French, Flemish and Dutch Pictures, Valuable Antique Marbles ... the Property of the late Duke of St Albans, Deceased, brought from His Grace's late Residence in Mansfield Street, Christie, Pall Mall, 27 March 1802.

H. H. Bolitho and D. Peel: *op. cit.*

Lady M. Coke: *op. cit.*

J. T. Godfrey: *op. cit.*

J. Langdon (ed.): *op. cit.*

R. Lowe: *General View of the Agriculture of the County of Nottingham,* 1794.

G. E. Mingay: *English Landed Society in the Eighteenth Century,* 1963.

G. Ormerod: *op. cit.*

R. R. Sedgwick: *op. cit.*

Henrietta Countess of Suffolk: *Letters,* 1824.

R. Thoroton: *History of Nottinghamshire* (revised and enlarged edn), 1790.

H. Walpole: *Correspondence,* 1937–1973.

---

1. Historical Manuscripts Commission *Report on American Manuscripts in the Royal Institution of Great Britain,* vol. II, 1906, 138; Charles Jenkinson to General Sir Henry Clinton, 7 June 1780.

2. Public RO PROB 11/1150/92.
3. W. J. Smith (ed.): *op. cit.*, vol. II, 311–312.
4. Arundel Castle MSS, Howard Letters 1760–1816.
5. H. Swinburne: *The Courts of Europe at the Close of the Last Century*, 1841, vol. I, 238.
6. H. Walpole: *Correspondence*, vol. X, 1941, 342–343.
7. M. Röthlisberger: *Claude Lorrain. The Paintings*, 1961, vol. I, 442–443.
8. Harrowby MSS, vol. XCV, 146–147; Earl of Eldon to Richard Ryder, 3 July 1810.
9. G. Elers: *Memoirs*, 1903, 244–245.

Chapter VI

A Man to be Reckoned With

It is a refreshing change from the folly of Hanworth to consider the career of Lord William Beauclerk, later to become eighth Duke. He was no saint, but a man of commonsense, pragmatism and energy. For the first forty or so years of his life, he had no strong expectations of succeeding to the title or Bestwood; but he had already consolidated the position of his line of the family by securing for it an estate larger than the one he was to inherit when he became duke.

This estate—at Redbourne, in Lincolnshire—was obtained through a prudent marriage. Even though that marriage had no surviving children, Redbourne still remained with him rather than with his first wife's side of the family. In other words, he had performed a feat very similar to Louisa's—only this time to the Beauclerks' advantage. He went on to marry again, within seventeen months, and by his second wife produced a family of seven sons and six daughters. From him the ninth to the thirteenth (and present) dukes descend. Almost all the remaining heirs to the title are his descendants. No good portrait of him in middle or old age exists, but from the fine portrait of him painted by Romney when he was a midshipman of seventeen it would be hard to deduce the lucid, dispassionate realism which seems to have informed his life.

As a midshipman he served in H.M.S. *Triumph* in the Channel, then in H.M.S. *Warwick* off America under the future Admiral Lord Keith, and later off the East Indies in H.M.S. *Crocodile*. Still off the East Indies, and now serving under Admiral (Andrew) Mitchell, he was promoted acting lieutenant. He was confirmed in rank in April 1788, and served under Commodore Parker in or off West Indies, presumably as his secretary. His active career in the Navy, which began in 1782, effectively ceased with his marriage to Charlotte Carter Thelwall on 20 July 1791.

He remained, however, on the Navy List until his death, and on 29 July
1822 was promoted commander on his retirement. This last promotion
was clearly an honorary one, and his retirement purely formal.

At the time of her wedding to Lord William, his bride was not merely
an heiress with substantial expectations; she was an orphan (like Jane
Roberts), and the actual owner of Redbourne Hall, near Brigg, with its
5,000 acres. This estate had come into the Carters' possession in 1703,
through the marriage of Thomas Carter to Elizabeth, eldest sister and
ultimate co-heiress of Sir Oliver Style; only in the three months during
which the latter was head of the family did Redbourne actually belong to
a Style baronet, having descended to him from his mother, an Armine of
Osgodby. The Carters had long resided at Kinmel in Denbighshire, but
that property had been sold in 1729 by Elizabeth Carter's son William.
The latter's son Robert, who was to become the father of Lady William
Beauclerk, was a younger son who after service in the Lincolnshire
Provincial Regiment in 1745 made his career in the Church.

The death of an elder brother without issue in 1768 meant that he
inherited the Lincolnshire estates; in 1774 he also came into the considerable fortune of his other brother Roger, an India merchant.[1] Shortly
afterwards he inherited yet another fortune, the Thelwall estate at
Bathafarn in Denbighshire, and changed his name to Carter Thelwall.

On entering into possession of Redbourne a year after his marriage
he resigned his twin livings of Waddington and Broughton and became
a bluff country squire, spending about three months of each year in
Denbighshire and the remainder at Redbourne which he made into his
principal home. In 1773 he undertook improvements to the Hall at
Redbourne, enlarged the parish church in 1775, and a year later—in
complacent thanks for the good gifts of God—built a Triumphal Arch.
In the same year he, his wife and daughter were painted by Stubbs.

Each year at Redbourne was held 'a kind of annual village feast or
fête champêtre' attended by all the tenants and cottagers and their wives.
The month originally chosen for these festivities was April, to coincide
with his daughter's birthday. Later, the occasion was transformed into a
harvest festival and held in October. One hundred and fifty people would
forgather in the grounds of the Hall; a banquet would be laid on, with the

tenants eating in the house and the cottagers (weather permitting) in the open air; after the meal there would be wrestling, sack races and other sports; and at the end of the day Squire Carter Thelwall would hand out £1 in prize money. Not until the time of the ninth Duke of St Albans was such munificence to be seen at Redbourne, though by 1830 it was munificence on a more lavish scale.

The girl who became Lady William Beauclerk in 1791 was the only child of Robert and Charlotte Carter Thelwall. For four years before her marriage she seems to have been brought up at the home of her father's sister Mrs Eleanor Vyner, at Gautby, about twenty-five miles south-east of Redbourne. Life must have been almost insufferably lonely for Charlotte Carter Thelwall as she approached adulthood. Her mother had died in 1780, her father in 1787, and marriage no doubt seemed the most delightful of all prospects when it offered itself in the form of a handsome naval lieutenant two years older than herself. After their marriage at Gautby in 1791 they settled at Redbourne and William made this, rather than the Navy, into his career.

Little disturbed the peaceful life of the estate which with its farming, field sports and social engagements went on much as in the time of Squire Carter Thelwall, except for the birth and death of a son, William Robert—the merest infant—in May 1794, and then the sudden devastating blow of the death of Lady William Beauclerk herself, on 19 October 1797, aged twenty-nine.

Not everyone had been as convinced of Lord William's attractiveness as his late wife. To some he had appeared too scheming, ruthless and cunning, especially perhaps to those who had been a little jealous of the exceptional good fortune of a young man of twenty-four in marrying so charming and wealthy a bride. 'Lord William was a *roué*, good for nothing', Sir Charles Anderson noted acidly in his memoirs as he looked back over a long life in the 1860s.

> He had got Redbourne by his first wife whom he used badly, and was not an acquisition in any way to the County.

The most jealous and disapproving of all were to be found amongst his wife's relations, of whom Sir Charles Anderson was one (being the grandson of Charlotte's cousin). Their disapproval became angry disappointment when the news broke that Lord William had become the outright owner of Redbourne and Bathafarn: Charlotte's marriage settlement had given her power of appointment to name the successor to her estates, if she died without surviving issue, and she had left them to her husband.

The principal parties to the dispute were William Beauclerk and Welsh cousins of the Carters, the Kenricks of Nantclwyd. Bathafarn, the object of dispute, was not in itself a very large property (972 acres, with a small though substantial Georgian mansion which still stands today), but the stake was high enough to justify going to law. Matters came to a head in 1799 when Lord William Beauclerk sold Bathafarn to the Rev. Roger Clough. The Kenricks disputed the soundness of Charlotte's will in the Court of Chancery, but it was held to be valid.

In view of this disaster the Lincolnshire cousins of the Carters were loth to try their strength against the 'good for nothing'; yet the doubts remained, and they centred around the will. Writing at a considerable distance of time, and admittedly with some partiality, Sir Charles Anderson notes: 'I have heard my mother say that there was reason to suppose a later will was destroyed'. The will which was found after Lady William's death (and which, incidentally, is missing today: it did not need to be proved as it was an appointment under a settlement) was, it seems, forced upon her by her husband; the solicitor who knew she had made it under duress afterwards committed suicide.

Throughout the brief six years of their marriage Lord William had 'treated her badly', but mental cruelty was not a crime in 1797 and in any case possession was nine-tenths of the law. All this might seem to be the carping, ungenerous attitude of a man unwilling to accept the loss of Redbourne to an outsider, were it not for the generally balanced tone of the Anderson memoirs and the fact that his grandfather Sir John Nelthorpe had been Charlotte's executor.

My grandfather [Anderson continues] went to Redbourne on the evening of Lady William's death from Scawby [the two estates are about four miles apart]. [He] found a packet or deed, which he had

seen before in a drawer and which he took to be one of her private
deeds, had been removed when he returned the next morning to
transact business as executor.

Faced with the disappearance of a will, if in fact one did disappear, there
was no redress for the Nelthorpes, Vyners and Carters but to seek out the
witnesses. There was not even any effective form of protest open to the
executor. The matter was heard in Chancery in 1799. Mary Carter,
Eleanor Vyner and Charlotte Nelthorpe, the heiresses at law, did not
accept that Lady William's will bequeathing Redbourne to her husband
could have been the last appointment under the marriage settlement.
Contrarily, if it was, they asserted that she was either forced to make the
appointment or else was of unsound mind. Lord William, however, was
triumphant; and, having also proved his title to Bathafarn and sold the
Welsh property, he put Redbourne at the centre of his life.

Whatever impression he made upon Lincolnshire society, he continued
to mix with it. In 1804 he was made lieutenant-colonel of the Brigg,
Caistor and Raisen battalion of the Norfolk Volunteers; he even served
as High Sheriff of the county in 1808. His next wife, Maria Janetta
Nelthorpe, was also from Lincolnshire. The fifth cousin of Charlotte
Carter Thelwall, whose mother had been a Nelthorpe, she was the only
daughter and heiress of John Nelthorpe, of Little Grimsby near Louth:
an estate which had been in the Nelthorpes' continuous ownership since
1688. On 4 March 1799 the marriage took place in the fifteenth-century
chapel of Little Grimsby, adjacent to the Hall and one of the smallest
chapels in England. The bride was twenty-four, the bridegroom thirty-
two. Not until 1811 did she actually come into possession of the Queen
Anne mansion with its 818 acres and village of tenants, shopkeepers and
cottagers who used the hall chapel as their parish church. It later became
the home of Maria Janetta's second surviving son, Frederick, in whose
descendants it continued until finally sold in 1918.[2]

The mansion at Redbourne was a Georgian structure in stone, brick
and slate, with sixteen bedrooms and an enormous drawing-room. It had
a smoking-room with panelling very similar to that in the Oak Room at
Chatsworth. Half a mile away from the Hall, across fields, was a church

whose patronage was in the gift of the Carters and later the Beauclerks; and in the grounds of the park itself were the ruins of a medieval chapel. The estate was divided into about twenty farms. The whole of the small village of Redbourne, along with the neighbouring village of Hibaldstow (two miles away), also belonged to Lord William. Quite apart from the Lincolnshire landholding at Redbourne and Hibaldstow, there was another Carter estate in the same county: Pickworth, near Sleaford, much smaller in acreage than Redbourne (just over 1,000 acres) and about forty miles away from the main seat. The small hall at Pickworth, built by a wool merchant in the early Tudor period, seems not to have housed Lord William's family at any time, largely because it would have been too small for his numerous children. Presumably Pickworth Hall was let. Like the Carters, the Beauclerks frequently mortgaged the whole of the Pickworth estate until they eventually sold it in 1864 to raise funds for the building of Bestwood Lodge.

As the children of Lord and Lady William grew up, the atmosphere of Redbourne Hall became very different from the sad, lonely years when Robert Carter Thelwall was a widower and his daughter an orphan. The Beauclerks were fond of throwing parties, usually of an informal, artistic kind. In 1812, a year before *Mansfield Park* was published, there is a record of amateur theatricals at Redbourne: a party which seems to have been less full of dissension and surprises than the one presided over by Lady Bertram. Sir Charles Anderson recalls the play *La Colombe*, which he claims was by Mme de Genlis. The stage management was in the hands of Mrs Andrew Robertson, wife of the celebrated miniaturist, who enterprisingly used a stuffed white fowl to represent the dove. After the play Lord William's eldest son, another William, danced a fandango with his sisters Maria and Charlotte, all of them dressed in peasant's costume. The evening ended in a ball, before which the children were sent to bed. Next morning, the harriers met in the park just by the hall and Anderson enviously admired the eleven-year-old Willie Beauclerk in his pink coat.

Another of these evening parties, also in 1812, is recorded in a water-colour by the Lincolnshire country gentleman and amateur watercolourist Charles Uppleby.[3] Andrew Robertson is there again, this time singing the favourite air of the day, 'The Beautiful Maid'. He is accompanied by

Landscape with Jacob, Laban and his Daughters: by Claude Lorrain, 1676.
This painting was once in the collection of Aubrey, fifth Duke of St Albans. It was
auctioned on 8 June 1798 at Phillips's in New Bond Street.

H.M.S. *Dryad* in Combat with the French Frigate, *La Proserpine*: by Thomas Whitcombe.
The *Dryad*, under the command of Captain Lord Amelius Beauclerk, R.N., captured the
Proserpine in this engagement, 13 June 1796.

The Earl of Burford, later Sixth Duke of St Albans: by Gainsborough Dupont, c. 1790.
Burford is wearing the uniform of a captain in the 34th Foot.

the governess on the piano, Uppleby on the cello, and Lord William himself playing the flute. Amongst the eleven others in the room are the water-colourist Benjamin Gale, the family physician Dr Metcalfe, and three relations of the first Lady William, her cousins Sir Henry and John Nelthorpe and Sir Henry's wife. (Incidental proof that if ever there was bad feeling between the Nelthorpes and Lord William, it did not lead to a protracted feud.)

Whether the artists Robertson and Gale were intended to be the lions of these particular evenings we do not know, but the Anderson memoirs record that Lady William was certainly 'fond of giving parties with queer people for lions'. Sir Charles Anderson has also left a somewhat unflattering portrait of his hostess. She 'was called a beauty', he writes. 'She had a handsome oval face with arched pencilled eyebrows, but dressed horridly'. Uppleby has also remarked on her beauty, but without disparaging her dress. On the evening of the amateur theatricals, she wore 'a blue habit frogged all over with braid and a Scotch cap with a black feather'. More damaging still is Anderson's comment on her personality: 'she was an uneducated woman, not without some wits', but perhaps some allowance must be made for his sense of grievance?

In a way remarkable for a man unused to Lincolnshire farming, Lord William seems to have ensured that Redbourne and Pickworth prospered under his management. In this, as in everything else, he showed an eminently practical sense. A Redbourne lease dated 16 January 1813[4] assigns 543 acres of the estate to George Siddall, at an annual rent of £568-1-0d for fourteen years. Reserving the timber and shooting rights for his own use, the landlord forbade Siddall to 'sow any woad-like or mustard seed [charlock] or let any cole [kohlrabi] or turnips stand for seed upon the said premises ... under the forfeiture to the said Lord William Beauclerk, his heirs or assigns at and after the rate of £20 per acre per annum'. He well knew that if white turnips were allowed to drop seed, they would spread in profusion, killing the crops beneath them and covering the land with weeds! Siddall was also forbidden to 'give, sell ... or otherwise dispose of any of the hay, dung, manure or compost that shall ... be made ... upon the said ... premises, but shall and will use, consume, spread and employ the same upon the said premises'.

This, a more usual requirement, ensured adequate fertilizing of the ground: it was an alternative to stipulating how many head of cattle should be kept on the farm. Last, Siddall was to take care of the hedges and not to cut any hedge under eight years' growth. In an area where nowadays hedges are the exception rather than the rule, Lord William was insisting that hedges should not be laid to a height of four feet or so before they had grown sturdy enough to prevent soil erosion and act as windbreaks for cattle.

Whereas in 1736 'the whole of the lordship of Redbourne ... consisted of large fields, pasture and sheep walks', it had become more arable by the end of the eighteenth century. From a lease dated 7 February 1799[5] it is clear that the farms were large by the standards of those times: a home farm of 316 acres was attached to Redbourne Hall, and other farms were 517, 506, 468, 460 and 378 acres in extent—at rentals of £194, £180, £156, £145 and £148 a year respectively.

Lord William Beauclerk seems to have been less active than his brother Amelius in the furore over the sixth Duke's death. He may have felt it indecorous to be too visibly involved when he had so much to gain; but we may be quite sure that he was kept well informed of developments—and even perhaps directed the family's moves, since he was of a less blustering, more calculating nature than the Admiral. The news of the baby seventh Duke's death came to him at Redbourne; his wife writes of

> an event ... which an *express* has just brought us from London this morning: the death of the infant Duke of St Albans and, melancholy to relate, that of his poor mother the Duchess a few hours after. How awful a visitation! The agitation of the moment scarcely allows my dwelling on any other subject but I trust we shall acquit ourselves of the *Devoirs* attendant on the change of circumstances so as not to discredit the elevation.

The change in the new Duke's circumstances was not so great. With the peerage he inherited very little, except of course for the entailed 3,700 acres at Bestwood, certain pictures and plate, and the office of Hereditary Grand Falconer of England with its net emoluments of about £600 p.a.

This meant that about £3,000 p.a. was added to the £6,000 p.a. that the new Duke derived from Redbourne and Pickworth (and to the £1,000 p.a. which the Duchess derived from Little Grimsby as from 1811). In 1818 his total annual income, combined with his wife's, was probably in the region of £10,000. The salient fact to re-emphasize in Lord William's career is that but for his fortunate marriage to Charlotte Carter Thelwall the dukes of St Albans might have been reduced to the bare level of a squire's income. Their £3,000 p.a. (£1,500 from Bestwood, £600 from the Grand Falconership and the remainder from investments) would not have been large enough for them to compete with Mr Darcy!

The ducal title brought with it a certain change in the habits of himself and the Duchess. Leasing a princely house, 21 St James's Square (later the town residence of the bishops of Winchester), they began to spend more and more time in London. Twenty miles out of the capital they leased a country retreat, Upper Gatton Park, from Sir Mark Wood. Capability Brown had designed lodge gates and laid out the park of just over a hundred acres. The handsome pedimented house, with its long front of windows, which still stands in the still parkland today is much smaller than the house lived in by St Albans. A contemporary illustration, 'The Surrey Foxhounds, 1824. Fox breaking cover at Upper Gatton, Seat of the Duke of St Albans', shows that at least one vast wing has been demolished.

In 1816, when St Albans first came to live there, Upper Gatton Park had three lodges, a large stable block and a gazebo. There was also a study or reading-room ('Burford Lodge') where Lord Burford—the former Willie Beauclerk in his pink coat—worked with his tutor, Monsieur Renault. The rent for the whole property was £695 p.a., payable half-yearly. Within easy reach of London, Upper Gatton was the perfect house for a peaceful weekend, and St Albans and his family frequently travelled up and down sometimes by carriage, sometimes *à deux* in a landaulet.

Box Hill, the scene of a memorable episode in *Emma*, was only eight miles from the house and the setting for a happier party than the one described by Jane Austen. It took place in April 1819, and is described by the Duke's daughter Lady Charlotte Beauclerk in lighthearted terms:

We set out a little before eleven though it had been raining the whole morning. . . . After rambling an hour or two on that beautiful hill, we returned to the Dun [the ridge of Box Hill], and thanks to Burford who was commander-in-chief we had a droll but excellent cold collation which everyone seemed much to enjoy. . . .

Both on Box Hill and at the Redbourne amateur theatricals, fiction is reflected with uncanny closeness in the habits of an aristocratic family in real life.

Real life was positively suffused with the fiction of medieval romance when St Albans appeared garbed as Hereditary Grand Falconer of England at George IV's coronation in July 1821. It was amateur theatricals on the grand scale. The doublet was of green velvet lined with apricot silk and richly embroidered with gold bullion and silver tinsel. The breeches were of green velvet with slashings of apricot silk, and gold bullion tassels at the knee; the tights were of dark green silk with yellow embroidered clocks; the boots of brown suede; the scabbard of green velvet; there was a cream velvet hawking-glove, a green velvet badge, a belt, a girdle, and a strange crown-like hat surmounted with a black ostrich plume. With the tights, and the slim waistline of the doublet, no garb could have been less suitable for an old, ailing man of fifty-four, but it was the wish of the Prince Regent, now George IV, and it is on record that many courtiers recoiled at the sight of the fancy-dress doublets and hose which the King expected them to wear. From the size of the Grand Falconer's costume, incidentally, it is clear that the eighth Duke of St Albans was not a large man. The hawking-glove was the last ever to be carried at a Coronation, and the whole costume is the finest specimen of Regency Gothic dress in existence.[6]

Like the entire coronation ceremony of George IV, the Duke's costume was strongly imbued with a sense of pageantry and medievalism inspired by *The Waverley Novels*. The predominantly green and brown velvet ensemble with lashings of gold braid is a dress one might have read of in *Ivanhoe* or *Anne of Geierstein*, except that it is much more lavish and ornate than what would actually have been worn in the more frugal and austere Middle Ages.

At the next Romantic pageantry inspired by Scott, at Edinburgh in August 1822, George IV appeared in Royal Stewart highland dress surrounded by courtiers dressed like characters out of *Rob Roy*; and the Duke of St Albans was also entitled to the Royal Stewart tartan, as a descendant in the male line of Charles II, because Scottish heraldry and genealogy have always been more indulgent to the rights of bastards than has been the case in England. St Albans may have felt rather out of place in Edinburgh in that tartan, as his family—Stuart though they basically were—had always carefully avoided too close a contact with Scotland.

Through all the fairy-tale fiction of the Coronation and the Scottish visit, the realism of St Albans's concern for 'a pledge of better times' persisted. When he was not too ill to attend to business, the latter years of his career (until his death on 17 July 1825) were spent in trying to increase the family fortune. Towards the very end of his life, after his wife's death in 1822, he seems to have considered the idea of a third marriage: again to an heiress, but a woman who would have been by far the wealthiest of the trio, the widowed millionairess Harriot Coutts. And two or three years before the Coutts project, his main design for Willie Burford had been that he should marry the young 'Gascoyne heiress', Frances Mary Gascoyne, a girl with expectations of a private income of £10,000 p.a.

The Duke's plan for his heir was keenly assisted by the Duchess, who had even looked forward to such a marriage years before her husband inherited. The friendship between the Beauclerks and Gascoynes began in 1810, when Charlotte Beauclerk and Fanny Gascoyne became intimates. There was constant visiting between the two families when they were in London, and Fanny used to be invited to Upper Gatton. St Albans and his wife had high ambitions for both Burford and Charlotte: he was to marry the Gascoyne heiress, and she the young Lord Cranborne, heir to Hatfield and the Salisbury marquisate! By November 1818 Burford was seventeen and Fanny sixteen, and the aspiring Duchess was beginning to plan for the match in calculating earnest.

As in a comedy of errors, however, an unexpected danger now loomed on the horizon as Cranborne seemed more interested in Fanny Gascoyne than in her beloved Charlotte. Maria Janetta herself had seen how attracted Cranborne was by the heiress's beauty. Meanwhile, attending dances at Hatfield and seeing the Salisburys in London, she did everything possible to distract Cranborne towards her own daughter. But Lord and Lady Salisbury were by no means as enthusiastic for an alliance between their son and needy Charlotte Beauclerk as was the Duchess.

Throughout 1818 and 1819 a spate of letters descended from Charlotte on Fanny, extolling the charms and merits of Willie Burford. He had distinguished himself, she writes, in the Rebellion at Eton in October 1818, when boys revolted against the headmaster's decision to change the hour of lock-up from six o'clock to five. Explosives were hurled about the school, masters' windows were broken, part of the Long Wall was demolished, Keate was hissed and boo-ed by his pupils and even had to abandon reading prose in Upper School; even his desk in Upper School was smashed to smithereens. But Burford was spotless, and his family recieved a personal letter of commendation from the senior master at Eton, Dr Drury. 'I cannot hide from you', Charlotte confessed to Fanny, 'the pleasure that we have just enjoyed by dear Burford's peculiar good conduct at that time'. In April 1819 she sent Fanny her account of the party on Box Hill at which Burford was 'commander-in-chief'.

In August Fanny was at Gatton again, after a long absence perhaps inspired by her interest in Cranborne. 'I often wished for you', Charlotte had written to her in the preceding April, 'but I wished in vain, as I know you have now such an antipathy to poor Gatton whose unfortunate inhabitants join with me in sincere love to you'. Early in September 1819 Willie Burford left on the first of his Grand Tours, and no sooner had Charlotte returned from seeing him off at Dover than she put pen to paper about it in a letter to her beloved Fanny. They set out from Gatton.

As the day was most beautifully fine, everybody of course turned out to see us set off, and bid His Highness a last farewell. The carriages now being ready, we ascended the phaeton, and Burford and Mr Lynch their coach and four, and then drove away from the mournful adieus in haste. . . . We slept at Canterbury the first night. . . . A fine day and a fair wind seemed to invite them across.

Accordingly we proceeded to the beach, where the packet boat was waiting for them. . . . We returned to our inn with heavy hearts. . . .

Later that month there was the Hatfield Ball, 'the usual grand ball' (she writes) 'given in honour of my Lord Cranborne's birthday'. But she was not a guest at Hatfield, staying instead at Lady Caroline Lamb's house at Brocket, five miles away.

We all set off from her door at about 9 o'clock in two carriages. Lady C. Lamb, Lady F. Beauclerk, Cousin Lamb's tutor and myself occupied one carriage, Lord Frederick, Mr Lamb and Augustus the other.

(Lord Frederick was her uncle, the cricketer, and Mr Lamb the future Prime Minister, Melbourne. Melbourne's son Augustus was her cousin because Lady Caroline Lamb's father Lord Bessborough and St Albans's mother were brother and sister.)

You cannot have an idea of the excessive foolish conduct Lady C. exhibited during the whole of the 5 miles to Hatfield House, first exclaiming they would be all robbed and murdered, then if they escaped that death they should decidedly be all overturned coming home as she was sure that Lady Salisbury made it a regular system of giving the servants too much liquor. However, we arrived in perfect safety and after dancing with six separate partners, Lord Cranborne at their head, we retired at ½ past 4 o'clock in the morning.

At this ball at Hatfield Fanny was obviously not present.

Meanwhile, Burford was in Italy. He had been presented at the Casino dei Nobili and

writes from Milan ... in raptures with the beautiful picturesque scenery he has passed through and seems fully sensible of the wonders Nature has displayed in the Alps, of which mountains he has not only given a very interesting account but has also enclosed a few lines of poetry of his own composition, which, we understand, faithfully describe the spot where his Muse tempted him to write them.

But a few words of her own composition are needed to account for the length at which she relates her brother's experiences. 'Pardon my thus long having dwelt on this eighth wonder of the world', she adds self-deprecatingly, 'but, to deal plainly with you, I do not find you are as yet sensible of the true worth and merit of his *curiosity*'.

This eighth wonder of the world—as, indeed, in a sense he was—went on from Milan to Rome and Naples, under the watchful custody of his tutor Mr Lynch. Early in December Charlotte received what she describes as 'the most delightful and satisfactory pledges of Burford's love'; these were for Fanny, and one of them was a necklace, 'a *don d'amitié et de noces* and the commencement of your acquaintance together on that score'. He was home by Christmas, 'everything our brightest hopes could have wished, and his tenderness and sincere affection to Mama unexampled'. With great intrepidity he had travelled from Italy alone.

After Christmas came the second leg of his Grand Tour. Rejoining Lynch on the Continent, he travelled to Rome. If it was his hope and plan to win the Gascoyne heiress, he was singularly ineffective in his approach. As he stood hemmed in and out of action on the chessboard, it was the queen's turn to manoeuvre.

> Manoeuvring [wrote the Duchess to Mrs Gascoyne] is not confined to the imagination of the Edgeworth family. I am curious to discover Lady Salisbury's *but* in asking an interview with you, unless it is to ingratiate her little agreeable Matadore into your dear daughter's good graces. But If I know her well, she requires more personal as well as mental qualifications before she bestows her hand and heart on so prompt a predilection, as the *Palais de Vérité* must take precedence of the *Palais de Hatfield*.

At Lord Verulam's seat, Gorhambury, in January 1820, she had seen Fanny and the Matador, Cranborne, falling in love.

By June 1820 the lovers had decided to marry. In the previous month Fanny had turned down a proposal from Lord Erroll. But, despite the continuing absence abroad of the eighth wonder of the world, the Beauclerks were not so easily dissuaded. First Charlotte swung into action:

Your resolution, my dear Fanny, afflicts me sincerely. My heart had chosen you for my sister, but since fate decides otherwise, may you be happy with him in whom you have fixed your destiny. Accustomed to see you, *depuis longtemps*, my affection for you made me desire your alliance with my brother. But he is absent. If he had remained with us, he would have been able to appreciate your good qualities, and would have rendered himself amiable to merit the preference. . . . I beg you to believe that this event will make no change in the sentiments of tenderness that I shall ever feel for you. —Receive, my amiable Fanny, the assurance of the wishes the most sincere of your *Friend* Charlotte Beauclerk. P.S.—May I address you some day by a dearer name. *Oh! que je serais contente!* For I acknowledge I do not yet lose *all* hope.

If the last sentence of this letter seems outrageously disloyal, worse was to follow in the Duchess's letter to Fanny's mother.

I fear [she wrote towards the end of June] you are a little cross concerning what I named about our friend Cranborne whom I think very delightful in most respects, but we all know him to be so great a *swain* that the sooner he gets married the better, and since this last *éclaircissement* which has so much amused the world where Lord Camden is concerned, I could not help laughing at your standing up for his chastity, as I dare say Lady S. would be glad to break up the little French establishment he now keeps.

At about the same time—probably a little earlier in the month—she had again dipped her pen into vitriol. 'Cranborne', she wrote to Mrs Gascoyne, 'we hear much of, as, when he comes to devote his *soirées* to Almacks, his *matinées* are passed *chez* Lady May Dewhurst who is an *old* love, I trust a Platonic one, but she will not allow us aunts to dictate her *liaisons*'. She did however bring herself to write Fanny a congratulatory letter on her engagement, albeit tinged with irony.

The Beauclerks still would not give up hope, lured on by the magic appeal of a private income of £10,000 a year: Fanny stood to inherit as large an income as the Duke's and Duchess's combined, drawing as much in any one year as he was to bequeath to any of his younger children for a lifetime! In August 1820 Charlotte wrote to Fanny of a great exploit in which Burford had distinguished himself. The young man was still abroad, but now on the way home from his second trip to the Continent. In the Mediterranean, sailing towards Marseilles, his ship was first caught in a violent storm, 'then becalmed and afterwards threatened by pirates. Although he does not boast of his exploits, we discover he has behaved with heroism and afforded assistance to his associates while others in the vessel were fastened down in the hold being frightened. I should not think it worth while to repeat these domestic *contes*, had you not appeared to enquire after Burford with a continued interest'. How they discovered he behaved with heroism, if not from his letter, Lady Charlotte does not relate.

Finally, when preparations for the marriage were fully in hand, Fanny actually received a marriage proposal from Burford. The young man who had seemed so strangely withdrawn from the arena whilst his mother and sister fought gladiatorially on his behalf now struck a blow as indecisive as it was dishonourable. Even his mother was distressed and ashamed.

> I am only just informed [she wrote to Fanny], and *that* by accident, of a circumstance which has given me great mortification, and therefore I must intrude on your time by writing an apology for an *exposé* which I hear Burford has made of his long concealed *tendresse* for you, which we never suspected *lately* to exist. . . . Pray excuse this boyish ebullition, by which he has so far undervalued himself that I am quite angry with him, and were he at my elbow I should give him a maternal lecture. . . . Love will hope where reason despairs. I trust you will not *après tout* withdraw your favourable opinion of him, as I hear he wishes for the more tender passion to be transferred into that of friendship, and that his indiscretion may be excused which, believe me, wounded my pride and shocked my feelings that at *such a period such* a declaration should have been made.

In a letter written to Fanny just a month before her wedding, from which (incidentally) we learn that the Duke and his family had spent the New Year of 1821 at Brocket with William and Lady Caroline Lamb, Charlotte Beauclerk asks her friend to return the 'inconsiderate *exposé*': which presumably she did, as it is not in the Hatfield papers. She also answered the invitation to become a bridesmaid:

> You, my dear Fanchette, have so long and so well acquitted your-self *dans les devoirs envers vos parents* that you will allow for my inclina-tions being in the required instance in obeisance to my father's wishes, who says we are all so domestically assembled *sous le toit paternel* at present that he does not wish us separated, and there-fore that I cannot comply with your request respecting being brides-maid on the approaching event. I need not explain, my dear friend, how much the relinquishment of this attendance on you costs me, but I trust it will not affect our friendship hereafter.

Fanny married Cranborne, and became the mother of the great Marquis of Salisbury. Lady Charlotte Beauclerk died a middle-aged spinster. Through a generous invitation ungenerously declined, the Gascoynes obviously forgave the 'boyish ebullition' of a man who always remained a boy.

NOTES TO CHAPTER VI

Naval Officers' Personal Records: Public RO (entry for 8th Duke of St Albans, 15 August 1817).

Diaries of Sir Charles Anderson: Lincolnshire RO AND 5/2/2.

Gascoyne papers in the Hatfield archives (letters of Lady Charlotte Beauclerk and her mother to Miss and Mrs Gascoyne).

E. Gillett: 'The Reverend Robert Carter Thelwall (1719–1787): an Eighteenth Century Husband', *The Lincolnshire Historian*, vol. II, no. 7, 1960, 37–43.

T. Allen: *History of the Counties of Surrey and Sussex*, 1829.

C. Oman: *The Gascoyne Heiress*, 1968.

W. White: *History, Gazetteer and Directory of Lincolnshire and the City and Diocese of Lincoln*, 1856.

---

1. Lincolnshire Archives Committee: *Archivist's Report*, 22 March 1956– 23 March 1957.
2. Abstract of Title of Mrs Vera Beauclerk to Little Grimsby estate, 1918.
3. *The Curious World of Charles Uppleby* (published by The Lincolnshire Association Museum of Lincolnshire Life), 7–8.
4. Lincolnshire RO RED 1/1/9.
5. Lincolnshire RO RED 1/1/7.
6. Inventory of Grand Falconer's Costume, Museum of Costume, Bath.

CHAPTER VII

Harriot Coutts

The mother of the first Duke of St Albans was an actress, as was the first wife of the ninth. Such matches, regular or irregular, were by no means confined to Charles II and his Beauclerk descendant. From the Restoration to the early twentieth century (with Lady Headfort, Lady Dudley and the Gaiety Girls), actresses fascinated the British aristocracy. Indeed, they have continued to do so, though in a less direct and lavish way! Actresses, complained Evelyn, were 'foul and undecent ... women ... which inflaming several young noblemen and gallants, became their whores, and to some their wives.' The third Duke of Bolton, Nassau Paulet's half-brother, married one in 1751, after fathering three sons on her. Eliza Farren, an actress comparable with Mrs Siddons, married Lord Derby towards the turn of the century, and Louisa Brunton became Countess of Craven just after it. Another actress, Mrs Jordan, bore William IV ten illegitimate children. Most of such women, far from being 'foul and undecent', resembled Nell in their youth, vivacity, beauty and charm: witness, for example, Lawrence's portrait of Eliza Farren. The unusual feature of the ninth Duke of St Albans's marriage to an actress was that the bride was neither young nor beautiful. At twenty-five years of age he chose a stout, middle-aged widow, rather pompous and coarse-minded, but with a heart—and a purse—of gold.

The woman who was to marry one of the very wealthiest of London bankers, and after his death the sixth in rank in the peerage, was born on 11 November 1777 in lodgings near Lambeth Palace. Like Eliza Farren and Mrs Jordan, she had Irish blood; she even spent part of her childhood in Cork, Eliza Farren's birthplace. It was her mother who was of Irish descent: the daughter of an Irish cottier who was first a milliner's assistant, then a theatrical wardrobe-keeper and finally a strolling player.

There are two stories about Harriot's paternity. According to one, she was illegitimate: born in the theatrical world in which she was to grow up, and make her name and fortune; her father an actor in a repertory company, her mother a domestic servant employed by the theatre manager. According to the other, he was Matthew Mellon, a lieutenant in the Madras Infantry, who met the cottier's daughter whilst on sick leave in Ireland; they became lovers, and were married at Cork. Then Matthew had to rejoin his regiment, leaving a pregnant wife whom he promised to bring over to India as soon as he could afford it. He was never heard of again, and it was rumoured that he died of the consumption which first brought him to Ireland. The second story is certainly the more moving one, and the one that has generally gained acceptance; and if it is true, Harriot resembled Nell Gwyn in the fact that she too was the daughter of a military man fallen on evil days, who had married rather beneath himself. At all events, she never knew her father.

Sarah Mellon and her tiny daughter led a vagrant life in the years following the actor's—or lieutenant's—disappearance. With no means of support, either for herself or Harriot, she relied on the theatre for a living. The little girl was hauled from town to town, furnished room to furnished room, theatre to theatre, in the wake of a succession of travelling theatre companies. Her mother graduated from the theatrical wardrobe to become an actress, and eventually married (or remarried) at Wigan in 1782, when Harriot was aged four. Her husband was Thomas Entwistle, a violinist who was leader of the theatre band. It was not a marriage which brought any improvement to Sarah's finances, but at least it gave her stability and provided Harriot with a stepfather.

A great deal of Harriot's early childhood seems to have been spent in Lancashire. It was at Ulverston that she made her first appearance on the stage, on 16 October 1787, in a farce known as *The Spoiled Child*. Harriot, a 'poor little player-child' (as she referred to herself in later years), played the part of Little Pickle. During the next seven years came many tours of the provinces, presumably in the company of her mother and stepfather. She played the Duke of York in *Richard III*, Arthur in *King John*, and other infant characters. She was in Yorkshire, at Otley, in 1789 or 1790 and in Skipton about the same time. According to local tradition, she lodged in Chancery Lane, Skipton with a milliner Elizabeth Rodwell; and much later, when she had become Duchess of St Albans, returned to the town and exchanged memories of the Skipton theatre with her old landlady.

In the autumn of 1794 Harriot's repertory company made a tour of Staffordshire; at the Red Lion Inn, Uttoxeter she was described as 'not less amiable and kind in disposition, than handsome in appearance, being in every way the opposite of her mother, who was . . . a vulgar virago'.[1] From Uttoxeter she moved on to Stafford, which presented her with a big opportunity.[2] She was now nearly seventeen and had found an admirer in a local banker, Mr Wright.

In October 1794 the opportunity of a lifetime occurred when Sheridan, author of *The Rivals* and part-owner of the Theatre Royal, Drury Lane, came to act as a steward at Stafford Races, and saw Harriot act when he attended the local theatre. He was complimentary about her performance, and Wright urged him to take her on at Drury Lane. But although Sheridan murmured some politely vague remarks, nothing further would have come of the matter if Harriot and Mrs Entwistle had been lacking in determination. Mother and daughter pursued their advantage and, accompanied by Mr Wright, went down to seek an interview with the great man in London.

Sheridan had completely forgotten them, in the pressures of running the Theatre Royal, writing plays, attending The Club to which Topham Beauclerk had once belonged, and playing an intermittent role in politics. Mrs Entwistle refused to be put off by Sheridan, and the reward for her perseverance was a firm promise to engage Harriot at 30/- a week. Harriot's first London performance was as Lydia Languish in *The Rivals*, on 31 January 1795. For twenty years she was to continue at Drury Lane, a competent but never a distinguished actress, and never identified with any particular parts. She was usually cast in comedy, and one of her best performances was as Mrs Candour.

Not long after her engagement at Drury Lane, she was described by a fellow actor as 'a remarkably handsome brunette, [who] did not look a bit like an actress. She was much more like one of the genuine beauties of a quiet village two hundred miles from town. . . . Blooming in com-

Lord William Beauclerk, later Eighth Duke of St Albans: by George Romney, c. 1784.
Lord William is dressed as a midshipman in the Royal Navy.

The Costume of Hereditary Grand Falconer of England: from the collection formed by Mrs Doris Langley Moore.

This costume was worn by the eighth Duke of St Albans at the coronation of King George IV, 10 July 1821. The doublet and breeches are of green velvet trimmed with apricot silk, the tights are of dark green silk, the boots of brown suede with tops of dark green morocco.

BELOW: An Evening Party at Redbourne Hall in 1812: a watercolour painted from memory by Charles Uppleby, 1813.

The eighth Duke of St Albans is seen playing the flute directly beneath the portrait of the Rev. Robert Carter Thelwall; the Duchess is seated in the centre; the governess is at the piano, with the artist Andrew Robertson singing beside her. Concealed behind Robertson and the Duke is Uppleby himself.

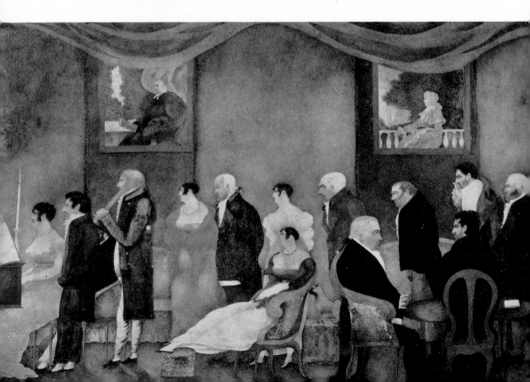

plexion, with a very tall, fine figure, raven locks, ivory teeth, a cheek like a peach, and coral lips'. Perhaps it was her beauty, rather than her acting ability, which on one memorable occasion at Liverpool, when she was playing the part of a woman pursued by creditors, roused a sailor to climb down from the gallery on to the stage, offering to go bail for her to any amount. For, though an established Drury Lane actress, she still continued her provincial tours. At York and Liverpool she became a great favourite, both with the public and the management.

During her time at Drury Lane she also acted as a coach in amateur theatricals, principally at Strawberry Hill near Hanworth, Horace Walpole's old residence which on his death in 1797 had passed to a friend's daughter the Hon. Mrs Damer. Anne Damer, a distinguished sculptress, was the centre of a brilliant social and intellectual circle that included Jane Austen and George IV's secret wife Mrs Fitzherbert. She was a friend of Joséphine de Beauharnais, Napoleon and Nelson. Between 1797 and 1811 Strawberry Hill regained the prestige it had enjoyed in Walpole's heyday: it became less of a curiosity and more of a salon; its character was less eccentric but equally exclusive, and here Harriot Mellon must have acquired many useful contacts and greater social poise. Thanks to her growing influence with the powers that be, her stepfather obtained the postmastership at Cheltenham.

It was at Cheltenham, in 1805, that she is supposed to have first met Thomas Coutts, during the time she was fulfilling an engagement at the local theatre. Mrs Entwistle, still the motive force behind her rise to fame, had applied to him for a subscription to Harriot's benefit performance. He sent five guineas, saw her act, and was introduced to her afterwards in the green-room. Then aged seventy, he was one of the richest British financiers of his time, perhaps even outstripping the Hoares and Drummonds; as friend and banker of the Royal Family, he had been lending the Prince of Wales money since 1792; and he was a friend of Sheridan.

His ailing wife, whom he had married in much humbler circumstances, was still tenaciously clinging to life; his three daughters, aided by their dowries and expectations, had all married into the nobility. He was lonely, and took a fancy to her. At Cheltenham he arranged to see her again in London, where he became a regular visitor at her house, 17 Little Russell Street, on his way home from the bank. He was generally to be found there for luncheon at two o'clock. He had in fact fallen in love with this woman of twenty-eight, in the full prime of life; but it was not an affair. Throughout the ten years of their friendly intimacy she kept an unblemished reputation. Though one of the most affectionate of women, she was not passionate. No love-affairs seem to have played a serious part in her life. When Thomas Coutts gave her money, she did not hide the fact—feeling no reason to be ashamed.

In 1807 he established her at Holly Lodge, Highgate, a villa 'by no means conspicuous either for its size or its architectural beauty', standing 'in most beautifully timbered and extensive grounds'.[3] This was only a leasehold property, however, and always remained so during Harriot's lifetime.[4] He also tried to put the friendship on an unassailable footing by getting his daughters to receive Harriot: Ladies Guilford, Bute and Burdett could not justifiably object to her lowly status, their own mother having begun her adult life as a domestic servant. Meanwhile, Miss Mellon continued to act; her new-found affluence was explained away by the rumour that she had won a large lottery prize; but there was equally a rumour that if ever Thomas Coutts became a widower he would marry the young actress.

On 6 January 1815, aged eighty, Thomas Coutts did become a widower and was as keen to marry Harriot at thirty-seven years of age as at twenty-eight. Like other notable people after him, he wished to be married in the utmost secrecy, particularly as the wedding was due to take place within a fortnight of Susannah Coutts's death. There was only one witness at the ceremony on 18 January, the bride's stage manager James Raymond, and the bridegroom tried to avoid any impression of unseemly haste by keeping the marriage secret until early March. He showed less than his usual shrewdness in the way he chose to make the announcement. *The Times* of 2 March 1815 carried the news that Mr Thomas Coutts and Miss Harriot Mellon had married 'on Wednesday at St Pancras Church', without actually stating the date. And so it came to light that not only was it a Wednesday six weeks before, but that the marriage was unfortunately invalid—there being only one witness instead of the required two. On 12 April the ceremony was performed all over again at the same church. Having married one of the richest men in England, Harriot now decided to bring her acting career to a close, though she did appear at Drury Lane at least once after the January wedding, when she played Audrey in *As You Like It*.

Despite the disparity in ages, it was an excellent match. The new Mrs Coutts may have been vulgar and ostentatious, especially in the early years, but she was devoted to her husband and he sought to please her in every way. There is a story that the Duke of York appeared at the coronation of his brother George IV wearing a magnificent diamond cross borrowed from his jeweller; the next day the jeweller called on Mr and Mrs Coutts as they were at dinner, and the banker bought it for his wife with a cheque for £15,000.

Inevitably, such lavish wealth aroused much envy and hostility. People were inclined to think that Coutts was becoming senile, and that his fortune-hunting wife was exploiting him. Her transformation from rags to riches was particularly hard for the envious to bear. Scurrilous lampoons appeared, the most notorious—and exaggerated—of them being the *Secret Memoirs of Harriott Pumpkin, or the Birth, Parentage and Education of an Actress, in which are developed a variety of interesting and amusing anecdotes; her Private Acquaintance for many Years; the Vicissitudes to which she was exposed; and her Extraordinary Marriage with OLD CROESUS!! to which is added the Art of making an ostentatious Show-off under the colour of Charity; the whole portraying her never-forgiving and malicious disposition.*

Not only did her brash display of wealth provoke such scurrility, it also invited blackmail. Edmund Antrobus, a young partner in the bank, did much to shield Thomas and Harriot from this danger,[5] and so earned his employer's lasting gratitude. The final insult that befell Thomas Coutts as a result of his second marriage was the rift between himself and two of his daughters, Ladies Guilford and Burdett; Lady Bute was always loyal to her father, and did everything she could to heal the breach; yet the eldest daughter Lady Guilford remained unreconciled until her father's dying day. Libel, blackmail and family dissensions did nothing, however, to mar the idyllic happiness of Harriot and her 'blessed, matchless'[6] husband: their union, he confessed, had 'proved the greatest blessing of his life, and made him the happiest of men'.[2] At his death on 24 February 1822, he made her his universal legatee: 'this is too much', was Henry Fox's sardonic comment.

The estate was proved at £900,000. Overnight she became 'the richest widow in Great Britain', and a dazzling prey to any fortune-hunter. She was wise enough, however, to lead a retired life during the first eighteen months of her independence. One of the most striking features of these years is her extreme generosity to the three daughters of her late husband —a generosity which may have been spontaneous, or otherwise designed to avert legal wrangling. She retained Thomas Coutts's controlling interest in the bank, and even seems to have had some say in its management. Her profits for 1822 were £36,208;[7] for 1823, £36,196;[8] for 1825, £32,821:[9] quite apart from other income, amounting in 1825, for example, to £15,660.[10] Out of a total income in 1825 of £48,481 she gave £25,815[10] to her three stepdaughters—regardless of Lady Guilford's longstanding hostility. About the same time she settled £10,000 p.a. on each of them. In 1823 she gave £20,000 to Lady Bute's daughter Frances on her marriage to Lord Sandon.[11] The following year, she settled £2,000 p.a. on Lord Dudley Stuart,[12] the only son of her favourite stepdaughter, so as to provide him with some luxury for his Bonaparte bride—of whom, however, she disapproved. During her lifetime she gave £30,000 to Lady Guilford[12] and £10,000 each to her two daughters.[12] Her total benevolence to Ladies Guilford, Bute and Burdett amounted to £335,000. In her will (14 March 1837) she states that she had already given Lady Burdett £118,602-15-0d. Even though her income in later years regularly exceeded expenditure by £40,000 p.a., it is still remarkable that she should have chosen to give the three daughters so much, when two of them had treated her disrespectfully until she had control of the purse-strings, and all had received so much from their father.

She also had time, energy and money for philanthropy. Amongst the charities she liberally supported were those for the famine-stricken Irish peasantry and the Spitalfield weavers.

She never [wrote Horace Smith] trusted to the representations, however sad and plausible, which were addressed to her every day in scores of letters, but subjected them, in the first instance, to the investigation of her secretary or treasurer, who made inquiries among such of the permanent residents as were best acquainted with individual cases of distress, as well as with the wants of public charities and institutions. Rarely, indeed, was the bounty withheld where the claim proved to be just.

By 1824 Harriot Coutts was beginning to emerge from the seclusion of her early widowhood. Because of her wealth she was keenly sought in marriage. Even the King's brother the Duke of York was reputed to be a suitor, though it is unlikely that he could have married her in view of the odium incurred by another of his brothers, the Duke of Sussex, upon his marriage to Lady Cecilia Buggin. The Royal Marriage Act did not affect the chances of that other widower, the eighth Duke of St Albans, however, and both he and the Dukes of York and Wellington were guests at a magnificent garden party given by Mrs Coutts at Holly Lodge in July 1824. Also in that year she invited St Albans and his heir Lord Burford to a dinner party at which the latter was to meet a wealthy young heiress, for whom he was 'intended'. The ideal arrangement, from the Beauclerks' point of view, would have been for the father to marry Mrs Coutts and the son to marry the beautiful young heiress. No one, in fact, was more astonished than Mrs Coutts when Burford (aged twenty-three) paid all his attentions to her, a woman exactly twice his age. An interest in Shakespeare was the bond which cemented this sudden, unexpected friendship, which within a few months had become a deepening intimacy.

Thomas Coutts had been born in Edinburgh, and it was partly this fact, together with a distant relationship to Sir Walter Scott and the general interest in Scotland stimulated by Romanticism, which prompted Harriot to make fairly regular visits north of the Border. During the autumn of 1824 she set off on a Scottish tour with a grand retinue of seven carriages, twenty-eight horses, two doctors, two bedchamber-women (one for the day, and one for the night), 'menials of every grade', and the dutiful Lord Burford with one of his sisters as chaperone. At Edinburgh she gave £150 to various charities and presented the Lord

Provost with a silver vase; her father-in-law, John Coutts, had been Provost of the city from 1742 to 1745. But when it was rumoured that she was about to receive the freedom of the city of Edinburgh, the Scots vehemently denied any such suggestion: believing their 'rulers ... incapable of so prostituting civic honours'. Undismayed by this rebuff, she proceeded with Burford and his sister to Abbotsford, only to meet with further humiliation.

As a distant cousin of Thomas Coutts and a visitor to his house in London, Sir Walter himself was all civility; but the same could not be said of the novelist's other women guests. For the Abbotsford detour Harriot had abandoned four of her seven carriages, but even the arrival of three carriages was something of an imposition. She made matters worse by not arriving on the evening when she was expected, after holding up dinner for two hours.

Even when she did reach Abbotsford, the visit bristled with difficulties. One of Scott's guests was Lady Compton, whose husband was heir to a marquisate and who scorned parvenu wealth. Though not actually discourteous to Mrs Coutts, she treated her icily, as did several other ladies. Lockhart gives a rosy account of the episode, suggesting that after short tête-à-têtes with the ladies Sir Walter put matters right. Probably much closer to the truth, the painter C. R. Leslie recalls that Mrs Coutts and her party left after only one night at Abbotsford instead of the intended three, and that when Lady Compton tried to accompany her on the piano Mrs Coutts was so choked with grief that she could hardly utter a note.

This, however, was not the last of Harriot's visits to Roxburghshire, nor was it the last of the rebuffs she was to receive under Sir Walter's roof. On a subsequent visit, after her marriage to the ninth Duke of St Albans, the problem arose as to whom Sir Walter should lead in to dinner. On this occasion his house-party included Lady Grey, wife of the Prime Minister. Etiquette clearly demanded that Harriot should precede Lady Grey; Sir Walter was in a quandary, since Lady Grey passionately objected to playing second fiddle to the former Harriot Mellon. Eventually the brain that had devised *Old Mortality* devised a cunning expedient. Engaging duchess and countess in the library before dinner, he became so animated in his conversation that apparently without noticing it he took each by the arm and all three walked into the dining-room together!

Mrs Coutts made a further tour of Scotland and the north of England in November 1825 again accompanied by the lovestricken Burford, who four months previously had succeeded to his father's dukedom. His sister Charlotte again acted as a kind of chaperone. Their movements were chronicled by the press in the manner of a Court Circular, as the duke and the millionairess made a royal progress via the George Inn at Leek (the scene, perhaps, of humbler moments in Harriot's life) to the Cheshire home of her banking partner Edmund Antrobus, at Eaton Hall,* two miles out of Congleton; thence to the now defunct King's Arms at Liverpool, and much further north to Lord Breadalbane's seat at Taymouth Castle, in Perthshire.

Yet for all the newspapers' malicious aping of the style of a Court Circular, Mrs Coutts's progress was far from royal in the eyes of many of the older aristocracy—even though she was accompanied by a duke. At Derby St Albans was cut at a county meeting by the Duke of Devonshire. At Alnwick the Duke of Northumberland merely wrote giving them permission to view the castle: he did not invite them to stay.

They did, however, stay at Abbotsford again, and a mention of this visit is to be found in Scott's diary entry of 25 November 1825, a fortnight later, when Mrs Coutts and her party called on him at his house in Castle Street, Edinburgh to bid him farewell. Scott records:

> When at Abbotsford [the Duke's] suit throve but coldly. . . . She had refused him twice, and decidedly. He was merely on the footing of friendship.

But in this friendship Scott was shrewd enough to discern the beginnings of a love-affair.

> I urged it was akin to love. She allowed she might marry the Duke, only she had at present not the least intention that way.

That very same day the Duke penned Mrs Coutts one of the strangest

* Not the Grosvenors' Eaton Hall, near Chester.

love letters imaginable:[13] a letter which surpasses any of the wildest flights of fancy in *The Waverley Novels*, but which certainly confirms Scott's judgement that 'if he marries a woman older than himself by twenty years, she marries a man younger in wit by twenty degrees'.

> My dear Mrs Coutts,
> You profess to have a sincere attachment for me which emboldens me to make the following declaration. We are in Scotland together now, and if you were to say that you acknowledge me as your husband, I would say I acknowledge you as my wife; this would not be binding, as there would be no witness present; consequently, it would remain a secret, never to be divulged by either. You could gain nothing by marrying me but rank, and if you want that, you may afterwards marry the Duke of Gordon. If you do accept my proposal, I hope you will do what you said you would to whomsoever you married, when you were walking on the road between the Tully Arms Inn and Dunkeld. I write this in strict confidence.
>
> Yours affectionately,
ST ALBANS

From her first invalid marriage when only one witness was present, Mrs Coutts was now liable to descend to a marriage with no witnesses at all, if the Duke had his way. As a last resort, if the strawberry leaves of a ducal coronet proved overpoweringly tempting, she could marry a duke two years older than Thomas Coutts had been when she married him: for the Duke of Gordon—with a castle in Banffshire as grand and melancholy as Combourg was to Chateaubriand—was actually aged eighty-two!

By 18 October 1826, however, St Albans was her 'pet Mr Duke',[14] and by 16 June in the following year (the day before St Alban's day, which that year fell on a Sunday) Scott's expectations had been fulfilled: at her town residence, 1 Stratton Street, the fifty-year-old widow was married to a man twenty-four years her junior. 'The ceremony took place in the great drawing-room', says a family memoir.[15]

A magnificent altar was erected covered with crimson velvet richly ornamented with gold lace and fringes, the chairs, the cushions all corresponding red, and the whole of the apartment was embellished with peculiar care.

The bride's gown was of Brussels lace costing 300 guineas; a diamond comb stood out against her raven black hair. Her wedding presents to the Duke were a cheque for £30,000[16] and a small country estate in Essex: the manor of Woodham Walter, near Maldon, reckoned by Lady Holland to be worth £26,000. The £30,000 cheque provoked a minor sensation, both in Mayfair drawing-rooms and in the popular broadsheets. In a contemporary lampoon, 'A Beau-Clerk for a Banking Concern', Harriot hands the Duke a cheque for £100,000 as he says to her:

you may depend upon it, Madam, I shall endeavour to give you every satisfaction. I shall be very attentive, and if I can't get through the business as you like, you are at liberty to employ an assistant.

She replies:

Why, you seem to be a good-looking, hard-working young fellow, but I must tell you my business is extensive and I shall expect you will employ your time day and night for the benefit of the Concern. You must also be humble and submissive. Should this be realized on trial, I will make you a sleeping partner. And here's a trifle for you to buy a pair of gloves.

Even so, the Duke's family considered that he was bartering himself for a paltry sum, whilst Harriot's stepson-in-law Sir Francis Burdett sat up till four in the morning on the day of the wedding trying to persuade her not to go through with it. When Creevey noted in his diary on 15 June that more than £30,000 might be forthcoming if the Duke behaved himself, he was (it seems) very far from the truth: as the family memoir explains, Harriot stood firm in her resolution not to give more, and the Duke did not hold out for a larger sum, 'fearful of losing the prize altogether'. Apart from their mutual affection (which was obvious enough), it was very definitely a marriage of convenience. As St Albans points out in his letter to Sir William Knighton of 20 June 1827, he even settled £1,000 p.a. on her, and wished her to be as financially independent of him as possible:[17] a fact which envy overlooked.

Harriot had gained the highest of titles, but no phoenix of a husband. Society remembered his foolish conduct with Fanny Gascoyne, besides which there was the ill-starred engagement to Lady Elizabeth Conyngham which lasted only a few days in May 1823: she 'has consented to marry the idiot Lord Burford', Henry Fox noted in his *Journal* on 19 May. And Creevey comments that the young man 'became so unmannerly and cross that the lady sent him a letter of dismissal last Saturday'. To Lord Broughton he seemed 'a retired, gentlemanly young man'. Lady Holland was hardly less critical than her son: besides noting his 'fixed, glazed eye' and expressionless though handsome face, she comments on the rapid change of liveries at the wedding breakfast: 'before the ceremony Mrs C.'s servants wore the Coutts livery; immediately after, they appeared in the St Albans yellow and black stockings' —looking, no doubt, rather like Malvolio. Those who took a kindlier view of the proceedings compensated for their small numbers by exalted rank. Recalling perhaps the financial help he had often received from Thomas Coutts, George IV, 'your very sincere friend', sent a message which was read out at the breakfast.[18] Scott penned a sincere letter of congratulation, to which Harriot responded with the hope that one day her 'true history' might be 'written by the Author of *Waverley*'.

If the author of *Waverley* had in fact written Harriot's life story, it would have been very different from the glittering procession of dinners, fetes, balls, breakfasts etc. recorded by newspapers and diarists. To outsiders, Harriot seemed a phenomenal being—even grander than in the days when Mrs Coutts had visited Scotland with seven carriages. Brighton, which the Prince Regent had made fashionable and which he still visited constantly as King, became one of the centres of the Duchess's existence. Until 1830 she lived in a large house on the sea front known as Byam House (138 King's Road), but finding this not large enough for her requirements she then moved into Regency Square, to a house with enormous stabling which she rechristened St Albans House. 'The splendid equipage of the Duchess of St Albans', writes the Brighton correspondent of *The Morning Post*,

is an object of much attention in our streets, where it is to be seen at almost every hour of the day. Her Grace occupies a house on the King's Road (Belle Vue House), which is by no means suitable to the reception of her extensive establishment; but there was no better to be got when she arrived here. On Sunday the entry of the Duke and Duchess, followed by *two* footmen, made quite a sensation in the chapel where they attended divine service; and at the theatre, the night before, far more attention was paid to them than to the stage.

From the unreal limelight of her theatrical days Harriot had entered on a life where fiction and reality coalesced.

But for the inner truth about her married life—a truth beyond the glare of publicity and glamour—we must turn again to the family memoir. On one occasion, not long after their wedding-day, the Duke actually ran away from Harriot. The storm broke at Portsmouth where Harriot, the Duke and three of his brothers were staying: we are told that Lords Frederick, Henry and Charles, all in their teens, breakfasted early at their hotel so as to go sailing; the table had not been cleared when Harriot arrived, and 'burst into one of her terrific fits of passion', for which not even her compliant husband would stand. She pursued him all the way to London, where some kind of reconciliation took place, though even after this St Albans wrote very disparagingly about her to his uncles, expressing 'disgust to her person and age'. The family memoir also suggests that whenever the Duke was 'permitted to hunt', Harriot sat waiting for him impatiently, with the temptation of a delicious lunch, at the point where the hounds were expected to leave off. Woe betide him if he ended up in another place!

None of this disturbed Harriot's pretensions for Stratton Street, which in February 1828 she was making even more splendid than in the lifetime of Thomas Coutts. A letter of the Duke to Lord Dudley Stuart[19] mentions that a statue of Apollo arrived from Italy in January of that year. It was almost as if they were making up for the vanished collections of the fifth and sixth Dukes. The most eminent of contemporary sculptors, Sir Francis Chantrey, had been called in and admired it. Dudley Stuart was asked to turn his stay in Italy to advantage, and find a companion statue of Venus. Within six months of her marriage Harriot had spent £21,000.[15]

Her pretensions were grander still at Holly Lodge, where she took to giving the most sumptuous parties some of which cost as much as £2,400.[15]

One of these was the *grande fête champêtre* to celebrate their first wedding anniversary. It was attended by the Dukes of Cumberland and Sussex and by Prince Leopold (shortly to become King of the Belgians). The Duke of Sussex proposed the couple's health, and St Albans, presumably overlooking the Portsmouth squabble and the hunting disputes, spoke of claiming the Dunmow flitch; as a second best, however, he had ordered a Dunmow flitch to be engraved on a silver fruit basket for the Duchess. She in return presented him with a six-oared cutter, appropriately named the Falcon. The entertainments went on well into the night, and concluded with waltzes and quadrilles in the illuminated gardens. Much popular envy was aroused, and in one poem published on 6 July 1828 in *The Age* the Duke and Duchess were mocked as 'Lord Noodle and Queen Dollabella'.

Despite the presence of some of the King's brothers at these parties, and some were even attended by the King's heir presumptive the Duke of Clarence, Harriot was still not fully accepted by the Court and London society. Perhaps such favour as the Royal Family showed was largely due to the fact that George IV and the Dukes of Sussex, Cumberland and York all banked with Coutts, whereas the aristocracy favoured Hoares, Childs and Drummonds. Two of St Albans's sisters, Louisa and Mary, found themselves shunned by the houses where they had formerly been welcome visitors, merely because they—still unmarried—were living under Harriot's roof. A further snub was administered when Harriot wished to invite the Duchess of Gloucester to her parties; after all, the Duke of Gloucester (George IV's cousin) was a regular visitor, but his wife, a sister of the King, was not so easily persuaded. The go-between was St Albans's aunt, Lady Frederick Beauclerk, who urged the utmost caution. A typical instance of Hanoverian double standards came to light when the Duchess of Gloucester told Lady Frederick that 'the Duke of Gloucester would not permit her on any account to become acquainted with the Duchess of St Albans'. So Gloucester always came to Harriot's parties alone.

At William IV's accession the climate seemed to have changed. First came the question of presentation at a royal Drawing Room: Harriot had never been presented at Court, a fact which in itself illustrates her extremely ambiguous social status, and royal etiquette demanded that she should be presented by a lady who herself had been presented—if at all possible, by a lady of her own family. Rather as in the Bible story of the wedding feast, Lady Guilford (Harriot's stepdaughter) put her £10,000 p.a. at risk by pleading ill-health, and Lady Caroline Dundas, St Albans's aunt, refused point-blank for fear of offending the Dundases—even though she offended her brother Amelius by her refusal. Eventually, the dowager Lady Salisbury (mother of the Cranborne who succeeded in marrying Fanny Gascoyne) was prevailed upon to present the unfortunate Harriot to whom Queen Adelaide actually spoke, commenting 'how splendid her dress was'.

The Queen's comment on the Duchess of St Albans's dress was not meant as a mark of favour. In January 1831 a ball with 830 guests was held at the Royal Pavilion but Harriot, though the highest in rank of the inhabitants of Brighton, was not on the invitation list. Creevey even comments on this in a letter to Miss Ord. It was a great setback, but worse was to follow. At a Court ball a month or two later the Duke of St Albans's presence was requested, together with that of his sisters Louisa and Mary; but there was no mention of Harriot. St Albans was unwilling to go without his wife. After establishing that the snub was deliberate, the sisters also refused to attend, much to the satisfaction of their uncle Amelius. The cruellest twist of irony came when Lord Amelius fell out with his nephew shortly afterwards over a bailiff's dismissal, and then threatened to take Louisa and Mary to the Queen's ball—in the Duke's carriage, probably paid for by Harriot, into the bargain! The fact that the girls did eventually attend the Court ball led directly to the rift between St Albans and his uncles which was to mar their happy family life for years to come.

William IV's coronation, on 8 September 1831, provided Harriot with a way out of her dilemma. No doubt in his capacity as Hereditary Grand Falconer, St Albans was invited to carry the Royal Sceptre with Cross, the last of the regalia to be conferred on the newly consecrated king:

it had been decided not to feature the Hereditary Grand Falconer in the garb his father had worn ten years before. At the Coronation service Harriot was dressed 'with great splendour, and stood third in her place, the two Duchesses of Richmond being before her' (duchesses of Norfolk, Somerset and Grafton were not present for the simple reason that in 1831 no such ladies existed; the Duke of Beaufort's wife was not at the Abbey).

As she stood behind the daughters of a duke and a marquis in the line of duchesses near the Throne, this must have seemed to Harriot the pinnacle of her career, a grander moment than any she had experienced in the make-believe of the theatre. Five days later she was again received at Court, and about the same time attended a dinner in honour of Talleyrand, then the French ambassador, at which the King made a somewhat *risqué* speech in French: Lady Holland comments in a letter to her son Henry Fox that the other ladies at the dinner gave Harriot the cold shoulder; 'how' (tongue in cheek) 'can women behave so to one another!' Much the same attitude was revealed by Queen Adelaide at social functions in Brighton not directly connected with the Court. The Queen acknowledged that Harriot should 'have the place of honour next to her', though 'she would not bring herself to speak to her, well knowing what her former life had been'.

Ironically, the Duke's position as Hereditary Grand Falconer nearly brought Harriot and Queen Adelaide into greater proximity in 1832, when William IV was seriously considering reviving falconry and establishing heronry at Windsor. As *The Windsor and Eton Express* put it, mews were to be built and the Duke and Duchess of St Albans were to take up their official residence at Cumberland Lodge (echoes of Cranbourne again!). Any favours that Harriot was to receive in the charmed circle of Court and society were entirely due to her husband's rank, not to her own wealth.

The situation was no different in the country, except that in Lincolnshire and at Brighton Harriot was more able to impress the common people. 'Even Coutts's money-bags could not buy the popularity of the Lincolnshire gentry', wrote Sir Charles Anderson to his friend Samuel Wilberforce in November 1828. Harriot and her husband reserved their grand entry to Lincoln and Redbourne until September of that year, fifteen months after their wedding. From Lincoln to Louth, where thousands lined the streets to the King's Head Inn and the constabulary had to be called in to offer Harriot protection, to Redbourne itself was a triumphant progress of a kind never before seen in the county, but marred by the vetoing of a public breakfast that was to have been held in her honour at Louth; the Louth bellringers demanded ten guineas for their exertions on her behalf but Harriot would only give them four; the Louth ladies pursued her from shop to shop with insatiable curiosity; on leaving the town, Harriot vowed never to set foot in it again.

At Redbourne a huge falconry display was laid on, to which the Duke invited all the notabilities of Lincoln. Falconers were imported from Germany, where with its large forests and attachment to its medieval past falconry was far from a dying art; in mock Gothic fashion, they were attired in green and orange velvet trousers, with long white gauntlets and steeple-crowned hats with bands of gold and adorned with black plumes. A champagne party, sideboard supper, fireworks and dancing regaled the guests until far into the night. On Lincoln racecourse there was an even more spectacular falconry display, attended by 20,000 people: on this occasion the Duke was dressed in his ceremonial costume of Grand Falconer, and escorted by a page in Lincoln green. Partridges were let loose, pursued at a short interval by hawks; but it was no ordinary pursuit, as the beauty of the hawk's flight came when it soared aloft and then stooped after its quarry; equally remarkable was the hawks' obedience to their trainers' skilful control.

At the end of the day, 'the Duchess of St Albans ... caressed the noble creatures as she sat in her carriage, and gave largesse to their attendants'. In appreciation of which the freedom of the city of Lincoln was conferred upon the Duke, and Harriot was toasted at the Mayor's Inauguration Dinner on 12 October and invited to become patroness of the Dispensary Ball—though with a warning to curb her lavishness, as otherwise it might be difficult to find a patroness to succeed her.

At another Lincoln ball Lady Brownlow was adamant that 'this ball was altogether a meeting for society, and not for any object of charity', and so it was 'peculiarly necessary that the ladies of the county should vindicate the honour of their sex from any commixture'. If Harriot attended, she would 'enjoy the highest seat in the Assembly, but otherwise without notice or regard': a stinging insult from a woman who, besides being younger than Harriot, was more recently married! And so, although a duchess, Harriot tasted the bitterness of being ignored by the Mrs Dymokes, Mrs Turnors, Mrs Birch-Reynardsons, Mrs Heneages and Mrs Massingberds who, although the wives of misters, enjoyed a firm place in county society. After a further visit to Lincoln, in 1830, it was reported that:

> The Duchess is disgusted with the city: no shout when she placed the falconer's cup upon the stand before the populace, with her own hands, her health not drunk at the Mayor's dinner, nor her contribution to the Races mentioned in any of the speeches. The novelty was over, and the entertainment value gone.

Brighton was also treated to falconry displays, in Regency Square, on the downs by the racecourse, and at Devil's Dyke. On the whole, they met with a more favourable response than at Lincoln, partly perhaps because she had lived there before her marriage and was not considered a showy intruder, and partly because of the more diffuse nature of Brighton society. A contemporary newspaper did, however, query whether this 'zoological foolery' was at public expense.

> There is something attractive about the pomp and dignity of a Grand Falconer to superintend the absurd birds, which, however, does not, we think, quite counterbalance the folly of making them a part of the national establishment. Perhaps, however, we are ignorant, and the rapacious hawk is only emblematical of some active officer, as the premier [Wellington] might be represented by a cormorant, or some other member of the administration by some equally rapacious animal.

The vogue of falconry was shortlived. By 1837 it was all but dead; in 1827 it had hardly come alive. It was a symptom of the same Romanticism which produced the Young England movement, the Eglinton Tournament, the notion of Merrie England and the medieval novels of Sir Walter Scott. There is an amusing story that shortly after

Harriot, Duchess of St Albans: by George Clint, c. 1827.

A Beau-Clerk for a Banking Concern: a lampoon on the marriage of Harriot Coutts and the ninth Duke of St Albans.

Harriot, Duchess of St Albans and Husband: a Lampoon for their First Wedding Anniversary, 16 June 1828.

The Duke of St Albans is the dwarf presenting the Dunmow Flitch; Harriot responds with the six-oared cutter.

his marriage to Harriot a letter arrived for the Duke at Cheltenham sealed with the Royal arms: his immediate attendance was required at Windsor, together with his hawks. Though Hereditary Grand Falconer, he had at this time neither hawks nor falconers. His aunt Lady Frederick Beauclerk urged him not to go to Windsor until hawks and falconers had been obtained from Sir John Sebright. 'It may be', she cautioned, 'a snare laid to discover if you really keep the hawks and if not, to make it a pretence to bring the inutility of your office before Parliament and to deprive you of it'. The letter turned out to be a hoax, but it must have given additional incentive to Harriot to set up a hawking establishment, thus combining the current taste for medieval chivalry with her own hard-headed practical sense and her pride in her husband's dignities and privileges.

Harriot was a strange mixture of realism and romanticism, common sense and sentimentality, warmheartedness and vulgarity, reticence and ostentation. Her contemporaries reacted to her in extreme ways: she was the sort of woman whom you loved or hated, but to whom you could never be indifferent. Scott liked her: 'I have always found her a kind, friendly woman, without either affectation or insolence in the display of her wealth, and most willing to do good if the means be shown to her'. To Henry Fox she was 'vulgar and purseproud', though not lacking 'a sort of frank good humour and hearty gaiety, which alone makes her sufferable'. Wordsworth and Southey both admired her. Wellington, who nicknamed her Queen Mab, spoke of her behind her back with haughty disdain. At a breakfast she gave in July 1835 he found her with Lady Aldborough, the Duchessa di Camizaro and Lady Stepney: 'all the demi-reps in town'. He refused to let her sit by him at table, though she did succeed in holding him by the arm for some time. Sir Francis Burdett, on the other hand, was deeply grateful to her for offering to pay the cost of his election campaign at Westminster in 1837, when he resigned his seat to test public confidence in the Melbourne administration.

For every appearance at Court she bought between £1,000 and £2,000 worth of diamonds; indeed, her entire jewel-box consisted of diamonds except for three large sapphires; yet, hearing of a lady who was living in great poverty at Brighton, she disguised herself, visited the lady and,

finding the report true, left behind a packet containing £300. On a visit
to Cheltenham she slipped out from the fashionable dinner party at which
she herself was the hostess, and returned an hour afterwards, her face
stained with tears. It was later discovered that she had been weeping
beside her mother's grave.

At a party she gave in Brighton 'the Duchess's great body covered
with white satin, and blonde, and surmounted by a large hat and
feathers, burst in among the waltzers as 12 struck, exclaiming, "Stop,
stop, supper is ready. Ladies and gentlemen, stand not upon the order
of your going, but go at once".' As in this quotation from *Macbeth*, she
loved to refer to her earlier life in the theatre. To Sir Charles Anderson's
mother she once remarked, as tea was brought in at Redbourne: 'Ah!
I never taste such good tea as when my poor mother used to make it out
of a kettle under the hedge'; perhaps because of this, she tended to prefer
stronger liquor: brandy and water was one of her favourite drinks. Her
love for her first husband was undoubtedly sincere: according to the
Duke of Gloucester, she had been Thomas Coutts's mistress, but this
was strongly denied by Lady Frederick Beauclerk. As to her love for her
second husband, it was more maternal—and material. Her career as an
actress fitted her for assuming such different parts.

One aspect of her relationship in which it is difficult to absolve her
entirely from blame is her treatment of the ninth Duke's family. Though
Lords Amelius and Frederick were initially opposed to their nephew's
marriage, they eventually relented and Lord Frederick even officiated at
the wedding. An antagonism began to develop as she expected her new
husband's family to fall in with her every whim. And the trouble was
exacerbated because Lords Amelius and Frederick still had a parental
attitude towards the Duke, whose weakness and instability they sadly
recognized. The crisis erupted when Lord Amelius took his nieces to the
Queen's ball; Harriot forced the girls to leave their brother's house;
Amelius, no more tactful now than in the Sinclair crisis, aggravated
matters still further by asking Harriot to finance a naval cadetship for
one of his protégés, which was refused; Harriot and her husband deeply
resented Amelius's conduct, and the Admiral fruitlessly asked his parson
brother not to have any further dealings with the Duke and Duchess 'on

this occasion'. When another Lord Frederick, the Duke's brother and then heir, wished to marry a businessman's daughter in 1837, Harriot strongly objected—forgetting that she herself had been the actress wife of a banker and the stepdaughter of an itinerant musician.

This animosity is reflected in her will, with its codicil dated 14 March 1837. The Duke was left an annuity of £10,000 for life, a life-interest in her 'cottage' Holly Lodge and its contents, a life-interest in 80 Piccadilly, rooms at Coutts Bank, £2,000 worth of plate, and her wine cellar—but only on one condition: that Lord Amelius and her brothers-in-law Frederick and Charles Beauclerk should not reside with the Duke for even as long as a week in any one year. The punishment was more merited in Lord Amelius's case than in either of his nephews'. Angela Burdett, a granddaughter of her first husband, inherited the bulk of her fortune, amounting to £1,800,000. At Harriot's death on 6 August 1837 the Coutts heiress was twenty-three. No one was surprised at this turn of events, since latterly Angela Burdett had been almost an adopted daughter: Harriot's appointed heir until 1835 had been another grand-daughter of Thomas Coutts, Lady Georgina North; and earlier still, it had been Lord Dudley Stuart, a son of yet another Coutts daughter, until he had disgraced himself (in her eyes) and forfeited his immense expectations by marrying Napoleon's niece.

The widowed Duke, still only thirty-six and twice as rich as before his marriage, looked round for another wife. First, however, we are told of his enterprise in seducing a servant girl, by whom an illegitimate daughter was brought into the world on 19 July 1839; there are still descendants today. As for a lawful successor to Harriot, Queen Victoria suggested Henrietta Beauclerk, the Duke's first cousin; but his own preference was for a beautiful twenty-six-year old Irishwoman, Elizabeth Gubbins, whom he married at Harby, in Leicestershire, less than six weeks after the mistress's confinement. The new Duchess, who had been orphaned at nineteen, was resident with her cousin Mrs Hartopp, wife of the Rector of Harby; her dowry of £15,000 helped to reduce the mortgage on Redbourne necessitated by the eighth Duke's bequests to his younger children.

Within ten years of his second wedding St Albans was dead, still only in his forties. The watershed in his life, Harriot's death, coincided with that watershed in British social and political history, the accession of Victoria. The glamour and gaiety of George IV's reign, which had continued at Brighton into the reign of William IV, gave way to a sober respectability, echoed in a minor key in the life of St Albans and Elizabeth Gubbins. He produced an heir, gave up falconry, gradually lost his sight,[20] and sustained a long and ultimately fatal illness as the result of a hunting accident. Most of his latter years were spent at Redbourne, where he founded the elementary school.

When Henry Fox commented in 1829 that he was 'a sad spectacle; but yet he seems partly to understand what is said to him, at least the sense of what he has heard an hour ago sometimes flashes across his mind', he was not far from the truth. A man who could ask, on seeing Siamese twins, whether or not they were brothers has so plumbed the depths of stupidity as to attain a kind of genius. To Henry Fox he made the improbable assertion that the third Earl of Chichester was the most intelligent man he had ever met. It was caustically observed when he took an honorary LL.D. at Cambridge in 1828 that an honorary L.S.D. would have been more appropriate.

The political innocence which made him only dimly aware of the most despotic of nineteenth-century tsars, Nicholas I, also led him to waver in his attitudes towards the two greatest English domestic issues of the early nineteenth century: Catholic emancipation and the Reform Bill. On the first of these he began by voting against enfranchisement of the Catholics but on the second reading, in April 1829, he voted in favour. The Reform question caused him still greater torture. Initially against electoral reform, he 'ratted' (in William Holmes's phrase[21]) on the bill's second reading in September 1831, and thereafter voted in favour. But at least his deep insecurity on these major issues had one compensatory advantage, and one which also gave him a liberal complexion, albeit accidentally: his non-interference with tenants' franchise. He admirably exemplifies Dr Johnson's maxim that the one great benefit of primogeniture is that 'it makes but one fool in a family'.

Angela Burdett-Coutts, for such she became by the terms of Harriot's will, had a career noted for its wise philanthropy. She emulated Harriot at her best, taking every care to ensure that her gifts were sensibly employed and quadrupling the money she inherited. Though lacking her predecessor's ostentation, she was better known and more generally liked and admired. With the London poor her name became a byword, whilst her thoughtful generosity was recognized at the highest level when in 1871 she was created a baroness—one of the first such titles to be conferred.

There was a rumour shortly after Harriot's death that she might marry the widowed Duke: but in a strange comment on his first wife, St Albans is said to have declined with the words, 'to marry once for money is more than enough'; and it is in any case far from certain that Angela would have accepted him. Her hero as a young woman was the field-marshal and statesman who so frowned on Harriot. But like her benefactress, she finally married a man less than half her age: compared with whom St Albans had the shining merit of never belittling his wife in public. Perhaps Harriot's greatest act of wisdom was in bequeathing her estate to a woman who was in every way worthy of inheriting it, though with all the advantages of vast wealth neither had the more usual blessings of a normal marriage and children to follow them.

NOTES TO CHAPTER VII

M. Baron-Wilson: *Memoirs of Harriot Duchess of St Albans*, 1839.

A. Dale: *Fashionable Brighton, 1820–1860*, 1967.

R. H. Gronow: *Reminiscences and Recollections, 1810–1860*, 1889.

J. W. F. Hill: *Georgian Lincoln*, 1966.

Earl of Ilchester (ed.): *The Journal of the Hon. Henry Edward Fox (afterwards fourth and last Lord Holland), 1818–1830*, 1923.

Earl of Ilchester (ed.): *Elizabeth Lady Holland to her Son, 1821–1845*, 1946.

J. G. Lockhart: *Memoirs of the Life of Sir Walter Scott, Bart, 1837–1838*.

H. E. Maxwell (ed.): *The Creevey Papers*, 1903.

W. Scott: *Journal*, 1890.

G. L. Strachey and R. T. B. Fulford (ed.): *The Greville Memoirs, 1814–1860*, 1938.

W. White: *op. cit.*

---

1. F. Redfern: *History and Antiquities of the Town and Neighbourhood of Uttoxeter*, 1886, 357.

2. Latymer Papers, L 449.

3. J. H. Lloyd: *The History, Topography, and Antiquities of Highgate, in the County of Middlesex*, 1888, 262.

4. *Survey of London*, vol. XVII, 1936, 71.

5. Harrowby MSS, vol. 1078, 305a–c.

6. Harrowby MSS, vol. LX, 203–204.

7. Latymer Papers, L 1164.

8. Latymer Papers, L 1166.

9. Latymer Papers, L 1168.

10. Latymer Papers, L 1169.

11. Latymer Papers, L 1078.

12. *Gentleman's Magazine*, October 1837, 419–421.
13. Latymer Papers, L 483.
14. Harrowby MSS, vol. LXI, 321–322.
15. The 'Family Memoir': a MS document in the possession of Mr Miles Acheson, and probably drawn up by Lady Frederick Beauclerk (1816–1877).
16. Harrowby MSS, vol. 1056, 149.
17. RA 24059.
18. RA Y57/50.
19. Harrowby MSS, vol. LXII, 39–40.
20. Diaries of Sir Charles Anderson, 1830–1845: Lincolnshire RO AND 5/2/3, 16 and 18.
21. A. Aspinall (ed.): *The Correspondence of Charles Arbuthnot*, 1941, 146.

CHAPTER VIII

The Victorian Patriarch

William Amelius Aubrey de Vere, tenth Duke of St Albans was only nine when he succeeded his father in the title. He was born on 15 April 1840; his sister Diana, the only other legitimate child of the ninth Duke, was two years younger. William and Diana were largely brought up by their mother, who found herself considerably poorer on her husband's death through the loss of his life-interest in Harriot's estate. In 1859 Elizabeth Duchess of St Albans remarried. Her husband, Lord Falkland, was also bereaved. His first wife, Lady Amelia FitzClarence, had been an illegitimate daughter of William IV, and so began that close connection with the Court to which Harriot had always aspired but never attained, and which was finally cemented when the tenth Duke married a daughter of Queen Victoria's trusted private secretary, General Grey.

After periods at Eton and Cambridge, and a tour of Italy with his mother in 1859 where he became increasingly friendly with the Prince of Wales, William St Albans came of age. Even before 1861, in rejecting the offer of Byron's old home Newstead for £6,000,[1] he had decided to make Bestwood his principal seat: not Redbourne or any established Nottinghamshire house. This was a bold, and some thought a foolhardy, step. His family had never had any close links with Nottinghamshire. The dukes of the Dukeries were Norfolk, Portland, Newcastle and Kingston; never a St Albans. Indeed, so slight was the Beauclerks' interest in Bestwood during the 18th century that the Duke of Portland had even offered to buy the estate from the third Duke. But where was the money for the tenth Duke to build a mansion? Although the Bestwood estate was to provide a colliery which would greatly replenish the Duke's bank balance, the mansion preceded the coal-mine. We have to remember that even in the ninth Duke's time the family fortunes had been greatly restored by the marriage to Harriot, whose bounty to her husband continued even after her death. She had given him the estate of Woodham Walter, in Essex, and this went towards the building of Bestwood Lodge. So, too, did the Pickworth estate in Lincolnshire, inherited in 1797 from the first wife of the eighth Duke and sold by his grandson in 1864.

Before a new house could be built, two existing ones had to be demolished. The half-timbered hunting-lodge, with its thirty-eight rooms and roof of tile and slate, was still standing. Now over 500 years old, it was in much worse repair than when Cromwell's commissioners had inspected it on 5 April 1650. In fact, even if its owner had chosen to renovate it, it was now almost beyond repair. Not far away was the strange architectural toy built by Lord Amelius Beauclerk with his brother the sixth Duke's permission: a 'naval castle' closely resembling a warship, and the exact length of a quarterdeck, with its rooms modelled on ship's cabins. Both these buildings had been pulled down in 1860, the year before St Albans came of age.

The way was now clear for something to be erected more in harmony with contemporary taste and more in keeping with aristocratic grandeur: it was, after all, to be the family's principal seat. Samuel S. Teulon was instructed to draw up plans for a spacious mansion in neo-Gothic style, on a site somewhat higher than the original houses and thus commanding a view of Nottingham. The favoured architect succeeded admirably in producing a house as like St Pancras Station as it is possible for any human habitation to be, which amply explains why in the 1860s and 1870s Bestwood Lodge was considered 'a very handsome and conspicuous object', whereas today it is a 'jarring ... composition' whose 'skyline defies description'; Teulon, writes Sir Nikolaus Pevsner, was 'one of the most ruthless, insensitive, and original of the High Victorians'. A similar though much larger mansion was built between 1870 and 1883 by the first Duke of Westminster, at that other Cheshire Eaton: the best and most flamboyant example of the Gothic Revival in England, now sadly razed to the ground.

For the first time in almost two hundred years the Beauclerks were putting down roots in the land granted to them by their founder, Charles II. It had taken ten dukes, and five generations, to achieve this result. Ironically, the work—when it did begin—was undertaken by a very young man who was still a bachelor. At a ceremony in October 1862 the first brick was laid by the Honourable George Cadogan; by 1865 the main building was complete. Meanwhile, the Duke and his mother spent some of their time in Italy; his sightseeing, particularly in Florence and Venice, inspired him with ideas for the decoration of Bestwood. No doubt his admiration for Ruskin dates from this time, if not from the actual appearance of *The Stones of Venice* in 1853. At the very end of his life we find him consulting Ruskin about more imaginative forms of employment for Nottingham workers.

The site of Bestwood Lodge, close to those of the medieval hunting-lodge and the 'naval castle', perhaps explains the Duke's preference of Nottinghamshire to Lincolnshire. Whereas the countryside around Redbourne is flat and uninteresting, with few trees to relieve its seemingly endless acres and none of the charm that appealed to Verlaine at Stickney about this time, Bestwood's finest feature is its commanding position and densely wooded setting. From the terrace were fine views over towards Nottingham, much less then than now a town of 'dark Satanic mills', whilst on two sides of the house the gardens fell away towards Arnold, which in 1862 was still a village, unaffected by urban sprawl.

The gardens themselves were a combination of styles, with an Italianate series of tiers leading down from the drawing-room terrace to a fountain, and an entirely informal English setting of undulating lawns shaded by majestic beeches and limes, almost the only old trees on the estate when the Duke began his work (the 'naval castle' had stood near them). Though there was a short drive leading from the Arnold lodge, the main approach in those days was along $1\frac{1}{2}$ miles of bumpy woodland tracks, winding steadily uphill. Plantations of trees, mostly firs, gradually replaced scrubland, filling visitors to Bestwood with romantic visions of Sherwood Forest—though the original Sherwood Forest would have been deciduous.

On emerging from the long woodland tunnel the visitor to Bestwood Lodge was confronted with a sight of which he had already gained some inkling from the brick triumphal arch suitably emblazoned with arms and cypher. Although it did indeed have an architect, the house seemed subject to no overall plan. A profusion of flying buttresses, pseudo-ecclesiastical windows (some even with stained glass), a mass of chimneys and steeples (one even with windows in it for good measure!) vied with mock crenellations and a high-roofed conservatory, steep gables and gargoyles of hounds, a ram's head, Robin Hood, Maid Marian and Friar Tuck to create a brick hybrid, which was part cathedral and part baronial mansion.

Such was the spell of the warm South that within two months of the first brick being laid at Bestwood the Duke and his mother were back in Italy, where they not only admired art but mixed with artists and connoisseurs. This taste was shared by Queen Victoria's eldest daughter and her husband, the Crown Prince and Princess of Prussia. 'All our friends were at the railway station', Princess Frederick writes to her mother on leaving Rome in December 1862: 'including Mr Odo Russell, Mr Pentland, the Duke and Duchess of St Albans, Mr and Lady Elizabeth Adeane, and most of the English artists'. It was also in Italy that the Duke acquired his passion for bric-à-brac, though unlike the Prince Consort he does not seem to have specialized in paintings.

This Royal friendship was further strengthened three months later at Windsor, when the Prince of Wales married Princess Alexandra of Denmark (10 March 1863). St Albans was one of the Prince's six special guests out of the nine hundred who attended the wedding, and Lady Diana Beauclerk, his sister, the prettiest of Alexandra's bridesmaids. Yet another three months passed, and Lady Diana's name was 'the talk of all London'.[2] Rumour ran that she was about to become engaged to Willem Prince of Orange, eldest son and heir of William III of the Netherlands; it was also rumoured, and with some foundation, that she had compromised herself with the Prince. Queen Victoria, whose uncle the Duke of Sussex had contracted a quasi-morganatic marriage by marrying an earl's daughter, dismissed talk of a future Beauclerk queen as utter rubbish: 'the Mother actually imagining he would and could marry her'.[2] She overlooked the Lady Craven who married a margrave of Brandenburg Ansbach in 1791, the Duke of Hamilton who in 1843 had married a daughter of the Grand Duke of Baden, and whose daughter was soon to become Princess of Monaco; she did not know, and could not have guessed, the irony that was soon to befall her own family, when one of her daughters married the future Duke of Argyll. With a wiser assault on the young prince, it would not have been impossible for the lovely Diana Beauclerk to become Queen of Holland.

As it was, far from marrying the heir to a throne, she was to remain painfully on the shelf for nine years and then marry an ageing judge, John Huddleston QC, Judge Advocate of the Fleet and a former Conservative member of Parliament for Canterbury. Not the least of his accomplishments was to become the last ever Baron of the Exchequer. Both during and after her marriage, her eccentricities were legion. She was insistent on what she believed to be her brother's hereditary privilege, as Grand Falconer of England, of riding in a carriage along Rotten Row: a privilege supposedly confined to the dukes of St Albans and the Sovereign. She even rode along it herself with her brother.

The road she ought to have ridden along, if she had been born a generation earlier, was the carriage-drive between Birdcage Walk and Buckingham Gate, which until 1828 was reserved for the carriages of the Royal Family and the dukes of St Albans. There never seems to have been any permission for the Duke of St Albans to drive in a carriage along Rotten Row. Lady Diana Huddleston was prone to such confusions.

The most amusing consequence of this foible came when, as a wealthy widow, she was travelling by train to London from her home in Brighton. So completely devoted was she to Baron Huddleston's memory that she would never be parted from his ashes, and even carried them on the train in a wicker basket. On one memorable occasion the picnic basket was confused with the basket containing his ashes, but the mistake was instantly rectified.

Although Lady Diana had married outside Royal circles, she and her brother remained the friends of Royalty. Her wedding present from the Prince and Princess of Wales was a gold bracelet set with diamonds and rubies. The Prince was a boon companion of Lady Diana's brother, whom Palmerston described to Queen Victoria in 1864 as 'young, unaccustomed to business and not over steady'.[3] In March of the following year the Prime Minister even felt it necessary to warn Victoria of her son's excesses, when the Prince lost £138 to St Albans, Lord Sefton and Sir Robert Peel in eight rubbers of whist. St Albans was then a bachelor aged twenty-four.

When the time came for him to settle down, two years after this gambling episode, he chose a wife from within the Royal circle, but not one who would lightly have approved his wayward excesses. Sybil Grey, eldest daughter of the Queen's private secretary and granddaughter of the Grey of the Reform Act, was a mere eighteen when she married the tenth Duke of St Albans on 20 June 1867. By special permission of the Queen the ceremony was performed in the Chapel Royal, at St James's Palace. The Prince of Wales, Princesses Helena and Louise, Prince Francis of Teck and Prince Edward of Saxe-Weimar were amongst the witnesses. The wedding present from the Prince and Princess of Wales was a gold necklace. The bride was a great favourite of Queen Victoria, though when the Duchess of Bedford wished to resign as Mistress of the Robes in 1869 Sybil St Albans was considered '*far* too young'[4] to fill the vacancy: and this despite the fact that there was no other suitable candidate in sight. Instead, her energies were channelled into the furnishing of Bestwood (only recently finished), the building of a church there, and the raising of a family.

Three children were born to her in rapid succession: a daughter named after Princess Louise, her godmother; a son and heir, to whom the Queen, the Prince of Wales and Angela Burdett-Coutts were godparents; and a second daughter, named after herself, to whose birth she owed her death. An aura of inescapable melancholy, and touching earnestness, surrounds this beautiful young woman who did not live beyond the age of twenty-two. Her son Charles was born as his grandfather lay on his deathbed, and the baby's name recalled his memory. It was a sickly child, over whose baptism on 10 May 1870 the General's death still cast a shadow. To the Queen, whose gift was a bust of the beloved private secretary, it was a 'very sad christening',[5] and after the brief formalities were over she hurried away. It would have been an even sadder occasion if Queen Victoria had realized the terrible destiny of madness that awaited the child. The earnestness with which Sybil devoted her brief life to religion was eminently Victorian. Though a chapel had been included in Teulon's designs for Bestwood, it was scarcely large enough for the tenantry and servants: the parish church was at Lenton, five miles away and on the other side of Nottingham; she urged her husband to endow a living at Bestwood itself.

The building of Emmanuel Church, in the grounds about a quarter of a mile from the house, took two years. Its five stained glass windows were painted by her in memory of her father; she embroidered its altar frontals, trained its choir each Wednesday evening at the Lodge, and chose its Sunday hymns. Her thoughts went further than the actual church building. She was seriously concerned at the small size of local congregations, and keen to enlarge them. Such practical evangelism was in the traditions of her north-country ancestors, though they would not have shared her desire for Holy Communion at least once a month. She was the second person to be buried in Emmanuel churchyard; inside the church is a marble bas-relief sculpted to her memory by Princess Louise; to Queen Victoria the young Duchess's death seemed 'a horrid dream'.[6]

Coalmining proved a distraction to the thirty-one-year-old widower, to whom the 'horrid dream' was made almost unbearably painful by the memory of a young woman's self-sacrifice in bringing a daughter into the world. The Duke tackled the exploitation of his Bestwood mineral rights in a most businesslike manner. Stirred on by the example of Lord Middleton's Wollaton pits, which supplied Nottingham with fuel, the ninth Duke had considered opening a colliery at Bestwood as early as 1825, but had decided it would be too risky a venture: coal had never been found east of the river Leen, and if it was there he felt that it would be so deep underground as to involve huge engineering costs. But the prospect of a huge colliery fortune was as dazzling to any Victorian landowner as that of finding diamonds in Griqualand, or gold in the Transvaal, to any landless man with a thirst for adventure. And there were entrepreneurs, such as the Lancaster family, to assist men such as the tenth Duke of St Albans in the search for coal.

John Lancaster[7] was the eldest of seven brothers, all of whom were in the same line of business. After a profitable spell in his native Lancashire, where he sank mines at Patricroft, Ince and Aspull, he became mineral agent to Lord Mostyn in Flintshire and in 1849 helped Lord Granville to plan a colliery on his estate at Shelton in north Staffordshire, of which he then became manager; from 1855 to 1858 he developed the Duke of Newcastle's Shireoaks Colliery at Worksop. In and around the Midlands huge increases of income were being enjoyed by those lucky enough to own the precious seams: the Duke of Portland had a mine on his estate at Welbeck; Sir George Sitwell leased the mineral rights at Renishaw; Lord Fitzwilliam had collieries on his Wentworth estate, outside Rotherham; so too did Sir Charles Wood (Lord Halifax) at Doncaster, on which he drew royalties of 6d. a ton. Much of the splendour of the dukes of Sutherland and Stafford House, St James's was financed by the Staffordshire coalmines. Moreover, the whole question of coal-development was very much under debate in the late 1860s, and with little hostility towards the colliery-owners. It was not felt to be rapacious greed if a man exploited the coal under his land and, like the Morgans or Winns, turned himself into a millionaire in the process.

Coal was needed in ever increasing quantities to power the railways and factories, to maintain industrial prosperity, and to provide jobs. A government inquiry reporting in July 1871 estimated that the attainable quantity of coal in known coalfields amounted to 90,207,000,000 tons, and the probable available coal in other places to 56,273,000,000 tons. Despite the ninth Duke of St Albans's doubts as to the wisdom of prospecting for coal east of the Leen, the moment seemed ripe for prospecting to begin; and John Lancaster began.

The Bestwood Coal & Iron Co. Ltd was formed in August 1872 to handle the Duke's mining interests, with both John Lancaster and St Albans on the board. Unlike his father in 1825, St Albans was not expected to risk much capital. His main contribution was the lease of seventeen acres of land to the Bestwood Coal & Iron Company, whilst the Lancasters provided the finance and expertise. And in the event, the gamble paid off for the Lancasters, as well as for the Duke, when coal was soon discovered just east of the river.

The sinking of mineshafts began in March 1873. Lancaster's plan was to run a colliery and an iron works side by side. By 1876 the colliery plant was in operation, connected to the outside world by a standard-gauge railway, an offshoot of the Midland line: J. &. G Tomlinson Ltd built the branch railway and junction for the Midland Railway Company

Bestwood Lodge, Nottinghamshire: Teulon's Idealized Projection, 1863: an engraving from *The Builder*, 5 September 1863.
This illustration was published in *The Builder* two years before the house was completed.

A Party at Bestwood, June 1881, to coincide with the Opening of Nottingham University. Prince Leopold stands in the middle; the Duchess of St Albans, in a dark gown, sits facing her husband who is seated on the extreme right. Next to the Duke of St Albans is Lord Fife, a future son-in-law of Edward VII; the Duke of Portland stands in the doorway, between Prince Leopold and a guest holding a puppy.

The Great Hall of Bestwood Lodge.

at a cost of £15,000; the colliery line and sidings were laid by the Best-wood Coal & Iron Company at their own expense. By 1884 720 men were employed at the mine—550 underground, 170 on the surface—and 350,000 tons of coal were being raised in a year.

St Albans's royalties from Bestwood colliery probably more than compensated for the income his family had lost with the expiry of Harriot Coutts's annuity on his father's death. Through the good fortune of happening to have coal seams on their Nottinghamshire estate, the Beauclerks had recouped the vanished bonanza from the bank. Whether the grime, hardship and danger of their new source of revenue was as morally palatable as the dividends obtained from managing other entre-preneurs' money in a private bank is a nice question. It is doubtful whether St Albans ever had time or inclination to read any of Zola's novels, but if by some chance he did come across *Germinal* (composed within a few years of Bestwood colliery's foundation) he would certainly not have classed himself amongst the callous, rapacious, complacent Hennebeaus, 'marquises, dukes, generals and ministers', ready to steal the miners' shirts off their backs, who are Zola's colliery managers and proprietors. Nor would he have thought of John Lancaster as such. Conditions were not as bad in English mines as in those on the Continent; as early as 1842 an Act had been passed prohibiting women from working in the collieries. Neither would Dickens's social propaganda have pricked his conscience because to him collieries such as Bestwood enriched both capitalist and working-man alike. D. H. Lawrence's picture of Bestwood in *Sons and Lovers* is much closer to the reality of that Nottinghamshire mining village. The fact that the capitalist took a larger slice of the cake than did his employees seemed justified on account of risk and enterprise. Though St Albans ran no risks himself (whereas the miners' risks were innumerable!) and though he showed less enterprise than John Lan-caster, both became much richer men thanks to the colliery at Bestwood.

Not that they would have been poor or even only moderately rich without the colliery. Both falconry and yachting were interests they shared long before they began to negotiate about coalmines. In 1864 Lan-caster, cruising off Cherbourg in his yacht *RYS Deerhound*, actually rescued the crew of the Confederate cruiser *Alabama* after she had been sunk by the Federal war-steamer *Kearsage*: a British business man yachting for pleasure had saved the lives of over forty Americans during the Civil War.

St Albans's yachting career never had the same adventure or excitement but already in 1863 he had owned the 135-ton schooner *Pilgrim*, though the expenses of building Bestwood Lodge had forced him to sell his ship in the following year. Not until his mining ventures began did he return to yachting as an owner rather than a mere guest on others' yachts, such as Lancaster's. It was a sport which provided an additional release from the pain of his wife's death. On his first yacht, RYS *Xanthra* (230 tons), which he registered in 1872, he soon made a minor and unexpected incursion into international politics. Cruising off the French coast in August of that year, he landed briefly at Trouville. Amongst St Albans's guests was the Prince of Wales and amongst Trouville's summer residents was Thiers, President of France. It was an unscheduled meeting between the Prince and the President, who had met once previously. Their principal talking-point was fear of a renewed German attack; it was only eighteen months since the end of the Franco-Prussian War. Thiers urged his visitor to inform the German Emperor of France's desire for peace. Even before Bismarck received the official report of this meeting, he was aware that it had taken place: it had been observed by a German spy.[8]

No such notoriety usually attended the Duke's voyages, though the steam yacht which replaced *Xanthra* (there had been a yawl for a short period in between) achieved fame and made its owner into an international social celebrity through lengthy cruises to the Scottish lochs, the Orkneys, Norway and the Mediterranean. Its name was the RYS *Ceres*; it was bought in 1875, displaced 305 tons, and had previously belonged to John Lancaster, who in July of that year proved much more cautious than his friend when each was sailing his yacht to Norway. A storm blew up off Lerwick, Lancaster put back to port, but St Albans continued aboard the *Ceres* until eventually a revenue cutter was sent out to look for him.[9] The yacht's skipper, Captain Jones, became a trusted friend of the Duke, and from the moment when he was taken on with the *Ceres* served him for more than twenty years.

Being a member of the Royal Yacht Squadron from 1862, St Albans quite often attended Cowes Week, where the *Ceres* became a centre of social life. The Queen herself came on board.[10] At Valencia, in September 1877, so did the Duke of Connaught.[11] Princess Louise, Duchess of Connaught, was another visitor to the *Ceres*, at Gibraltar in April 1879.[12] The Duke of St Albans and his family would often put in at Venice to visit churches, palazzi and antique-shops, and to admire and buy works of art. He cruised so often with his children that at least one of them, Moyra, became thoroughly disenchanted with his expensive hobby.

It was almost inevitable that a man widowed so young should remarry, and this he did in January 1874. His bride, Grace Bernal Osborne, was a young Irish heiress eight years his junior; her father was a Liberal Member of Parliament. Her home, Newtown Anner in Tipperary, belonged in fact to her mother, Catherine Isabella, who came from a long line of Osborne baronets and was the heiress to her only brother. It was a splendid inheritance, with a fine Georgian house near Clonmel restored and enlarged by Catherine's father. The Newtown Anner estate amounted to 13,000 acres, including land in Co. Waterford around Glenpatrick. In 1815 it produced a rental of £8,000 p.a.—very large by Irish standards.

After the breakdown of her engagement to Sir Jacob Preston, Catherine Isabella married Ralph Bernal in 1844, who assumed the additional surname of Osborne a week before the wedding. Bernal's father was a wealthy Spanish Jew whose fortune was derived from West Indian sugar plantations, and who acquired a European reputation as an art collector. The Bernal Osbornes had two daughters, of whom Grace (afterwards Duchess of St Albans) was the younger. Edith, the elder, was on the worst of terms with her parents who disinherited her for committing the unpardonable sin of marrying a mere commoner—who however lived to revenge himself by becoming in turn Governor of the Bahamas, Newfoundland, Jamaica, Hong Kong and Ceylon. Happily, the two sisters' friendship remained unclouded by Mrs Bernal Osborne's favouritism.

This marriage, apart from providing the Duke with five more children (one of whom was to inherit the title), established a link with Ireland—though Grace did not actually succeed to the 6,000 acres at Newtown Anner until her mother's death in 1880. The new Duchess was very different from the first, a woman of abounding energy, an activist on behalf of the causes she believed in, impulsive and straight to the point, more worldly and mature than Sybil, with a wider outlook and strong literary and musical leanings. It was a difficult task for one of her background to follow Sybil, whose connections with the Court were so close: Queen Victoria, quite unlike her eldest son, had a positive dislike of Ralph Bernal Osborne, and vetoed his appointment as a Foreign Office minister.

It was also difficult to bring up children who were not her own. But these tasks she discharged most ably, and was a brilliant hostess at Bestwood. In September 1877 Gladstone writes hoping to stay at Bestwood whilst transacting some business in the county;[13] other visitors included Tennyson, Browning, Bright, Joseph Chamberlain—and even Randolph Churchill and Disraeli, despite their Tory allegiance. For the opening of the Midland Counties Art Museum, at Nottingham, in July 1878 the Prince and Princess of Wales stayed for three days, and planted cedars. When the University was inaugurated at Nottingham three years later, Bestwood received the visit of a younger son of the Queen, the Duke of Albany, and on 1 July 1881 a fancy-dress ball was held in his honour, at which Leopold appeared as Louis XV. The Prince of Wales also paid many visits to Bestwood incognito, walking up to the house from Daybrook station. Another Royal visitor in later years was the Duke of Clarence, the ultimate heir to the throne. Beside gala occasions there was a regular stream of bazaars, fancy-dress children's parties, private theatricals, children's concerts, and cricket, hunting and shooting parties. A former Cabinet minister, writing to the Duke in 1897, refers to 'the many very happy days I have spent at Bestwood'. Matthew Arnold excuses himself from a stay at Bestwood in 1887, solely on account of an article he is writing on Tolstoy for *The Fortnightly Review*. St Albans and his wife also entertained at Alt na Craig, the house near Oban rented in the summer of 1893.[14]

The Irish link was to have important consequences for both Duke and Duchess. It gradually propelled William into the vortex of Irish politics, making a cleavage between his hereditary Liberal convictions and his passionate Unionism; the social prestige of Grace's marriage added weight to her defence of the Unionist cause. As early as 1880, in a letter to his friend Hartington, St Albans records the growing disillusionment of many Liberals with Gladstone's policy of Home Rule. Perhaps because of his displeasure with the Gladstone administration of 1880–1885, he turned down the offer of the Garter in June 1885,[15] his friend Lord Sefton being appointed instead: with the result that only two dukes of St Albans, the first and the second, have held the Garter, a record amongst English ducal families only surpassed by the dukes of Manchester.

It was not, however, until 1886 that St Albans deserted Gladstone for Hartington's platform of Liberal Unionism. In that year, as Gladstone was forming his short-lived (third) administration, a minor crisis blew up over the new appointments to the Royal Household, potentially as serious as the Bedchamber crisis which had forced Peel's refusal of the Premiership in 1839 except that *this* was defused. Opposition to Home Rule made it well-nigh impossible to find Liberal peers and peeresses to staff the Household. Seven peers refused to become Lords in Waiting.

As to the all-important position of Mistress of the Robes, no Liberal duchess could be found for it. The Duchess of Roxburghe, who had held it at the end of Gladstone's previous period of office, now refused on her husband's advice. Grace St Albans was invited, but being 'alien and averse to a Court appointment'[16] got her husband to decline on her behalf at an interview with Gladstone. The next day (13 February 1886) St Albans saw the Prince of Wales, feeling that the circumstances as reported by the Prime Minister called for an explanation; he also wrote the Prince a letter,[17] which was passed on to Victoria. The Queen's reply to her son completely exonerated the Duchesses of St Albans and Roxburghe and the seven Liberal lords.

> While I much regret not being able to have the Duchess [of St Albans] in my Household, I honour her for what she has done. ... It is atrocious of Mr Gladstone, or Lord Granville even more, to expose *me* to having only half a Household.[18]

She felt Lord Granville had been 'altogether very untruthful in this Household business.[18] The Colonial Secretary's next suggestion, the Duchess of Leinster, was totally unsuitable so far as the Queen was concerned; his ultimate attempt to cut the Gordian knot, with the appointment of a marchioness, was utter anathema: 'this has never been done in my time or in Queen Adelaide's.[18] Finally, three duchesses (Bedford, Argyll and Leinster) were prevailed upon to share the duties of Mistress of the Robes on a rota basis during the six tricky months that Gladstone was in power. In a country which was at the heart of a world-empire it is amazing, to us very nearly in the last quarter of the twentieth century, that a Prime Minister in the last quarter of the nineteenth was expected to cope with such trivialities of protocol—and cope personally. And it is yet one more illustration of the intractability of the Irish problem from every angle. But the important point is that this was a Gordian knot which Gladstone could loosen, if not cut. The Duchess of St Albans and her like-minded colleagues did not force him into the dilemma of Sir Robert Peel.

It was just as well that Grace St Albans declined the Mistress-ship of the Robes (only once held by a St Albans duchess, the first), since in the years of Gladstone's third and fourth administrations she became increasingly militant against Home Rule. She enlisted to this cause many of the most influential names in the land, including the historian J. A. Froude. Froude's comments on the Irish situation are vigorous and doom-laden. 'A gale of wind is blowing which may rise to a hurricane', he prophesied gloomily to the Duchess.[13]

> There are breakers all round: and the ship is full of lumber and an idiot is at the helm whilst the crew claim to be divinely inspired. But the poor crew have been intoxicated with poisonous vapours of national chloroform. . . . There are so many possibilities of evil that one can have no confidence. All I can say is that I believe Ireland ten years hence will be as quiet as she was under Cromwell.

How inspired and unintoxicated Gladstone and his crew were, subsequent events in the history of Ireland are still revealing.

The Duke's political influence was local rather than national, despite the fact that as early as 15 February 1869 he had been created a Privy Councillor; this honour accompanied his captaincy of the Yeomen of the Guard, which he held throughout Gladstone's first administration but not during the later three. The local influence was exerted at Bestwood rather than Redbourne. Although he served as a Deputy Lieutenant for

Lincolnshire from 1860, and was Provincial Grand Master of Lincolnshire freemasons from 1862 to 1878, the decision to make Nottinghamshire his home was sealed with the first brick laid at Bestwood. Admittedly, he did not sever his earlier links altogether. He revived falconry in Lincolnshire in the late 1860s, the last time any Hereditary Grand Falconer of England has practised the sport, and was painted by James Hayllar in his official costume. Towards the end of his life he himself seems to have accepted the (at least temporary) decay of the hawking tradition, when in 1891 he commuted the £965 p.a. net pension of Hereditary Grand Falconer for £18,335: about £7,500 less than the Treasury had been prepared to offer before Charles Bradlaugh raised vehement objections in 1886.

Redbourne was not let but kept in readiness for the occasional visit. St Albans took an interest in the affairs of Redbourne village, presenting the church with a new organ and lectern, appointing two incumbents to Redbourne as patron, and lecturing about a holiday in the Dolomites at the school his father had founded. We even find him staying with Lord Yarborough at Brocklesby in 1879 and 1884, but it was at Bestwood that he felt pride of possession, and gradually exerted considerable weight in local affairs.

In 1880 he was deemed sufficiently 'steady' (in Palmerston's phrase) to succeed Lord Belper as Lord Lieutenant of Nottinghamshire, an office which he held until his death. He was a magistrate for the county from 1869, if not earlier, and an active member of Nottinghamshire County Council for many years: a County alderman, chairman of committees, and a Justice on the Standing Joint Committee for Police. A more important political role in Nottinghamshire was to act as a shrewd go-between, interpreting influential local opinion to his ministerial friends in Whitehall. Writing to Hartington (now Duke of Devonshire) on 27 January 1894,[19] he voiced the anxiety of Liberal Unionists around Nottingham that the Gladstone government would give way to the Lords' opposition to the Employers' Liability Bill. Rather than accept Lord Dudley's amendment to clause 4, permitting employees to contract out of the Act wherever adequate private insurance arrangements covered industrial injury, he felt that Gladstone should dissolve Parliament and go to the country: on the issue of employers' liability the Government 'would get a majority in these parts'. As leader of the Liberal Unionists, Devonshire should insist on opposing 'the dictates of the Tory peers', and not jettison the bill at any cost. Otherwise, he and like-minded Liberal peers might find themselves in the position of voting against the whips in support of the will of the House of Commons. In St Albans's eyes, Hartington was the bulwark saving Gladstone from the folly of capitulating to Tory pressure in home affairs, and using his political splinter group as a brake on the Prime Minister's reckless haste over Ireland.

In another letter to Devonshire dated 30 December 1895, he claims responsibility for converting the Liberal member for West Nottingham, Charles Seely, to Unionism; Devonshire had just informed him of the baronetcy about to be conferred on Seely—at whose house in the Isle of Wight St Albans was to die on 11 May 1898. A further bond between St Albans and Devonshire was their position as Lords Lieutenant of neighbouring counties. In May 1897 he wrote to consult his Derbyshire colleague about the appointment of Ernest Hooley as a magistrate for Nottinghamshire. 'The thing is impossible', he asserted, but wished to check whether Devonshire had finally bowed to Tory pressure to give Hooley a similar appointment in Derbyshire. In the event, Hooley was not appointed to the commission of either county, although he was already a magistrate for both Huntingdonshire and Wiltshire. The general impression of St Albans's political stewardship is that he discharged the lord lieutenancy with meticulous care, whilst as a peer he remained basically loyal to the Liberal Party though obviously sympathizing with the Tories on the Irish issue rather than with Gladstone.

A contemporary description of him as 'a cheery, sensible, steady, kindhearted man of business' is perhaps the best tribute to his sober Victorian qualities except that it leaves out of account the literary interests which he shared with his second wife: thus, towards the end of his life he corresponds with Rosebery about the Irish character of Goldsmith's writings, particularly *The Deserted Village*; he also engaged Philip Bagenal to write a biography of his father-in-law, privately published in 1884. From small beginnings he brought the Bestwood estate up to a thriving community, with a colliery, an iron works, a church and a school. His interest in cricket led him to lay out a cricket pitch for the village within sight of his own drawing-room windows. He helped to introduce his tenants to the latest agricultural methods, including those practised in Canada and the United States. He foresaw the importance of cooperative marketing in agriculture. The Bestwood Agricultural Society, which he encouraged, was a forerunner of the local farming associations which gradually merged into the National Farmers' Union.

For a duke in the mid-nineteenth century, he was surprisingly in tune with the mentality of middle-class business men, the men with whom he worked on the board of Bestwood colliery and on Nottinghamshire County Council. Yet he was still an aristocrat: a member of the Jockey Club from 1863 until his death, with a string of racehorses most of which he had sold by 1865, though he always had one or two in training; a collector of works of art; and the builder of a stately neo-Gothic mansion. Indeed, the building of Bestwood Lodge exemplifies his blend of aristocratic idealism and practical middle-class common sense. The racehorses perhaps had to be sold to help pay the builder, yet the house and park were planned as securely as the founding of a dynasty.

The principal rooms were filled with works of art collected from his European travels: marble mosaic tables and mantelpieces from Italy, paintings and china figurines from Spain, and a vast congeries of jewels, embroideries and bric-à-brac, together with the family pictures and other heirlooms: Van Dycks, Lelys, Knellers, Reynoldses, Gainsboroughs and Romneys, a Fragonard and a Teniers, the ring given to Bishop Juxon by Charles I just before his execution, a fan belonging to Nell Gwyn, and a small drawing by Horace Walpole dated 1735.

Outside, St Albans was a great planter of trees: firs, including a fine Corsican variety, Austrian and Corsican pines and other species which, besides their sound commercial value as timber, gave a solid foretaste of futurity, repeopling—as the dukes of Newcastle and Portland had also done—the desolate scrubland of parts of the former Sherwood Forest. Bestwood seemed to be rapidly turning into a commercial and agricultural empire, the stronghold of the family for generations to come.

In his will St Albans laid down that the entailed estate should pass to whomever inherited the title. Yet two grave misfortunes were to wreck his hopes. In the late 1890s it became increasingly clear that Burford, his son and heir, was a nervous invalid, whose attacks of melancholia were growing more severe and prolonged. He could not marry, and had to abandon his military career. As Hereditary Grand Falconer, he loved to march about his grounds blowing a hunting-horn slung from a green baldric. He was not well enough, as Duke, to attend the Coronations of 1902 and 1911. Though never certified as insane, he was to spend the last thirty years of his life, until 1934, in a small private house in the grounds of a Sussex 'clinic'.

The second disaster that befell the family was the great fire at Bestwood in 1893, in which twenty-five pictures and many family records were destroyed. Amongst the lost works of art were: a full-length portrait of Prince Rupert, by Van Dyck; a portrait of the first Duke of St Albans by Kneller (another portrait of him by the same artist is at the Metropolitan Museum of Art, New York); Diana, Duchess of St Albans, also by Kneller; Charles II as Prince of Wales, by Gerrit van Honthorst; and The Twentieth and Last Earl of Oxford, by Sir Peter Lely. Most if not all of these twenty-five paintings are identifiable in the 1786 sale catalogue and would seem to have been bought by the fifth Duke at the Brussels auction. Having survived the third Duke's vagaries, they perished during the lifetime of his earnest constructive successor. The widespread mourning at the tenth Duke's death—from tenant farmers and coalminers to business men, politicians and even the Royal Family to whom he had not feared to speak his mind—showed the depth of public regard for his attempts to combine aristocratic privilege with practical service.

NOTES TO CHAPTER VIII

Will of 10th Duke of St Albans.

A. C. Benson and Viscount Esher (ed.): *The Letters of Queen Victoria. A Selection from Her Majesty's Correspondence between the Years 1837 and 1861*, 1907.

G. E. Buckle (ed.): *The Letters of Queen Victoria. A Selection from Her Majesty's Correspondence and Journal between the Years 1862 and 1885*, 1926–1928.

G. E. Buckle (ed.): *The Letters of Queen Victoria. A Selection from Her Majesty's Correspondence and Journal between the Years 1886 and 1901*, 1930–1932.

R. T. B. Fulford (ed.): *Dearest Mama. Letters between Queen Victoria and the Crown Princess of Prussia, 1861–1864*, 1968.

L. Jacks: *The Great Houses of Nottinghamshire, and the County Families*, 1881.

P. M. Magnus: *King Edward the Seventh*, 1964.

D. Spring: *The English Landed Estate in the Nineteenth Century: its Administration*, 1963.

F. M. L. Thompson: *English Landed Society in the Nineteenth Century*, 1963.

Private information.

----

1. W. S. Blunt: *My Diaries*, 1920, vol. II, 258.
2. RA Queen Victoria's Journal 21 June 1863.
3. RA A33/25.
4. RA C62/99.
5. RA Queen Victoria's Journal 10 May 1870.
6. RA Add. A17/494.
7. *Rugby Advertiser*, 26 April 1884; *Wigan Observer*, 25 April 1884; *Journal of the Iron and Steel Institute*, 1884, 557–558.
8. S. Lee: *King Edward VII. A Biography*, vol. I, 1925, 337. Cf. H. Malo: *Thiers, 1797–1877*, 1932, 538.
9. *Wigan Observer*, 16 July 1875.

10. Private information (Mrs M. J. Owen).
11. RA Add. A15/2696.
12. RA Add. A15/8445 Diary of Princess Louise Margaret, Duchess of Connaught 14 April 1879.
13. Archives of Newtown Anner, Clonmel.
14. *Dictionary of National Biography:* article Thomas Heazle Parke.
15. RA Add. A12/1154.
16. RA C37/302.
17. RA C37/308.
18. RA C37/310.
19. Chatsworth Archives 340.2535.

CHAPTER IX

Obby

Eccentricity has been a privilege of dukes. From the fifth Duke of Portland who lived underground at Welbeck and who ordered any housemaid he happened to meet in his corridors to go out and skate on silver roller-skates, to the third Duke of Dorset whose guests always had to eat in complete silence, to the sixth Duke of Devonshire who sent out a naval expedition to the Indies when taking up botany, there are many forms this eccentricity can take. But it is becoming increasingly rare. The pressures towards conformity are nowadays very great. It is not so easy to be eccentric with a modern estate to be run, and a house that is too large with too few servants—and no spare money to pay for more servants if more were available. Wild eccentricity flourished when there was an abundance of money, and all business problems were left in the hands of a steward or agent.

The twelfth Duke of St Albans—'Obby', as he was known to his friends—was the last of a dying breed. To a greater degree perhaps than any other aristocrat, he carried eccentricity into the twentieth century, and made no apologies for the fact. He was of course eccentric long before becoming a duke at the age of fifty-nine, but his peculiarities hardened with the years. He behaved more and more as he thought people expected him to behave, and revelled in eccentricity as it came into sharper contrast with the ways of life around him. From a spontaneous display of zaniness it became something akin to affectation. The man who even in the 1960s could say to Martin Newman, the hall porter at Brooks's: 'wind up my watch for me, there's a good fellow', was acting a part.

As a young man in the late Victorian and Edwardian eras, he had many qualities. Like his half-brother Burford, he was extraordinarily good-looking. Unlike Burford, he had a sharp brain—though he rarely put it to its fullest use. Besides wit and humour, he had charm—when he wished to turn it on. Even by ducal standards, he was well connected: the best connected of any of his namesakes, related by the end of his life to most of the people who mattered. Harold Macmillan was his nephew. So was the Lord Salisbury who resigned from the Cabinet over the release of Makarios from the Seychelles. Lord Balniel, recently second-in-command at the Foreign and Commonwealth Office, was a great-nephew. The Lansdowne who was Viceroy of India and Foreign Secretary became his father-in-law, and the Duchess of Devonshire was his wife's sister. A niece became Duchess of Buccleuch, and her daughter Duchess of Northumberland. His wife's cousins numbered the Dukes of Marlborough, Leeds and Gloucester. Such an entrée to the greatest country houses in England and Scotland would have given him every opportunity to make a rapid career for himself, in politics or in business.

And yet there was something lacking. His qualities of character were so assorted at birth by some Wicked Fairy that he was destined to achieve nothing. Indeed, in the long course of his life he did considerable harm, both to his inheritance and to people who knew him. Though sometimes constructive as a young man, he was essentially destructive in everything he undertook. All his charm, good looks, humour and brilliance were undermined by a deep instability, of which he himself was only too well aware. He feared the madness that had afflicted his two brothers and his great-uncle Charles Gubbins. Sometimes he would feel within himself the approach of something strange and overpowering, threatening to rob him of his self-control; and to avoid its attack, would escape from the house to the solitude and peace of the home farm.

If the tenth Duke was a totally different man from his father the ninth, Obby was quite as different again from the earnest Victorian patriarch. His father worked; Obby was indolent (and with some excuse, since from the age of nineteen or twenty he could expect the reversion of the dukedom). His father had a word for everybody, and as a colliery-owner and county councillor was on good terms with middle-class industrialists; Obby seemed to despise the 'square-toed middle class', the new rich who were unacceptable because they derived their money from trade. In this his father, though a Victorian, was far more attuned to the modern world than Obby himself. The enterprise of 'square-toed middle-class' industrialists made the wealth on which everyone's prosperity depended; and their lineal descendants, well-dressed tycoons in jet air-craft, are nowadays envied and acclaimed as popular heroes. Even to those of his own class Obby could be insufferably haughty. To a man now prominent in the Conservative party but who was then only at the outset of his career, he delivered the crushing retort: 'young man, you talk too much'. Politics bored him. After only a few sentences, any politician—old or young—had said enough. In this detached, disillusioned view of politics he was not only close in spirit to Topham Beauclerk but also in fact surprisingly modern: and quite the opposite of his father, who had stable political convictions. Obby loved to be perverse, the devil's advocate in any political wrangle.

On one memorable occasion in the late 1950s he was on a visit to his nephew John Wakehurst, Governor of Northern Ireland. Outside an Orange hall he saw a group of Protestant Unionists, the very sector of Northern Irish opinion so vigorously defended by his mother. He rushed up to them proclaiming himself a Papist: foolhardy, and quite untruthful, conduct which could have met with a savage reaction today. After the imposition of direct rule, and all that has come to be associated in people's minds with Sunningdale and the Council of Ireland, Orangemen would not have Obby's sense of humour, nor his conviction that the whole Irish problem was a stupid muddle whipped up by meaningless religious dogma.

Whereas, like most Victorians, the tenth Duke was a man of deep sentimental emotion living in what he took to be a rational, well-ordered universe, Obby had few refined emotions but much cruelty. His sharp mined enabled him to see through the frailties of others. If people had a weakness in their characters, Obby instantly divined it—and could mercilessly exploit it. People were often afraid of him, and few bold enough to put him in his place. His personal world polarized into those he idolized and those he detested; and there were many more of the latter than the former. To Lord Wakehurst he was never crueller than when he saw him rigged up in the trappings of political dominion at Hillsborough. It is the custom for a Governor-General or Governor to lead the way into the dining-room; but, not to stand on ceremony during Obby's visit, Wake-hurst allowed the ladies to precede him into dinner. He well knew how much Obby disliked ceremony but did not expect to be rebuked by his uncle, in front of the guests and servants, that as Governor of Northern Ireland he did not even know correct social form.

As between his sisters and half-sisters there were violent partialities. He loved his sister Moyra and her children. He detested one of the daughters of his half-sister Sybil. Robert Somerset, eldest son of his sister Katherine, was always a favourite. 'He is a hero', Obby maintained—long before he died a hero's death in a yachting accident.

With his ancestors it was just the same as with his sisters, nephews and nieces. Some he admired, but most he was indifferent towards or even disliked. He used to say that he felt no pride at all about his Beauclerk ancestry, maintaining that as a rule they had not married 'well'. The few ancestors of whom he was really proud were the de Veres (the first Duke had married well!), and his descent through the Osbornes from the ancient Kings of Ireland. Even in the genealogical aspect of things Obby's sharp gift for finding out weakness had hit its mark. The dukes of St Albans, on the whole, have not married 'well'—though they have usually married heiresses. Their wives have not usually belonged to the very highest families in the land; but Obby was wrong not to be proud of the Bessborough connection: the Cavendishes, Russells, Butlers, Cecils, Howards, St Johns, FitzGeralds and Staffords were his ancestors through Catherine, wife of the fifth Duke. Here as elsewhere he picked and chose perversely. With his sharp, brittle mind, he recognized and admitted the many unexciting lines of ascent in his family tree. But the things that did stir him he felt with passionate romanticism: his descent from the Irish kings, and the poetry and pathos of the de Veres. Who knows whether his fondness for the latter did not partly stem from the ninth Earl of Oxford's being Duke of Ireland?

Perhaps it was his Irish ancestry which gave him his capacity for poetry. He could love and idealize so long as he did not think too deeply. Self-awareness killed the poetic feeling. Despite all his strictures on Irish bigotry, he did have a sense of the dignity and holiness of religious things. He attended church regularly at Killaloan, near Newtown Anner. But he

'Obby', Twelfth Duke of St Albans: a drawing by Douglas Anderson, 1961.

The Present Duke and Duchess of St Albans: a photograph by Graham Murrell.

had no time for liturgy, doctrine or stuffiness. Like some latter-day Sir Roger de Coverley, he would exclaim: 'Rubbish' during the sermon, if he felt that any of the minister's points needed to be contradicted. And he would only give 2/6d for the collection.

The same mixture of moods was to be seen at an infinitely higher level with the Coronation. The first he was entitled to attend (his half-brother had been Duke in 1911) was that of George VI; this was a ceremony he attended, in ducal robes and wearing the gold chain of Hereditary Grand Falconer of England. He had surrendered to the poetry of the occasion. But when the next Coronation came round, in 1953, he was aware of another aspect of the same ceremony: its formality, out-of-dateness and interminable detail. He responded to the changed impression with impish humour. The gold chain of Hereditary Grand Falconer was no longer enough. He wished to bring with him a live falcon, and requested this permission from the Earl Marshal's office. No doubt he foresaw the flurry this would cause in bureaucratic circles—and the raucous cries with which the bird might compete with Handel, Parry and Vaughan Williams in the unlikely event of permission being granted. We are told that the Earl Marshal's office gave permission for a stuffed falcon to be brought to the Abbey; but this was an inadequate gesture, and Obby stayed away. In 1937 he had been in a mood to enjoy the uplifting grandeur; his skittish lucidity kept him away in 1953.

Throughout his eighty-nine years he ploughed a lonely furrow. No greater contrast can be imagined than between the tenth Duke and his three sons (by two wives): the father, a trusted friend and adviser of the Royal family and a pillar of the Nottinghamshire community; and Burford who suffered from melancholia, William whose life's achievement was to set a building at Eton alight before entering on the darkness of total insanity, and Obby who was not the trusted friend and adviser of anybody, and who was the pillar of no community.

Thanks to his sons' incapacity, the legacy which the tenth Duke had been building up was run down. In June 1917, during Burford's time as duke but with Obby as the remainderman, the 5,412 acres of the Redbourne estate were sold for £106,030. It comprised the Hall, eighteen farms, a fully licensed inn (the Red Lion) and thirty-two private houses, in addition to shops and labourers' cottages in the villages of Redbourne and Hibaldstow. Thus, the Lincolnshire influence was lost.

On 10 June 1940, a singularly bad time for selling land, the Bestwood estate was disposed of: its Lodge, with fine hall, three reception rooms, ballroom, billiard room, conservatory, gun room, nineteen principal bed and dressing rooms, seventeen secondary and servants' bedrooms, and nine bathrooms; its fifteen farms, colliery sidings and cricket ground; its twenty-five houses and cottages; its parkland and timber; and over 500 acres of building land, 'in parcels from 5 to 109 acres, adjoining recent development within the [Nottingham] city boundary'.

Bestwood had been in the family's ownership for 253 years. Its sale was no doubt a wise, and inevitable, decision. War is the greatest catalyst of social change; many estates were dismembered either during or just after the Second World War, whose aftermath changed the whole pattern of aristocratic life. The beauty that Obby's father had created at Bestwood, and which Grace Duchess of St Albans had maintained during the early years of her widowhood, was being marred by encroaching industry— which the tenth Duke had done so much to assist and promote.

In 1915 the Lodge and grounds were let to Sir Frank Bowden, whose Raleigh cycle company which he had founded at Lenton about thirty years previously was by now the largest manufacturer of bicycles in the world; with the outbreak of war, it had become a large supplier of munitions. In 1921 Sir Frank died and was succeeded by his son, who presided over an exceptionally active and cheerful period in the history of Bestwood when there were large weekend parties (to which Obby sometimes came), big shoots (in which Obby joined), woods well stocked with game, four keepers and an enormous indoor staff.

Here Sir Harold Bowden continued to live on the grand scale until 1940, but even before the estate's actual sale the Beauclerks had been trying to sell it for some years. Temporarily at least, the Bowdens seemed to have halted the encroachments of heavy industry; and who better to do so than they, since they controlled it? but because of its closeness to Nottingham, the break-up of Bestwood was inevitable.

Throughout this time Obby's home was in Ireland, where political circumstances after 1921 practically debarred him from exerting any local influence—though his neighbour Lord Donoughmore became a senator. Neither nationally (at the House of Lords) nor locally did he seek, or wish, to influence the course of politics. His world was the more real one of personal human relationships, many of them strained. One of his closest and happiest friendships was with Sir Mark Sturgis; another, with Sir Neville Anderson. Obby had few near friends, however. Few trusted him. He was as variable in mood as he was lacking in concentration. It is remarkable how few friends he had amongst the men of his own class. Indeed, many of them positively disliked him, and his detestation of them was just as cordial. But to servants and others of a lower social class than himself, especially if they were in any kind of need or distress, he could be friendliness itself. In 1950 he asked an old acquaintance if he was in financial difficulties over his wife's death; and offered to help. At Brooks's members popular with their fellow-members were not necessarily popular with the club servants; in fact, the reverse was often true: Obby's own brother-in-law the Duke of Devonshire was fierce even towards Martin Newman but the soul of affability to his social equals. Whereas Obby was one of Newman's 'top favourites' at Brooks's, and the same sentiment is echoed by many others whom he charmed with the courtly politeness of a *grand seigneur*.

Over the female sex he exerted not only charm but a tremendous fascination. He had many mistresses, or so he claimed. His taste was for smartly dressed, *soignée*, fashionable women, like Mrs Wilfrid Ricardo, but he was not averse from the more transient relationship. He once excused himself for not turning up to an invitation to tea by getting someone to telephone: 'tell them I'm having much more fun with the French maid'. 'Doesn't he realize that all our grandmothers were chambermaids?' he remarked on another occasion, referring to the Duc de La Rochefoucauld.

In a life littered with failure his amorous conquests were his one achievement. On his women friends he spent the time and energy others might have devoted to a career—or a marriage. He claimed to be the father of many illegitimate children, and sometimes was embarrassingly frank about it. A baronet and his foreign wife once came to luncheon with him in Ireland and throughout the meal Obby repeatedly asked a friend sitting next to him: 'what do you think? what do you think? Is he one of mine?'—in a whisper that was alarmingly audible. Neither the baronet nor his wife suspected anything, but the lady very probably retained an abiding impression of the oddities of the Anglo-Irish aristocracy. There are several titled women alive today of whom he claimed to be the father.

It is, however, doubtful whether some of his stories are entirely correct. Some who knew him are of the opinion that he romanticized, or even idealized, this aspect of his life—rather than bring to it the cold, lucid, dispassionate analysis he brought to so many others. But two things are indisputable: his relationship with Norah Ricardo, lasting over thirty years, was the only true love of his whole life; and whatever the complete facts of the matter, there is at least one child of his alive today.

Even in procreation, however, he showed his usual selfishness. The fact that he did not marry until he was forty-three was due to his fear of passing on the hereditary madness; but he did not scruple to risk passing this on to those who were merely natural children. Even in old age his deepest friendships were with women. Like Disraeli, he had a craving for feminine company and his happiest relationships were with women other than his wife. Both had the same mercurial instability, though Disraeli disciplined his; both had the same romantic temperament (born perhaps of Jewish blood), though Disraeli channelled his into more productive outlets. For both, women were the greatest source of peace; there was no better solace for jangled nerves.

In his early years he was much under the spell of his remarkable mother, from whom he perhaps gained most of those qualities—or attributes—that so distinguished him from the tenth Duke. Though Grace Duchess of St Albans was of Spanish Jewish descent through her father, it was through her mother's Irish father Sir Thomas Osborne that Newtown Anner came into Obby's possession. From Ralph Bernal, her paternal grandfather, she inherited artistic taste—but not his distinguished collection of paintings by Bronzino, Holbein, Cranach, the Flemish Primitives, Hals and Boucher auctioned at Christie's in 1855. She was the friend of artists, such as Leighton (who painted her portrait), and a talented amateur artist herself. She was a woman of great charm, vivacity and sex-appeal: all qualities that Obby inherited. Like him, she was utterly devoid of money sense; but unlike him, always insisted on buying the best. She was a woman of great literary interests, not merely confined to the big Victorian novelists and poets but also extending to historians, journalists, playwrights and actors. Her correspondence includes letters from Froude, Lecky, Creighton, Buckle, Lord Lytton, J. L. Garvin, Irving, Ellen Terry and Arthur Pinero, many or all of whom she invited to lunch or dine with her at 49 Cadogan Gardens.

Her absorption in politics was equally great, at a time when it was still possible for duchesses to exert undue political influence. The Unionism which had precluded her in 1886 from becoming Mistress of the Robes under a Home Rule administration became more ferocious as the pressures for separatism mounted. Inevitably, Hartington was her hero: she would have been Mistress of the Robes for him, if he had become Prime Minister in 1880, as was expected. There are many letters in her correspondence from him and from Joseph and Austen Chamberlain. Even young Neville Chamberlain was her guest at Newtown Anner in August 1902. Lord Randolph Churchill, who had threatened in 1886 to 'play the Orange card', was another of her political contacts. But her finest energy was reserved for the later leaders of Ulster Unionism, Carson, Craigavon and Edward Saunderson.

She was a keen worker for the Irish Loyal and Patriotic Union, which she supported with money and advice. With Carson and Craigavon she was involved in the events of 1912, conducting on their behalf a sort of public-relations campaign at the London end. Like them, she believed that true loyalty to the Crown lay in resisting the calamitous disregard for Ulster shown by Asquith and Birrell. It came as a great blow to her to see the partition of Ireland which took place four years before her death in 1926.

In these attitudes she was, of course, at variance with her son Obby, who was perfectly happy living south of the border in a partitioned Ireland. It may partly have been her dogged Unionism which led to rifts in their relationship in her latter years. As she grew older, Obby was sometimes horribly cruel to his mother. The truth was that he could not give himself wholly to any cause, whereas she could do so with zest and realism. Obby, in fact, was a throwback to her father, Ralph Bernal Osborne, a brilliant Member of Parliament who was too much of a dilettante to make great headway in the House of Commons: though attaining junior ministerial rank, he was never taken particularly seriously; the Queen disliked him, believing he would be a bad representative of his country in any Foreign Office post; his fellow Members of Parliament considered him lacking in concentration and stamina; and Disraeli even mocked him for the long list of the constituencies he had represented.

Obby never drew up an account of his life, with its lengthy succession of surface experiences, its travels to almost every corner of the globe. He lived only for the moment. Within five minutes of receiving a letter, he would have torn it up after writing a reply. This hatred of continuity and involvement can be seen in the outline of his life. After Eton he joined the 17th Lancers, in which he rose to no higher rank than a captaincy. In December 1899 he fought in the disastrous actions at the Modder River and Magersfontein during the advance on Kimberley. After the relief of that city in February 1900 he was assigned to operations in the Orange Free State (February–May 1900), the Transvaal (July–November 1900), Orange River Colony and Cape Colony (June–November 1901, March–May 1902). His services were rewarded with the Queen's Medal with six clasps, and he resigned from the 17th Lancers in 1902. Then began a series of peacetime journeys, to Persia, Russia, Tibet and other countries in the Middle and Far East. He also became friendly with Wilfrid Blunt, a still greater eccentric than himself, whose homosexuality he does not seem to have suspected.

It was in June 1908 that Lord Osborne Beauclerk cycled the forty miles from London to Newbuildings Place, in Sussex, where Blunt was then living; he came on the introduction of a mutual friend. Blunt was the poet, dandy and explorer who had established a stud of Arabian horses on his estate at Crabbet, and whose wife was the granddaughter of Byron. He was a much older man than Obby—sixty-seven to the latter's thirty-three—when they first met, but there was much that they had in common. Blunt in his younger days had been a tireless explorer: he had navigated the Euphrates across Mesopotamia, knew Persia and India intimately, and had lived in Egypt, Algeria and Turkey (including Palestine). Even in 1908 he still had a house in Egypt, where he spent the winters.

What could not have pleased Obby's mother, as the young man's visits to Newbuildings became more frequent, was Blunt's intense denunciation of colonialism, whether in Egypt, India or (as he saw it) in Ireland. In 1886 he had stood for Parliament as a Liberal Home Ruler, though unsuccessfully. He had even gone to gaol for urging tenant farmers in Galway to withhold rents from Lord Clanricarde. To Grace St Albans, as an Irish landowner herself, Blunt's attitude must have appeared a class-betrayal, an incitement to general sedition. In fact, however, Blunt had the gift of attracting visitors and friends of very different outlooks. He dazzled them with his talk, but by no means always converted them to his opinions.

The Crabbet set was as brilliant in its day as the 'Souls' or the Cliveden set and until his death in 1922 Blunt remained a magnetic social figure. 'He is a pleasant young man', was Blunt's first reaction to Obby, 'who has travelled much in Asia, and has ideas about horses, poetry and ethnology. . . . I showed him the stallions and gave him a copy of the *Golden Odes*. He says he will come again'.

The friendship was interrupted by Obby's shooting expedition to Persia in the autumn of 1908, in search of wild sheep east of the Caspian Sea. As soon as he was back in England he gave an account of this expedition to Blunt, who was impressed by the descriptions of a great forest of elms and sycamores on the mountainous borders of Persia and Turkestan, and of scrubland covered with juniper trees running away towards the deserts of central Persia. But he was less confident of Obby's political judgement: 'Beauclerk's ideas . . . are rather vague, and I had difficulty in persuading him that the Meshmed of Eastern Persia was not the same as Meshmed Ali'. On a further expedition to central Asia in 1909 Obby shot ibex, *ovis karelini* and wapiti. After his return home he became a still more regular visitor both to Newbuildings and Blunt's London house in Chapel Street; Winston Churchill, George Wyndham and Hilaire Belloc were some of his fellow guests. In fact, as early as April 1910, during a weekend party at Newbuildings, Obby and Wilfrid Blunt were even

offered peerages by Churchill on condition that they would assist the
passage of the Parliament Bill through the House of Lords, where it was
threatened by a large Tory majority; nothing, however, came of the
offer either for Blunt or Beauclerk because despite the Lords' stalling
tactics the proposed deluge of new Liberal peers never needed to be
created.

On another occasion Obby brought Lord Ronaldshay to luncheon
with Blunt. All three shared an interest in India, where Ronaldshay
aspired one day to become Viceroy: an ambition in which he was disap-
pointed, though for five years he had Cabinet responsibility for India
until dismissed by Churchill in 1940.

In the privacy of his diary Blunt summed up Obby with sympathy and
some shrewdness.

> Without being quite intellectual he is extremely intelligent, has
> seen much and thought much, has every good impulse and desire,
> and is feeling his way how to live up to them. He is hardly at all
> educated, but has a large experience of men and cities, or rather of
> wild places which are not cities. He has been at Eton and under-
> stands its snobbery; he has been in the Army and understands its
> futility; he is a landlord and understands its duties; he is without
> pretension and has a kindly heart.

Just as his father had been tempted by the El Dorado of coal beneath
Bestwood, so Obby succumbed in 1911 to the temptation of a literal
El Dorado: the prospect of gold in British Columbia. Fifteen years
previously gold had been discovered at Klondike in Yukon territory,
holding out hopes of much greater deposits than eventually came to
light. The vogue of Klondike was, in fact, fairly short-lived though
prospectors were still turning up in sizable numbers at the time of
Obby's venture. He seriously believed he would make a fortune, but not
in the more traditional Yukon area. After travelling for two and a half
days by ocean steamer from Vancouver, he began his adventure of a
lifetime by prospecting along the Stikine River, some 150 miles south of
the border with Yukon.

Soon he had moved his camp seventy-five miles further north to the

Cassiar district of British Columbia, where near the junction of Thibert Creek and Boulder Creek he helped to finance and supervise the Boulder Creek Mine. It was not the first time that prospectors had visited Thibert Creek, but somehow—every gold-digger being a Micawber at heart— Obby hoped for better luck at a spot a short distance away from the earlier site. The Boulder Creek goldfield did not lie in the river bed and so a pump and pipeline flumed water from Boulder Creek to the deposit, where sluices sifted the pressurized alluvium to reveal, alas! that the grains were neither pure nor plentiful enough to place the business on a sound commercial footing. By 20 October 1911 Obby had written up his General Report on the failed project, before leaving the Rocky Mountains for England where on 12 November he was dining with Wilfrid Blunt. It was a sad farewell to hopes of instant riches.

Although, according to Blunt, Obby had understood the futility of army service even during the Boer War, he was not so sceptical as to remain aloof in 1914. All one may assume is that, for all his adventurous spirit, he approached war with less than the mystical patriotism of a Kipling or Rupert Brooke! He rejoined the army as a major in the South Nottinghamshire Yeomanry and was appointed A.D.C. to Haig, who keenly appreciated his brain and wit. Indeed, not only his wit but his mere appearance and presence would sometimes convulse the General with laughter, and in more serious mood he accompanied Haig to Kassel in 1917 when George V invested the newly appointed Field Marshal with the Order of the Thistle: but the lighter mood returned in the evening when Obby joined Haig in a celebration dinner. In Haig's despatch dated 7 November 1917 Obby was one of some 1,700 officers, ladies, NCOs and men serving under the generalissimo from 26 February to 20 September 1917 'whose distinguished and gallant services and devotion to duty he considered deserving of special mention'.

He showed equal military zeal in enlisting as a private, and later becoming a corporal, in the Home Guard during the Second World War. His duties involved long hours as a sentry in Whitehall—and by that time he was approaching seventy. In the words of a friend: 'he had the opportunity to shirk three wars but in fact always served to the best of his ability in whatever capacity he was acceptable.'

When the First World War had only another three months to run, Obby married Beatrix, the widowed Marchioness of Waterford, who was forty-one years of age to his forty-three. She was a neighbour living with her six children at Curraghmore, eighteen miles from Newtown Anner. Beatrix Lady Waterford was one of the most gracious women of her age, whose misfortune had been that her first husband was a mental invalid. To different people Obby's story had varied as to how he and Lady Waterford came to marry. In the latter years of his life he claimed that he was trapped by her into marriage. According to his earlier story, she at first refused him but three or four years later changed her mind, and wrote accepting his offer. At any rate, it seems that between his first proposal and the eventual engagement his feelings for her had changed: he had ceased to love her. The Lansdownes, Lady Waterford's parents, did not consider him a valuable addition to the family, nor was he popular with many of the Beresfords. Only rarely, if ever, did he stay with his sister-in-law at Chatsworth. At a party given by Lady Lansdowne in 1930 to celebrate her grandson Lord Waterford's engagement to Juliet Lindsay, Obby made matters no better by his disparaging comments on Miss Lindsay's new family connections.

During the early years of his marriage to Beatrix, Obby lived at the Waterford home, Curraghmore (near Waterford). Until her death in 1926 his mother was still living at Newtown Anner; Lady Waterford's eldest child was only nineteen at the time of her second marriage, and her eldest son did not marry until 1930. During the time at Curraghmore Beatrix St Albans became pregnant, but much to her husband's relief—out of fear of the hereditary insanity transmitted perhaps from the Gubbinses—all ended in a miscarriage.

At Newtown Anner Obby found himself without a role (he had been a Deputy Lieutenant and even High Sheriff of Waterford before Independence). He became increasingly self-indulgent and cynical. The Tipperary property which had been in his mother's family for three hundred years ceased to interest him. It became too much of a bore to administer. From its original size of 3,500 acres at the death of Grace Duchess of St Albans, it had dwindled to a mere 500 acres thirty years later. Woods, shooting rights, cottages and farms had simply been frittered away:

mostly given to local people or sold at rock-bottom prices, though many of the woodlands had been leased to the Irish Forestry Department to bolster his liquid assets.

Being short of ready money he had to dispose of about 500 acres of farmland in order to keep going, but the other difficulty he faced in 1926—the fact that Irish agricultural land was rated—could have been overcome by a more enterprising man. (Farmland in England was rated until 1928). Obby could have farmed his land himself, as is now done by most landowners in southern Ireland, where the rating of agricultural land still applies. He would not have been alone in such enterprise; many Anglo-Irish families took to farming their own land after Independence. Obby took an easier way out. By selling farmland at rock-bottom prices in a period of agricultural depression, he at least avoided having to cope with tenants who were unable to afford both rent and rates. If cottagers refused to buy their homes, he could always find some means of persuading them, even on one memorable occasion writing a spoof letter on Dublin Government notepaper saying that the cottages would be compulsorily purchased if not renovated (which he, as landlord, refused to do).

The house at Newtown Anner gradually fell into decay, though weekend parties were still given, a good cook was employed, and there were excellent supplies of claret and port. At some of these parties guests recall bats and cobwebs but amongst those who accepted Obby's invitations to stay was Harold Macmillan. In Killaloan churchyard at the lodge gates a similar decay crept over the Osborne mausoleum, which Obby—the representative of the family—refused to have repaired.

In the years immediately following his succession to Newtown Anner, Obby spent much of his time in Ireland: hunting with the local Clonmel Harriers of which he was Master for a short while; a member of the Irish Turf Club (the equivalent of the British Jockey Club); owning a stud farm and a well-known stallion Tonton; and breeding many winners on the flat in the early 1930s. As time went on, however, he and Beatrix St Albans increasingly lived apart, she in Ireland and he in London. When at Newtown Anner their strained relations were sometimes painful, both to guests and servants. Yet she loved him with exemplary devotion. The fault for the breakdown of their marriage was not hers, except for such peccadillos as unpunctuality. One day when she was late for luncheon, he gave her empty chair at the dining-table to a man who had come to check fire-extinguishers, and denied her a place at luncheon when she eventually did appear in the room. He was unfaithful to her, and cruel as he had been cruel to his mother and even to Norah Ricardo, who loved him passionately for thirty years but committed suicide.

Gradually Obby came to a kind of arrangement with his heir Charles Beauclerk, a man whom he never liked and only once invited to stay at Newtown Anner. Though considering him a 'distant relation' who had to be kept 'at arm's length', he did not object to the family Trustees paying for three of his sons' education at Eton, and even for a time gave his heir an allowance. Obby was dilatory in making complete provisions to reduce estate duty. Partly through his nephew Richard Cavendish and partly through Hedley Strutt, arrangements were devised for Charles Beauclerk to buy Obby's life-interest for a cash sum. He lived just two years after these arrangements, instead of the five that were then necessary for full tax benefit. Because he survived the leap day of 1964 by two days, his estate qualified for a 15% remission of tax. The main asset was a Lincolnshire farm bought from New College, Oxford for £182,000 in March 1961, on which 55% remission of duty was allowed under section 28(1) of the Finance Act 1949. This was auctioned by Charles St Albans a year after he succeeded to the title. But Obby had not always scrupulously observed the laws of entail. In the late 1950s he sold a Fragonard portrait of Mme du Barry to an American collector. For £500 apiece he sold Sir Frank Bowden portraits of Charles II and the Duke of Monmouth, though— 'conscience-stricken', apparently—he repurchased 'Monmouth' for £300. His trustees, he claimed, would not permit him to spend any more: he had an eye to business! Sir Frank Bowden also recalls that Obby would have parted with two tapestries for £1,200, but here his salesmanship was unavailing. Mercifully, he did not dispose of any of the paintings in the Quadt bequest, inherited by the eleventh Duke in 1913 from a Bavarian countess who was a granddaughter of the fifth Duke's younger surviving daughter Lady Caroline Dundas. This bequest was a more recent—and, in a sense, marginal—entail than the trust settlement of the tenth Duke, or otherwise some or all of the works by Romney, Reynolds, Liotard and Hudson might well have gone the way of the Fragonard. To give Obby his due, however, he did lend thirty-nine of his pictures to the Ministry of Works for display in Government buildings; and one to this day (coming from the Quadt bequest) hangs in the British Embassy at Lisbon.

The death of Beatrix St Albans in August 1953, after two years of heart disease, was more distressing to Obby than his treatment of her had led people to expect. To those condoling with him on her death he had sent the harsh reply: 'Salt of the earth, Bertie, but such a bore'. Newtown Anner, where she had made her home for the last twenty-six years, became more and more distasteful to him. He decided to settle in Majorca, and built a villa at Andraix, near Palma, to which he transferred furniture and paintings from Ireland. In the words of Peter Ustinov, the present owner, 'he insisted on only the most plebeian materials being used in the building of the house, although, in the true English manner, there are fireplaces in all the most unexpected and useless locations'. But after seven weeks' residence there he tired of the villa and gave it to a nephew, Robert Somerset. Back in Ireland, he became a lonely unsettled widower. On 10 June 1956 a news report appeared in one edition of *The Sunday Dispatch*:

I'D LIKE TO MARRY SOME LOVELY GIRL, SAYS LONELY DUKE, AGED 82 [In fact, Obby was eighty-one].

The Duke of St Albans sank back into a deep armchair in his Tipperary mansion, took another sip of brandy, and told me: 'I am very lonely. I'd like to get married again. . . . There are many lovely girls I'd like to marry. However', he added ruefully, 'I think I'm too old'.

. . . The deserted palatial old mansion that is his ancestral home seemed to emphasize his loneliness . . .

He shook his head as if to answer an unspoken question: 'No, I don't think matrimony is for me at my age'.

But he spoke as a man who invited contradiction . . .

—and who obtained it, for whether invited or not contradiction and reassurance were quick to respond. Although this feature item had not appeared in all editions of *The Sunday Dispatch*, it elicited no less than sixty-eight offers of marriage—many from surprisingly eligible women. They amused and flattered Obby but did not stir him to action. He was basically uninterested in the matter; the *Sunday Dispatch* reporter had gatecrashed anyway; and he handed the passionately penned appeals to his gardener's wife, Mrs Thornton.

After the marriage of Juliet Waterford's elder son in July 1957, Obby invited her and her second husband to move from Curraghmore to Newtown Anner. John Silcock ran the farm and footed most of the bills, both indoors and out. A year later Obby made Newtown Anner over to them for life, and then bitterly resented giving them a life interest in it, like a child giving away a favourite toy. Before long he had left his old family home, never to return—taking with him only the bare necessities of life. He then embarked on his last world journey, travelling by banana boat to America, across the United States by Greyhound bus, and thence to Latin America, where the adjacent and furthest away countries of Peru and Chile were the only ones he had not already visited. Wherever he went he travelled second class.

As during most of his married life, the flat at 90 Piccadilly (shared with Captain George Spencer-Churchill) was still his headquarters, and Brooks's a 'temple of delight'. 'He enjoyed sitting in his club or a hotel', a friend recalls, 'and would make contact with those who came into the room. It was not long before they became classified as "rather a moderate fellow" or "an excellent fellow". When once this distinction had been decided there was no going back on it because it had been realistic and factual in the first place'.

Most afternoons he could be seen playing bridge at Brooks's, often with Sir Richard Molyneux, Sir John Coke or the former Lord Chancellor, Gavin Simonds. A fairly frequent lunch guest was the late Lord Salisbury. Juliet Silcock would sometimes come over from Ireland, and they would lunch at the Turf, Prunier's or the Mirabelle. Whenever she came, he always thought of something for her to bring from Newtown Anner: presents for friends in England. A set of golf clubs went to one young friend; two umbrellas with ducks' heads to Richard Cavendish's son Hugh. On one visit Juliet Silcock asked him if he needed a pair of valuable cuff-links which were still lying in the dressing-table drawer where he had left them at Newtown Anner; and received the reply: 'Woolworth's will do for me'. He had always been something of a Bohemian, hating encumbrances. One friend recalls a visit to Lord Dunraven and Mountearl, at Adare (forty-five miles from Newtown Anner), where he arrived walking across the lawn with a brown paper bag containing pyjamas and a tooth brush.

When the lease at 90 Piccadilly ran out in 1959, he moved nearer Brooks's to a three-roomed flat in a sidestreet off St James's. The house was the last set of gentlemen's chambers in London; it had solid mahogany panelling, a stately lift with interior seats, and rapid, courteous room service. Most occupants of the forty flats were transatlantic visitors on short rentals, paying (at that time) about £7 a day; but pleading poverty, Obby was allowed a basement flat at the special concessionary rate of £5 a day. He was the only permanent resident, and exceedingly popular with both manageress and staff.

His visits to the country became more frequent; his niece Elizabeth Salisbury and her brother Richard Cavendish were his favourite hosts. With the Salisburys he stayed oftener at Cranborne than at Hatfield; at Holker Richard and Pamela Cavendish made him a second home. Both at Cranborne and at Holker he was amongst the families of his favourite sister, and the paintings and antiques which he had lent them whilst Newtown Anner was still his. More and more time was spent at Holker, until eventually in 1961 he announced his intention to settle there permanently—keeping the basement flat at 7 Park Place as a *pied-à-terre* for the occasional visit to London.

He had always mixed in well with the Cavendishes' children, gardeners, estate workers and the general life of that tiny village in north Lancashire—though at the news of a visit to the Cavendishes from Princess Margaret in October 1958 he had felt a line must be drawn and was away in London for its duration! In his will he bequeathed many paintings and prints to Richard Cavendish. The question of Newtown Anner's ultimate ownership was a long time in being resolved. He was always talking of changing his will but it seemed clear that the estate would finally go to some descendant of his sister Moyra. For a promisingly long while one niece was in view; then it became a son of the Salisburys; the Silcocks, however, are still life-tenants. Thus Newtown Anner, never really the Beauclerks' property, has passed out of their control, and will eventually return to a descendant of the Osbornes.

Obby died on 2 March 1964, in the ground-floor bedroom his mother used to occupy at Holker. 'Bury me where I drop', had been a constant plea from the time of his wife's death. And so he was buried beside his mother at Flookburgh, Holker's parish church, whilst Beatrix St Albans—who had refused burial at the Waterfords' Clonegam—lies at Killaloan, in a closed-down churchyard, near broken stained-glass windows, with the Osborne mausoleum mouldering beside her.

CHAPTER X

The Belated Entrepreneur

... They married and gave in marriage,
They danced at the County Ball,
And some of them kept a carriage,
And the flood destroyed them all ...

Hilaire Belloc's verse recalls the solid, established, rather unimaginative way of life of the English aristocracy and gentry—rigidly conscious of their hallowed position within the social hierarchy, even when afflicted with the chronic malady of genteel poverty—such as it was at the turn of this century, and such as to Obby it always remained. But even when he wrote these lines, Belloc knew that the days of the traditional aristocracy were irrevocably over, a fact to which Obby in his futile life never attuned himself. How, if at all, in the second half of the twentieth century can the concept of aristocracy be filled with meaning? Was it only ever the ritual 'seed-time and harvest, love and death' of farming and farm-owning, inheritance and the marriage market?

To Obby's successor, Charles St Albans, 'keeping one's head above water' is one of the main necessities in an age of high taxation; which makes the practice of any of the aristocratic virtues all the more difficult. Belloc, of course, suggests that the general tenor of nineteenth-century aristocratic life was hardly less futile than Obby's. Between the ostentatious largesse of Harriot Coutts, the ethical paternalism of the tenth Duke, and the muddle of a man who found it too much of a nuisance to attend to his farmland and houses, a happy medium needs to be found.

Paradoxically, the time-consuming complexities of modern life seem to go hand in hand with a greater sense of responsibility than was the case in times of easy affluence; but it is *family* responsibility as much as a sense of the widest social responsibility, although the two are far from being mutually exclusive. And this is natural when the State has taken over most of the tenth Duke's paternalism, and when one is no longer so sure that the idea of the extended family—extending from generation to generation—will continue to have validity, even in aristocratic circles. Certainly, the concept of the extended family and its responsibility is not backed by the State. There is a real possibility that the extended family will become as anaemic a concept as heraldry, an academic absolute divorced from human reality, and resembling heraldry in its purely notional legal force.

* * *

Charles Frederic Aubrey de Vere Beauclerk, the thirteenth and present Duke of St Albans, was born in 1915. The eleventh Duke was still alive, and Charles Beauclerk was his second cousin; he stood in exactly the same family relationship to Obby. In 1915 he was ninth in line of sucession to the dukedom and estates; and at that time there still were estates, including the 5,412 acres at Redbourne not sold until two years later; by 1921 he was sixth in line of succession. The fact that from about the age of nineteen onwards he never knew 'from one day to the next' just when he might inherit the title presented him with some difficulty in his choice and organization of a career.

Except for a disappointment on a ranch in Canada, there might not even have been a Charles Beauclerk to inherit the dukedom in 1964. His father, Aubrey Beauclerk, nearly sixty-five years his senior, had remained an incorruptible bachelor until he was turned sixty. Resembling Obby in the need to fend for himself financially and in various adventurous but abortive quests for that crock of gold at the rainbow's end, he had emigrated as a young man to South Africa where he acquired a goldmine but was eventually forced to abandon it, lacking the necessary capital to turn it into a big business, which it now is. After a similarly inconclusive spell in Australia he fetched up in the splendid though salaried job of managing Fitzwilliam properties in Canada. His sister Laura was the wife of Lord Milton, eldest son of the sixth Earl Fitzwilliam, and he expected to be given or to inherit one of the ranches he managed on the Fitzwilliam estate. Either he was expecting too much, or labouring under a misunderstanding—perhaps even, the Fitzwilliams had changed their minds; but no ranch materialized.

At a time when most men begin to think of the past, it was time for him to think of the future. Aubrey Beauclerk hastened to England in quest of a bride, the financial solace of his old age, and was rewarded in the person of Gwendolen Hughes, a minor heiress twenty-nine years his junior; her father, Sir Frederic Hughes, who was already dead, had been a captain in the 7th Madras Light Cavalry in the service of the East India Company, knighted for his personal reconnaissance of Russian troop movements in Circassia during the Crimean War, after which he retired to his 960 acres in Co. Wexford.

Charles St Albans still remembers his father's aged Bohemian appearance: long, slightly curly hair, a mustard cloak with a scarlet lining; and the faint embarrassment his father's appearance would cause him whenever he chose to turn up at school. He was a mild, gentle, ineffective man, old enough to be the boy's great-grandfather: not a rebel in his way of dress, but just completely out of touch. He and his wife spent the nineteen years of their married life wandering—often with de Vere, as he was then called, in their tow—from house to house and even hotel to hotel, across France, England, Belgium and Germany. Their longest place of residence in the boy's pre-Eton days was at Dinard and its neighbouring Saint-Briac.

After preparatory schools in Switzerland and England, and four years at Dobbs's and Mayes's house at Eton (1928–1932), came Magdalene College, Cambridge—with allowances of £100 a year from Obby and £50 a year from his cousin 'Billy' Fitzwilliam which continued long after his time as an undergraduate. Even more so than his father, however, Charles Beauclerk had to fend for himself. He read Modern Languages (French and German) in the first half of his Tripos, obtaining a II 1; then chose Law because it seemed to him to be more 'relevant'. It certainly must have been relevant to keeping track of the intricacies of Obby's estate.

Until 1934, and indeed for two years after that, Charles Beauclerk had no legal voice in the management of the St Albans property. As the tenth Duke had left his real estate entailed to whomever should be Duke of St Albans, Obby was heir during the lifetime of the enfeebled eleventh Duke and Charles Beauclerk was 'infant tenant in tail'. Charles Beauclerk's father had absolutely no say in the sale of the Redbourne estate in 1917, nor was either Aubrey or Charles consulted when the Trustees of the eleventh Duke applied in 1927 for a Court order permitting the sale of family jewellery. Obby's succession in 1934 meant that, apart from two men (the tenth Duke's youngest son Lord William Beauclerk together with his own uncle), Charles was now immediately in line: forty years younger than Obby, Charles Beauclerk was in fact almost bound to inherit, as his uncle was a man of eighty-seven with no surviving male issue and Lord William Beauclerk was a bachelor of somewhat limited intellect to whom marriage would have been an impossibly hazardous enterprise.

In November 1936, just after Charles had come of age, Obby (as tenant for life) applied to the Chancery Division of the High Court requesting permission for the sale of settled chattels—pictures, drawings and plate. It seems not 38 years ago but 138 when one turns through the inventory of 109 lots consisting of around 700 items of 'silver and plate executed prior to 1830 and proposed to be sold in England or in America by public auction or private treaty': a pair of George IV asparagus tongs valued at 18/-; eighteen George III dinner plates with shell borders (476 oz.), valued at £119; two pairs of George III grape scissors, one silver gilt, jointly valued at £1; five antique marrow spoons, £1; and an intruding *Victorian* épergne weighing 418 oz. and not to be sold for less than £36-11-6d! The total estimated value of these 700 or so items was put at a mere £602-12-0d. Chancery judges are generally in favour of movement when applications for redisposal of settled assets come before them; permission for the sale of the plate, pictures and drawings was granted; but attempts were then put in hand to establish Charles as eventual remainderman. Nevertheless, when an application was made for permission to sell the Bestwood estate in 1940, Charles Beauclerk still had to sign his agreement.

The protection afforded him by his status as remainderman was more apparent than real. Under the terms of the Settled Land Act 1925 Obby, as life tenant of the settled estates, was able to dispose of them as he chose providing the proceeds of sale were paid to the Trustees of the tenth Duke to be applied by them according to the requirements of the Trust; however, Bestwood—as principal mansion house—could not be sold by the life tenant unless he had either the Trustees' or the Court's consent. Consent for the sale of the whole of the Bestwood estate was given by the Trustees of the tenth Duke.

As remainderman, Charles was approached by the Trustees before they came to their decision; but his only power of actual veto was over the sale of the mansion house—not the 3,424 acres of land other than the gardens and site of Bestwood Lodge. The thinking behind the legal advice which the young man received amounted to this: 'You are asked to give your agreement to the sale. You can, of course, refuse; and in that event the Trustees will probably also refuse their consent. Obby will then apply to the Chancery Division. This will mean further expense and delay, and it is extremely likely that in the present state of Obby's finances—quite apart from the War—the Court will agree to the mansion house being sold along with the rest of the land. As remainderman to the estate you have no right to object to the sale of the land as such, but only to the sale of the mansion house'.

Obby was, and always remained, entirely free to sell settled *land*. 'This was one of the great disasters for the family', Charles St Albans observes ruefully today, even though the Nottinghamshire property produced around £250,000 for Obby's settled estate. 'Bestwood was losing money just then, and Obby didn't feel that the rents were sufficient to meet the cost of necessary repairs. It was a great pity, because the estate was so close to Nottingham and included 500 acres of building land. Today they would have been worth millions'.

Naturally, Charles Beauclerk was not to know that inflation would push land values to astronomical heights, and it would be a facile distortion of the truth to argue that this young remainderman of twenty-five stood idly by as his prodigal cousin squandered the ancestral fortune. If repairs had been needed at Bestwood Obby should have arranged for them to be done between 1934 and 1939; but in 1936 he had made a sworn affidavit that he was short of funds, and by 1940 labour and materials were all dedicated to the war effort and repairs on a large scale had become impossible. The difficulty essentially was that Obby and Charles Beauclerk could not agree a long-term course of action between themselves. It was an instance of one generation not talking to another. 'I always realized', says Charles St Albans, 'that something more sensible could have been worked out if the wish to do so had been there'.

For a young man graduating at Cambridge in 1937 it was an unusual background, a stark contrast between wealth and modest means, against which to look for a job. 'I wanted to get married, and absolutely needed an income', he recalls. 'I was on bad terms with my mother, who opposed my marriage. I was completely on my own'.

His only sizable asset was a house at Aldeburgh given him by Lady Latymer—a great-granddaughter-in-law of Thomas Coutts by his first wife—who felt that the Beauclerks had profited too little from Harriot's estate. Charles received this house around 1923; his mother had an interest in it until he was twenty-five; even after 1940 she continued to live there, until it was finally sold in 1955. Their immediate neighbour at Aldeburgh was Benjamin Britten, who used hopefully to play 'God Save the King' after bouts of prolonged screaming from Charles's infant daughter.

Following up a lead from the Cambridge University Appointments Board, Charles Beauclerk became a journalist in 1937. The first publication for which he worked was *The Studio*, nowadays *Studio International*, a monthly 'illustrated magazine of fine art, home decoration and design'; but most of the time he was with *The Studio* was spent on a subsidiary, *Art and Industry*, now extinct. It was a job which kept the wolf from the door though it was not vastly well paid. As a sub-editor he turned his hand to any work that came his way, sometimes producing copy himself, sometimes handling the advertising. 'It searches the world for ideas which are valuable to modern commerce', declared *The Studio* in an advertisement of its offshoot, 'it shows you the men who produce them, it helps your own creative ability, showing you new avenues to explore and new lines to work upon. It stimulates the established designer, and guides the tyro; it is useful to teacher and student'.

The Star, to which he moved in 1938, offered much better prospects.

At that time it was one of three London evening newspapers: of Liberal complexion, owned by the Cadburys, associated with *The News Chronicle*, and boasting a circulation of 700,000. Of those three newspapers it has been the casualty, enjoying neither *The Evening News*'s mass circulation nor *The Evening Standard*'s advertising revenue; with the result that it was taken over by Associated Newspapers Ltd in October 1960, suffering the same fate on the same day as its national daily counterpart.

In 1938, however, it was still bursting with dynamic liberalism. Charles Beauclerk even describes himself as a 'keen and energetic' acquisition to the staff, and he was sufficiently valued to be kept on by *The Star* throughout the War, though he was not, of course, on their 'active list'. At £7 a week he was really well paid in 1938–1939. He worked on special features, not news or political reporting. Even as a journalist, to some extent he was insulated from the build-up of European events to the climax of September 1939.

His civilian career had been only of two years' duration; he had entered on that particular work almost by accident; yet it is true to say that he had made good progress in his accidental field of employment during those two years. The Second World War marked still more decisive progress in a military career beginning with the rank of private in the Somerset Light Infantry, then rising to that of colonel in the Intelligence Corps, with special duties some of them of so confidential a nature that they still cannot be discussed.

From a private in the Somerset Light Infantry he was promoted lance-corporal, corporal and instructor; then transferred to Sandhurst from which he was commissioned into the Intelligence Corps, serving with the Royal Irish Fusiliers on detached duty. After a 'short but rather ludicrous' time as a Military Intelligence Liaison Officer with Fighter Command at Bentley Priory he underwent a spate of courses: War Intelligence and Air Photo Interpretation at Matlock; German Interrogation at Cambridge; and other courses both at Cambridge and Oxford. A spell of duty as an Intelligence Officer first at Second Corps Headquarters, then at Newmarket, was followed by recruitment into the Political Intelligence Department of the Foreign Office, with service in Gibraltar, North Africa, Malta and Italy.

His most continuous, of not most important, function in political intelligence was directly related to his experience as a journalist and linguist. He headed propaganda networks operating on civilian populations and against enemy troops. From November 1942 to March 1943 he was at Algiers, controlling the radio station then in the hands of the Giraud government and also handling propaganda films. Harold Macmillan was in Algiers at the same time as Minister Resident at Allied Force Headquarters in North Africa, and took a close interest in the Psychological Warfare Branch.

In the Tunisian south Charles Beauclerk was also attached to the personal staff of Patton's Second United States Corps at Tebessa, where he was in charge of political intelligence and propaganda. He and his driver were the first people to get through by land from the First Army in Tunisia to the Eighth Army under Montgomery, who entered Tunisia from the south after his victories in Libya. Montgomery was never very favourable to propaganda broadsheets of any kind, and was happiest about the newspaper which Beauclerk ran for the troops; there were also French and Arabic newspapers for the local population, but for Montgomery—and consequently for Charles Beauclerk at this time—propaganda directed against enemy troops always came a very poor third.

Back in Algiers from Tripoli (which had fallen to the Allies in January 1943) he worked under the late Richard Crossman, then Deputy Director of Psychological Warfare at Allied Force Headquarters in North Africa; in September of that year, after a spell of activity in Malta, he took part in the Salerno landing and, under Mark Clark's command, produced *Fifth Army Advance* and *Il Corriere di Salerno*. These, he recalls, were actually printed and distributed under gunfire before the fall of Naples. Meanwhile, the Eighth Army had advanced from the toe of Italy to north of Bari, and after a period of service with G (Special Operations) Allied Armies Italy, Beauclerk was put in command of the Psychological Warfare Unit at Eighth Army, attached to Army Advanced Headquarters. He remained there for the rest of the campaign, eventually moving up with the British troops into Austria.

His next job was a projection in Austria of what he had been doing during the War. He was in charge of information services in the British zone of Austria—Styria and Carinthia—before transferring to Vienna where he remained with the Allied Commission for Austria (British Element) as deputy controller, then controller, of the Information Services and Public Relations Branch of the Allied Commission. He was the British representative on certain quadripartite committees.

Except that the War had now ended, it was a familiar pattern—with a news service, printing-presses, a film section and a photographic section under his control as well as a British daily newspaper (*The British Morning News!*), an Austrian daily newspaper (*Die Weltpresse*, which is still flourishing), other publications and a radio broadcasting network with stations in the British zone and Vienna. His staff, consisting of forty-eight British officers and 311 Austrians, discharged the most crucial function of the British Element. Demobilized in 1948, he belonged to the Foreign Office German section. In August 1950 the Military High Commission was abolished and its staff, including civilians such as himself, either became fully integrated with that of the Legation or ceased to have any functions at all. Though the Foreign Office suggested he might like to stay on in Vienna in a diplomatic capacity, Beauclerk preferred to return home—and found himself instead at the Central Office of Information though, as he candidly admits, he 'didn't really mean to go there'.

The War had placed intolerable strains on many marriages, and Charles Beauclerk's was no exception. His first wife, by whom he had one son, divorced him in 1947. His second wife, whom he married in the same year, was a civilian member of the Political Intelligence Department who had been posted to Vienna after serving in Italy and Trieste where they had never met. Of his offspring by the two marriages his eldest son and heir, Lord Burford, is now a chartered accountant working in the City and specializing in taxation problems; his second son, Lord Peter Beauclerk, lives on a farm near San Francisco; John, his youngest son, after working in journalism has transferred himself to Peru; whilst his daughter Caroline has married a former BBC man who is still active in radio.

For fourteen years, until his inheritance of the dukedom in 1964, the Central Office of Information was the focus of his working life, and—however accidental his arrival there—the logical extension of all his information and propaganda activities in the War. The first eight of his fourteen years were spent in the Publications Division where, as Chief Books Editor, he superintended 400 to 500 publications a year: anything from a 300-page book to a single-page leaflet. 'Publications for the home market were the more massive, but more interesting was the overseas work. A great many books and pamphlets concerned the colonies, but on behalf of a whole range of Government departments we dealt with anything from the desirability of having your tyres pumped up a bit more firmly to why you should be quicker in completing your Income Tax returns'. Charles Beauclerk commissioned authors, such as Eric Linklater, and managed a staff of designers and writer-editors.

The move to Chief Films Production Officer in 1958, the founding of a radio division producing recorded material for use by overseas broadcasting stations, and finally his work as Director of the Films and Television Division involved further applications of what was basically the same expertise, an expertise which, like advertising, was creative to the extent that it demanded an imaginative approach to the Government's public relations. The projection of a national image to overseas readers, listeners and viewers was a very different operation from the work of gilding the messages of Government departments to the longsuffering British public.

All this is to say that in the present Duke of St Albans we have the first example of a really modern duke. As Anthony Sampson has observed, he is the first of his kind to have actually worked in a regular salaried job. In fact, even as Duke of St Albans he continued for six months at the Central Office of Information before finally resigning his post. His years in military propaganda and Government public relations had given him a practical understanding of administration and communications completely lacking in Obby or, for that matter, in most if not all of Obby's ducal contemporaries. On his inheritance, the problems facing the new duke were twofold: how to restore the fading family fortunes; and how to maximize the opportunities now offered to his unquestionable ability.

Obby frequently used to delude himself that he had been a faithful steward of the ancestral wealth. 'I shall leave as much money as I inherited', he used to argue, overlooking the fact that inflation had slashed the value of money between 1934 and 1964 (from £1 to about 30p), and that—sometimes with Charles Beauclerk's consent, and sometimes without it—he had also disposed of so many heirlooms. Charles St Albans was one of the two or three poorest dukes in the British peerage in 1964.

Two years and one day before Obby's death Charles Beauclerk had received from his cousin an estate whose value was estimated in the press at nearly £300,000. This consisted of a 1,752-acre farm at North Ormsby in Lincolnshire worth approximately £200,000, together with heirlooms and securities roughly amounting to another £100,000. As early as 24 June 1940 Charles had executed a disentailing assurance, ending any entail which still remained under the trusts of the will of the tenth Duke. His eldest son Murray Beauclerk executed a further disentailing assurance to coincide with the transfer of the family assets. In return for Obby's life-interest in the estate Charles is said to have paid about £40,000— enough to provide his eighty-seven-year-old cousin with an annuity of £12,000 or so. These arrangements ensured, even if only by two days, a 15% remission on Charles Beauclerk's estate-duty liability. After allowing for the special estate-duty relief for agricultural land together with the additional remission of 15%, estate duty in the region of £75,000 must have been payable by Charles even though Obby's will had been proved in England at less than £24,000 (there was separate Osborne property in Ireland). Thus, if we deduct £40,000 from the value of the net estate, Charles would seem to have been left with an entirely disposable capital of £185,000 or thereabouts.

In the depressed equity market of the mid-1960s Obby's successor realized that if he was to go into business, the best outlet for his money would be property development. Linked with this, in his mind, was the rapidly growing importance of travel as a leisure industry. But though property has been one of his main interests as a businessman, he does not show the slightest desire to invest in an agricultural estate in England despite the estate-duty advantages which still exist in the autumn of 1974, though they may soon be eroded. Eight years ago he did make an approach to buy Castle Hedingham, with its Georgian mansion and twelfth-century keep towering over one of the loveliest of Essex villages; but only because it was 'family property' in the sense that it was the de Veres' principal seat until 1625. In any case the negotiation failed, and in addition to his claim to be the only duke to have had a regular salaried job he is also the only one of his ilk to own no country estate—and no freehold town property either. However, he insists that if a suitable family property did come up, not too far from London, he would be in the market for it.

From a leasehold town house, 57 Oakley Street, Chelsea, inherited from his father's sister Blanche Evans as long ago as 1948 but not actually his to live in until four years later, Charles St Albans launched into business and within seven or eight years had handsomely increased his inheritance. Not that everything he has touched has prospered. Some ventures, such as Informat, the public-relations company he founded in 1967 and wound up in 1970, were embarked upon more because they were things he wished to do than things he wished to make money. 'I have never', he confesses, 'wanted to be entirely restricted to doing one thing. And having seen the weaknesses of PR, I thought perhaps I could do something in it. So much in public relations is frivolous; I wanted a serious approach. But though I thought I could do a convincing job in PR, the commercial difficulties were too great'.

Similarly with the Mayfair art gallery largely run by his wife but bought and financed by him. Between 1965 and 1972 a great deal of money was laid out on the Upper Grosvenor Galleries, and hundreds of thousands of pounds worth of pictures by contemporary artists were sold. And yet the business continued to lose money and closed down when the lease came up for renewal. Perhaps the trouble was that it had specialized in figurative contemporary art just before the vogue for this really began.

'These things were done because they were things we wanted to do', is the Duke's philosophical summing-up. Ironically, the businesses most closely associated with his nineteen years of Government service were not commercially viable—even though they were more demanding than the successful ventures in that creativity and imagination which St Albans and his second wife certainly have in large measure.

To date, Grendon Trust Ltd has proved to be his main financial interest—and greatest success. He has even earned considerable notoriety from the Grendon affair of September–December 1973. In June 1968 he had become chairman of the property company Grendon Securities Ltd, of which he was a founder shareholder with a substantial holding. He had also been chairman of an investment trust, Industrial Midlands Investment Trust Ltd, since January 1968 although in this company his shareholding was more modest. Having already acquired the old-established company Hudsons of Victoria Ltd, which had recently developed an interest in the servicing of North Sea oil, Industrial Midlands rapidly proceeded to take over Grendon Securities in October 1972; and Grendon Trust Ltd was the name of the new holding company.

In a further takeover Grendon Trust acquired the Monotype Corporation Ltd in March 1973. Monotype, in addition to its activities in printing and typesetting, also owned 133 acres of valuable agricultural land near Redhill. Now Grendon's combined interests consisted of investment, property, printing, brickfields, road transport and the provision of onshore facilities for North Sea oil. The company continued to take over smaller property and investment companies but by the summer of 1973 it had itself become attractive as a takeover prospect; indeed, a number of offers were actually made to Grendon. In particular, it attracted the keen attention of twenty-eight-year-old Christopher Selmes's private company Eastminster Trust.

By the time Eastminster's interest in Grendon had been revealed (September 1973), it appeared to have already built up a 35% shareholding in the company through piecemeal acquisition by subsidiaries including the purchase of a 5% holding from First National Finance Corporation. With the announcement that 35% of Grendon's equity was now in its control, Eastminster was able to gather a further 10% of the shares. St Albans was then approached with a view to the purchase of his personal 4%. The Duke's sale of all but 500 of his Grendon shares, for a price approaching £800,000, produced heated argument in the City, his critics maintaining that but for his premature action in giving Eastminster virtual control of Grendon it would have been possible to obtain a higher takeover price than the one finally offered for Grendon shares in the deals that gave Eastminster complete control. It was alleged that in disposing of 264,400 of his shares to Eastminster the Grendon chairman had forestalled tentative counterbids for the takeover of the company. Feeling ran high at Grendon; St Albans resigned as chairman and ultimately gave up his seat on the board. The Duke is adamant that he acted throughout in the best interests of the company, its 3,000 employees and its shareholders. 'Despite rumours to the contrary, there was no sign at all of a firm counterbid. But if we hadn't clinched the matter with Eastminster there and then, it might all have fallen through. We certainly mightn't have had such a fair offer'.

Before selling the bulk of his shares to Eastminster, the Duke had informed his co-directors of his intention to do so, inviting them to follow his example. Having bought St Albans's holding at 300p, Christopher Selmes—through another company, CST—raised the bid for remaining shares to 315p. To sum up: St Albans, having turned down Eastminster's initial offer of 295p, improved not only his own selling price but also the base figure for every other shareholder.

Whatever the rights and wrongs of St Albans's final move in the Grendon affair—and the Duke's action was criticized by the City Panel on Takeovers and Mergers under Lord Shawcross—two things are undeniable: he himself disposed of his Grendon shares at the very best moment, just anticipating the collapse in property values; but equally, the shareholders of Grendon Trust Ltd prospered both during his five years as chairman of Industrial Midland and Grendon Securities and in the disposal of their shares. The consolidated accounts show that group profits before tax rose from £473,000 in 1971 to £1,103,000 in 1973, though the ratio of earnings to profits after tax was on the decline. Grendon Trust's attractiveness to Eastminster and others lay first and foremost in the potential both of its developable assets and of its increasing turnover.

Tourism is another of St Albans's major business concerns. Partly through his chairmanship of another company Travelworld Olympic and partly through his friendship with the then Turkish ambassador, he was invited by the Turkish Government to undertake survey work in that country. This has led him into trying to obtain permission for an important development on the southern Turkish coast north of Rhodes, together with a satisfactory agreement from the Turkish Parliament. 'I hope', he explains, 'to build villas, hotels, a casino and a marina'. To provide all the necessary financial backing, he has formed a small international consortium. International uncertainty, quadrupled oil prices, and the decline in British prosperity caused by a sharp imbalance in our terms of trade have posed serious threats to the travel and package-tour industries—and not only to Court Line. Within the last two months the investment potential of the eastern Mediterranean has been damaged by the Cyprus *coup d'état* and the continuing tensions between Turkey and Greece over the island's partition. 'I see all this as delaying our plans for Turkey by from two to five years', says Charles St Albans. 'But in the longer term these plans must be right. The development strategy remains the same, though there has been an inevitable change in tactics'.

From even a brief personal contact with St Albans, the impression that emerges from beneath the geniality and warmth of his manner is one of shrewdness and intelligent calm. Whatever the level of his financial expertise at his beginnings in business only nine years ago, he has turned his associations with Industrial Midlands, Grendon Securities and Travelworld Olympic into as undoubted a success as his earlier associations with army propaganda and the Central Office of Information. Above all, he has a practical awareness of the possible. He clearly saw—at a time of incipient recession in the mid-1960s—the growing importance and long-term investment potential of property development and the travel industry. As for the Upper Grosvenor Galleries and Informat, he frankly admits that 'one can't succeed in everything'; yet the knowledge of this does not deter him from future ventures in the lines he is making his own—nor, perhaps, from ventures into other fields. He still has to re-employ the capital and energy released from Grendon.

Energy is the second characteristic of this relaxed, unassuming man; but energy productively concentrated on particular points. Since inheriting from Obby he has never believed in intervention in his business concerns on a routine, daily basis. He refuses to become an executive director. But he is there to deal with essential matters as they arise, and to deal with them effectively and immediately, even if it involves dealing with a personally delivered letter over the luncheon table. And the remarkable thing about his energy is that it was not deployed in business until he was nearing the age of fifty; he is now fifty-nine, and full of further entrepreneurial ideas. In his awareness of the possible, he realized that even the golden energy of youth was not actually enough to launch him into an entrepreneurial career from hard-up beginnings; yet the mental and nervous energy was still in him when he inherited the tangible gold. This energy and finesse explain his highly successful adaptation to a great change in financial circumstances, even though that change came rather late in life.

What most differentiates St Albans from the prosperous entrepreneur or impresario he has essentially become, is that—for all his preoccupation with large-scale business schemes for the future, and despite his remoteness at birth from the title and long years in the wilderness of civil-service routine—he shows a deep, and increasing, sense of responsibility towards his ancestral family. In April 1973 he bought an ancestral portrait in a sale at Christie's: that of the first Duke's brother 'Lord James Beauclerk as a Child', from the studio of Kneller. Three years earlier he was at Sotheby's, buying a dozen paintings by Topham's wife Lady Di.

One of his latest interests is the restoration of Redbourne Church, including its mausoleum where two dukes and three duchesses of St Albans lie buried. Harriot Coutts is a duchess whose remains lie on a shelf forlornly beside the scattered ashes of the ninth Duke's second wife in a vault into which there is not even any ingress now, as the door from the graveyard has jammed; because of the Coutts connection, St Albans (as patron of Redbourne Church) hopes to persuade the Bank (as Harriot's representative) to contribute to the renovation. It is hoped there will be a public appeal at Redbourne, in addition to which St Albans will match every pound advanced by Coutts.

At the present time the living is vacant, but the Duke hopes to find another incumbent. He is reluctant to envisage Redbourne as yet another of the amalgamated parishes. 'The church must not be allowed to fall into greater disrepair', he argues. 'It dates from the fifteenth century; and, who knows? Redbourne may in the course of time become, or become close to, an important centre of population'. The contrast between a man eager to repair the Lincolnshire mausoleum, partly out of funds from his own pocket and partly by obtaining funds from other interested parties, and the man in Southern Ireland content to let the Osborne mausoleum fall into decay is more than striking: it is a nice symbol of the opposed attitudes to life of two successors in the dukedom, and perhaps also of the opposed attitudes to life of two generations.

Even in his eminently practical search for a country seat with family connections St Albans reveals a sense of responsibility towards the continuing destiny of his family. So, too, in his determination to prove beyond any doubt his genealogical claim to the dukedom after Obby's death. It took him and his solicitors almost four years in all, cost over £1,350 and demanded immense tenacity and patience; over 400 letters were exchanged, and more than forty certificates produced. The Crown Office, which is part of the Lord Chancellor's Office at the House of Lords, insists that every possible step must be taken to ensure there is no nearer heir to a title than the one claiming the succession; and Charles Beauclerk was only a second cousin to Obby, descended from the sixth son of the eighth Duke whereas Obby was a descendant of the eighth Duke's eldest surviving son; and it had to be established that the heir-in-line to the dukedom until 1916 had left no sons, only two daughters; and there were cousins in America whose lack of male posterity had to be proved; and Charles Beauclerk's father was born in Brussels and old enough to be his great-grandfather. . . . The difficulties were endless!

Interestingly enough, Coutts Bank, as Trustees for the tenth Duke's will, admitted Charles Beauclerk's claim to the trust money three years sooner than the Crown Office admitted his claim to the peerage title—so meticulous was the standard of evidence, so numerous the affidavits demanded. The services of the College of Arms had to be enrolled. Pedigrees had to be brought up to date, and genealogical links verified. The kings of arms and heralds could support the claims he was asserting at the Crown Office.

The important fact, however, about this labour of Hercules is that it was not undertaken with any strong view to political advantage. Indeed, in the throes of the struggle the hereditary House of Lords was very nearly abolished by the then Labour Government! The legal right to the dukedom was established with a view to the future, in the desire to tie up all the loose ends of the succession for posterity's benefit. Sitting—very rarely—on the cross-benches of the House of Lords, St Albans does not cast himself in any political role. He has applied for his Writ of Summons (an application which is made only once in a lifetime), and in at least one Parliament has accepted the writ and exercised his vote; he has never spoken, however, nor has he taken part in committee work, and in the recent Parliament he applied for leave of absence. Like many successful businessmen impatient of shadow-boxing and unfulfilled promises, he is less and less interested in the histrionic aspects of politics and the power-lessness of the Upper House. As a young man, on the other hand, he was fairly active in politics and during his lifetime he has moved across the political spectrum from right to left, before coming to rest on the cross-benches.

Like all successful businessmen keen on settling essential issues, he is actively concerned with the decision how best to settle what money he has made, and is still making, since 1965. 'The difficulty with re-entailing', he confesses, 'is the estate-duty problem. Besides which it is now only possible to entail for two lives. But it is vital to have some continuity'.

Not only has St Albans realized himself in a new personal context, he is realizing the role of a duke in the vastly changed context of the last third of this century. Except for his preoccupation with family continuity, he is to all intents and purposes an articulate, polished, prosperous, upper-middle-class businessman. Far from having 'sunk', however, from the social stratosphere to which dukes are popularly supposed to belong, he has come out of the backwoods into the light of day—and the light of publicity. When they are in England, and not at their house in Vence, he and his charming wife, authoress of a volume of autobiography *The Mimosa and the Mango* and a painter who has exhibited at the Royal Academy, are often to be seen at Royal Academy banquets, or dinner with a Cabinet minister, or a Foyles Literary Luncheon. He has served on the committee of the St James' and also belongs to Brooks's and the Beefsteak; the first two of these he regularly uses. Robert Graves is one of their literary friends. He has succeeded Compton Mackenzie as Governor-General of the Royal Stuart Society. He is Vice-President of the Ancient Monuments Society and a Trustee of Southwark Cathedral, just as his wife is Vice-President of SSAFA. As chairman of the Appeals

Committee of the Hanover Housing Association, he is responsible for raising money in aid of a charity which has built almost 3,000 dwellings for the elderly all over the country. He is tremendously proud of his nine-year-old grandson and ultimate heir, Charles Vere of Hanworth, and has scored a discreet triumph in the leasing, restoration and furnishing of 30 Cheyne Walk. For the first time in half a century the family pictures and other heirlooms have been gathered together under one roof. Just one achievement eludes, or insufficiently excites, him: the freehold of an English property that will re-endow the Beauclerks with the nucleus they have lacked since the sale of Bestwood in 1940.

To the apocalyptic gloom of Hilaire Belloc Charles St Albans opposes a more fertile concept of aristocratic life. In all probability, his own brave attempts to salvage and restore his family's fortunes will founder in the restless uncertainty of the modern world. It will not be an immediate process, nor one that can be predicted with any certainty as likely to occur in this century. Indeed, such is the resilience of families that it may not in fact happen at all; but whatever the future holds for the retreating concept of aristocracy, the pattern of life adopted by Charles St Albans is not one that grudgingly concedes its long-retained, taken-for-granted privileges, clutching to each until it is either wrenched away or meaningless. His is an adventurous, open, forward-looking vision of life, constructive in its contributions both to society and history.

CHAPTER XI

Conclusion

In a conspectus of three hundred years, the resilience of families is scarcely shown in a more vivid manner than with the Beauclerks. The ups and downs of the family, particularly of those very close to the dukedom, have been enormous. To begin with, their origins and the origin of the title were highly unusual: they began from the top and so, perhaps, were in an equivocal position, near and yet very far from the seat of power; not for them the slow, arduous working-up to a dukedom as was the case with most noble families (in 1679, Gervase Pierrepont bequeathed £10,000 to 'the first member of his family who should obtain the honour and title of a duke': a bequest which came into effect within forty years).

They began as cousins of the King: indeed, had Nell Gwyn been Charles II's legitimate wife, the first, second, third and fourth Dukes of St Albans would all have been kings of England, and the King of England today would be George Drummond. However, their 'spurious' kinship with the Stuarts made them all the keener to assert their loyalty to the House of Hanover.

The erratic succession of the dukedom was accompanied across the centuries by a lamentable failure to secure money. The problem of the *menses* of the sixth Duke's widow filled the junior members of the family with alarm that the title might go to a non-Beauclerk. Marriages to heiresses misfired, as when the third Duke parted from Jane Roberts and Glassenbury slipped away, or when the great inheritance of Sir John Werden passed from the fourth Duke to the Drummonds. Likewise, Hanworth eluded the Beauclerks on the death of the sixth Duke; and it is immensely to the credit of the eighth that, through his careful provisions and even calculation, he rescued the family from the embarrassing financial status of the minor gentry. This systole and diastole of fortune has been repeated in our own time with Obby and Charles St Albans, and once again the title has been secured against financial difficulties.

In the strange contrasts between father and son the seemingly eternal action and reaction is evident, as the interplay of human character runs independently of the fluctuations of wealth. What greater contrast than between the tenth and the ninth Duke, or the ninth Duke and the eighth! Obby, again, was strikingly different from the Victorian patriarch, resembling his Irish mother rather than his English father. Perhaps this is the explanation of much of the action and reaction in human character, that a man may take after one parent more closely than the other; but problems can arise when the continuity of estates and a ducal title is involved. Between Nell and Harriot, on the other hand, there is a curious sameness, though one was a mistress twenty years younger than her sexual partner whilst the wife was a mother-surrogate. The contrasts are vast; yet the line continues, and in it too continues the line of the de Veres, dating back unbrokenly to the eleventh century. Despite all the resilience, financial, generative and otherwise, that the Beauclerks have always shown, it is not however perhaps too rash a prospect to envisage the dukedom's possible extinction, as after the four sons and one grandson of the present Duke only one other father and son are in remainder: Topham's two surviving descendants in the male line.

Considering the family as a whole, one is strikingly impressed by its variety of outlooks and responses. Topham, for all his personal dissoluteness, presents no real point of contact with the third Duke, his cousin: he is a connoisseur, an artistic, intellectual figure, whose descendants number some of the more sensitive, civilized people the Beauclerks have produced. Louisa, second wife of the sixth Duke, is a quite different personality from Maria Janetta, her sister-in-law. Obby was eccentric, his brother and half-brother mad, but sanity seems to have prevailed amongst his three sisters and two half-sisters; the three sons of the tenth Duke produced no legitimate children, but amongst the descendants of his daughters are persons of real distinction, including one prominent Conservative politician and the late Lord Wakehurst.

The variety in outlooks, attainments and responses, the variety in fortunes and temperaments, is symbolized by—and perhaps the reflection of—the fact that the family have had no fixed or stable seat. Burford House, which came from a king, went back to a king—for a mere £4,000. Bestwood was the *majorat* of the Beauclerks, a place of last resort, the ultimate refuge (for the third Duke) in a financial crisis; it was not a nucleus or a home, except for the comparatively brief period when the colliery boomed and the tenth Duke believed that it would be fitting to have a seat in the Dukeries. After 1898, the year of the tenth Duke's death, it rapidly fell out of favour with the family, who still kept it, however, until 1940—and sold it too soon. Otherwise, Newtown Anner was Osborne property, even more briefly a home of the Beauclerks than Bestwood; Redbourne came with the eighth Duke, departed with the eleventh, and was only really a home of the eighth and ninth; Hanworth, which might have become a fixed seat of the family—the Syon of the Beauclerks—was burned down, rebuilt, but then lost to them through being conveyed by Louisa Duchess of St Albans to her side of the family: its loss was the most serious the Beauclerks sustained, for in the long run the loss of the Strand, Cheshire, Lancashire, Yorkshire and Berkshire estates was only to be expected as Sir John Werden was not an ancestor of the fifth Duke. The dukes of St Albans still are descendants of the Chambers and Beauclerks who owned Hanworth. As for Tidworth, Crawley, Cranbourne and Charlton—the stately hunting retreats of the second Duke—they were rented or grace-and-favour properties, mere passing moments (though serene at Tidworth) in the family's history.

The outcome of this instability is the virtual landlessness of the present Duke. Although until recently the chairman of a property company, he is entirely without freehold property of his own in England. Even his new home in Cheyne Walk is on a fairly long lease. No other ducal family in Britain, even in 1974, has the same rootlessness; but such rootlessness can nowadays be an advantage, as the family are not tied down by unmanageable responsibilities towards an unwieldy mansion. The rootlessness of Cheyne Walk gives St Albans mobility and freedom to manoeuvre.

The Beauclerks take little into the future except themselves—few enough now in the male line—and what has been carved out for them by the present Duke's ability. The minor heirlooms, too, are few enough, though displayed to advantage in his drawing-room. An ivory plaque that must once have been fixed to the coach of a duke of St Albans (probably the second's): 'Park Gates, Duke of St Albans Hereditary Grand Falconer's Coach'; it has a nostalgic echo; keys giving access to the various Royal parks, a fan belonging to Nell Gwyn, a death-ring bearing the head of Charles II, the de Vere Roll (the family pedigree), the ring given by Charles I to Bishop Juxon, a recipe book belonging to Thomas Chamber, two Grand Falconer's seals, a peach stone 1½ inches high carved by Nicolas Briot with the face of Charles I . . . these, and a few others including the sale catalogue of Topham's library, together with the fine collection of family portraits by Romney, Reynolds, Kneller, Lely, Zucchero, Wright and others, are the pledges of ancient times carried into an uncertain future. The family's motto, '*Auspicium Melioris Ævi*', so often defied by the turn of events, is still less sure of fulfilment in the next fifty or hundred years of the Beauclerks' history, when the gains and losses of fortune could be greater than in the past.

Somerset Maugham, in a celebrated mock-heroic passage on ducal titles, envisages 'the dukes of Manchester writing poems of a didactic and moral character, the dukes of Westminster composing stirring odes on Duty and the Responsibilities of Empire' whilst Marlborough would produce idylls and Devonshire elegies and love lyrics. It is possible, in the same half-fanciful mood, to imagine the dukes of St Albans if not writing sea shanties then at least naval poems of a more elevated character. If there is any continuity at all in the eight or nine generations of the Beauclerks, it must rest in the sea: with Lord Aubrey heroically killed at Cartagena, Lord Amelius winning the victory of the Dryad, Lord Vere of Hanworth the greatest admiral of his day apart from Anson, two sons of the eighth Duke naval captains, the elder of these rescuing a drowning woman near Dublin, another son of the eighth Duke losing his life at Scarborough in an attempt to rescue a lifeboat, the eighth Duke a naval commander, and the tenth (in a descant to the main ode) navigating the Mediterranean in his yacht; yet the sea is a region of ceaseless flux, and that is precisely its greatest affinity with the Beauclerks. From it, too, Obby may have derived his restless nomadic homelessness.

On the firm ground of sober reality, the pattern of the eight or nine

generations has in fact been one of service—ecclesiastical, naval, military
or political—in the younger sons, the marriage market for the daughters,
and for the successive heads of the family the precarious retention of an
established position. The retention of this position has been of even
more concern to them than the keeping of established property. For them,
too, it was a question of the marriage market, though they followed up
their favourable beginnings more clumsily than many of their less colourful equals. Court duties stressed their loyalty to the Hanoverians,
symbolized their status and added to their income. Field sports and
racing were their only diversion from the routine: although the eighth
Duke took some interest in Redbourne, farming in the main did not
interest them either as business or hobby, with the notable solitary
exception of the tenth Duke.

To Goethe, in a famous couplet from *Faust*, inherited possessions
could only really be possessed when they had been earned all over again
through a habit of service. The pattern of service is certainly strong in
the younger sons of the Beauclerks: it was a financial necessity; but, of
the heads of this sluggishly Whig family, only one or two have practised
that service at any significant level. The running of the social order at a
county or local level is, however, a service in itself, and if it is true—in the
words of Proust which are the epigraph to this book—that the history of
the aristocracy enshrines that of society as a whole, then by the Beauclerks it is enshrined at the level of Speke and Redbourne, Laeken and
Nottingham as, in the prosaic realism of the eighth Duke, the artistic
sensitivity of Topham and the third Duke's ludicrous revelry, they take a
solid but mysterious place in the fabric of English and Flemish history.

FROM *BURKE'S PEERAGE*

An updated and revised extract from Burke's Peerage
1970 *on the Beauclerk family, reproduced by permission of*
Burke's Peerage Ltd.

ST ALBANS

THE 13TH DUKE OF ST ALBANS (Charles Frederic Aubrey de Vere Beauclerk O.B.E.), Earl of Burford, co. Oxford, Baron Heddington in the same co., and Baron Vere of Hanworth, co. Middlesex, Hereditary Grand Falconer of England, and Hereditary Registrar of the Court of Chancery, only son of Aubrey Topham Beauclerk (*see p.* 238), *educ.* Eton, and Magdalene Coll. Camb. (B.A. 1937, M.A. 1947), Col. Intelligence Corps (1946), served in World War II 1939–45, in Somerset Light Inf. 1939–41, in Mil. Intelligence 1939–48 and in Mediterranean in Psychological Warfare 1941–45 (O.B.E. Mil. 1945), Controller, Information Services, Allied Commn. for Austria 1946–50, Central Office of Information, Chief Books Editor 1951–58,

Chief Films Production Offr. 1958–60, Dir. of Films and Television Div. 1960–64, resigned 1964, Chm. Travelworld Olympic Ltd., Amalg. Developers Ltd., Dir. Herbert Greaves Ltd., and other cos., Pres. Fedn. of Industrial Develt. Assocs., Gov.-Gen. Royal Stuart Soc., Vice-Pres. Ancient Monuments Soc., Chm. Appeals Committee Hanover Housing Association, Patron of two livings, *b.* 16 Aug. 1915, *s.* his second cousin 1964, *m.* 1stly, 21 March 1938 (*m.* diss. by div. 1947), Nathalie Chatham, (who *m.* 2ndly John Trevor Eldrid of London) dau. of the late Percival Field Walker, of Rythe Court, Thames Ditton, Surrey, and has issue,

1. ◆MURRAY DE VERE, *Earl of Burford,* A.C.A. (1962), Freeman of City of Lond., and Worshipful Co. of Drapers 1969, Dir. of cos. (*100 Campden Hill Road, W.8; M.C.C.*), *b.* 19 Jan 1939, *educ.* Tonbridge, *m.* 1stly 31 Jan 1963 (*m.* diss. by div. 6 May, 1974), Rosemary Frances, only dau. of Francis Harold Scoones, M.R.C.S., L.R.C.P., J.P., of Rosecourt, Greenford, Middlesex, and had issue,

   ◆Charles Francis Topham de Vere, *Lord Vere of Hanworth, b.* 22 Feb. 1965

   ●Emma Caroline de Vere, *b.* 22 July 1963, *educ.* Roedean.

He *m.* 2ndly 29 August 1974 ●Cynthia Theresa Mary (formerly wife of Sir Anthony Robin Maurice Hooper, 2nd Bt), yr dau. of Lt-Col. William James Holdsworth Howard D.S.O. of Scarsdale Villas, London W.8.

His Grace *m.* 2ndly, 19 March 1947, ●Suzanne Marie Adèle, dau. of the late Émile William Fesq, of Les Mas Mistral, Vence, A. M., France, and by her has had issue,

2. ◆Peter Charles de Vere, served in R.N.R. 1966–69 (*Beauclerk Ranch, Evans Ridge Road, Anapolis, California 95412, U.S.A.*), *b.* 13 Jan 1948, *educ.* Eton, *m.* in U.S.A. 17 May 1972 ●Beverlie June, dau. of late Alva Edwin Bailey of California, U.S.A., and had issue,

   Robin de Vere, *b.* 24 Dec. 1971, accidentally drowned 10 June 1973.

3. ◆James Charles Fesq de Vere (*20 Sloane Gdns., S.W.3*), *b.* 6 Feb. 1949, *educ.* Eton.

4. ◆John William Aubrey de Vere (*St Albans, 30 Cheyne Walk, SW3 5HH*), *b.* 10 Feb. 1950, *educ.* Eton.

1. ●Caroline Anne de Vere, *b.* 19 July 1951, *educ.* Queen's Gate Sch., *m.* 11 July 1970, Neil St John ffrench Blake (*Barn House, Midgham, Woolhampton, Berks.*), son of Lt Col Robert Lifford Valentine ffrench Blake, D.S.O., of Midgham Park Farm, Woolhampton, Berks. (*see* BURKE's *L.G. of Ireland*), and has issue,

•Clare Eleanor de Vere, *b.* 15 Jan. 1972.

2. a dau., *b.* and *d.* 15 Nov. 1963.

CREATIONS—Earl etc., 27 Dec. 1676. Duke, 10 Jan. 1684. Baron Vere of Hanworth, 28 March 1750. Hereditary Grand Falconer of England 1685, Hereditary Registrar of the Court of Chancery 1698.

ARMS—Quarterly: 1st and 4th, counter quartered, 1st and 4th, France and England, quarterly; 2nd, Scotland; 3rd Ireland; (being the Royal Arms of KING CHARLES II) overall a sinister baton, gu., charged with three roses arg., barbed seeded ppr. 2nd and 3rd, DE VERE, Earls of Oxford, quarterly, gu. and or, in the 1st quarter a mullet arg. *Crest*—on a chapeau gu., turned up erm., a lion statant guardant, or, crowned with a ducal coronet, per pale, arg., and of the first, gorged with a collar of the last, thereon three roses also arg., barbed and seeded ppr. *Supporters*— Dexter, an antelope arg., armed and unguled or; sinister, a greyhound arg., each gorged with a collar, as in the crest. *Motto*—Auspicium melioris aevi.

TARTAN: Royal Stewart

RESIDENCES—St Albans, 30 Cheyne Walk, SW3 5HH; Villa St Albans, 29 Rue Gambetta, Venc, 06, France, *Clubs*—Brooks's, St James', Beefsteak.

LINEAGE (of BEAUCLERK) ------- SIR CHARLES BEAUCLERK, 1st DUKE OF ST. ALBANS, K.G., F.R.S., of Burford House, Windsor and Bestwood, Notts., natural son of King Charles II by Eleanor Gwyn, Lady of Queen Catherine's Privy Chamber, 1675 and formerly a celebrated actress (*d.* 14 Nov. 1687), 2nd dau. of Thomas Gwyn, by Eleanor, his wife, *b.* 8 May, 1670, created Baron Heddington, and Earl of Burford, both in co. Oxford, 27 Dec. 1676 (with remainder, failing male issue, to his brother Lord James Beauclerk, who was *b.* 25 Dec. 1671 and *d.* in Paris, Sept. 1680), created DUKE OF ST. ALBANS, 10 Jan. 1684, constituted Chief Ranger of Enfield Chase, 12 June, 1684, Hereditary Master Falconer of England, 31 Jan. 1685, Capt. of the Band of Gentlemen Pensioners 1693–1712 and again 1714, Lord of the Bedchamber 1697–1702, Hereditary Registrar of the Court of Chancery, 29 June, 1698, Lord Lieut. and Custos Rotulorum of Berks. 1714, invested K.G. 31 March, 1718, elected F.R.S. 1722, Freeman and High Steward of Windsor from 1716, and of Wokingham from 1718, Col. Princess Anne of Denmark's Regt. of Horse (8th Horse) 1687, served under the Emperor Leopold I and distinguished himself at the taking of Belgrade 1688, served in the Low Countries under King William III and was present at the Battle of Landen (Neerwinden) 1693, Amb. Extraord. to France on the occasion of the marriage of the Duke of Burgundy 1697, granted a pension of £800 p.a. by the Irish Parliament. His Grace *m.* 17 April, 1694, Lady Diana de Vere, Mistress of the Robes and Lady of the Stole to Caroline, Princess of Wales (later QUEEN CAROLINE) 1714–17, 1st Lady of the Bedchamber to QUEEN ANNE and the Princess of Wales 1705–17 (*d.* 15 Jan. 1742) eldest dau. and eventually sole heiress of 20th and last Earl of Oxford, K.G. (*see Lineage of* DE VERE), and had issue,

1. CHARLES, 2nd Duke (*see page* 229).

2. William, Capt. R.H.G., 1721 M.P. for Chichester, Vice-Chamberlain of QUEEN CAROLINE'S Household 1728; *b.* 22 May, 1698, *educ.* Eton, *m.* 13 Dec. 1722, Charlotte, Lady of the Bedchamber to Anne, Princess of Orange (*d.* 3 July 1770), 2nd dau. and co-heir of Sir John Werden, 2nd and last Bt., of Burton and Cholmondeston, both in Cheshire, Leyland, Lancs. and Holyport, Berks. (*see* BURKE'S *Extinct and Dormant Baronetcies*), and *d.* at Bath 23 Feb. 1733 (*bur.* in Westminster Abbey), leaving issue,

   1. William, *b.* 26 May 1726, *educ.* Eton, *d.* there, 28 Nov. 1738.

   2. Charles, Page of Honour to the Duke of Cumberland 1740, Lt.-Col. 3rd Foot Guards 1761, formerly in 107th Regt. of Foot, Gov. of Pendennis Castle, Cornwall, *m.* Elizabeth Jones (*d.* 5 Dec. 1768), and *d.* 30 Aug. 1775, leaving issue, an only surv. son,

     (1) GEORGE, 4th Duke (*see page* 230).

     (2) Charles William, *d.* 24 Feb. 1763.

   1. Charlotte, eventual heiress of her grandfather Sir John Werden, 2nd Bt., *m.* 22 Dec. 1744, John Drummond, M.P., of Stanmore, Middlesex, son of Andrew Drummond, of Stanmore, Banker, and *d.* 7 March 1793, leaving issue (*see* PERTH, E.). He *d.* 25 July 1774.

   2. Caroline, *m.* 23 Feb. 1756, Major-Gen. Sir William Draper, K.B., C.-in-C. of the Expdn. to Manilla and the Philippine Islands, and *d.* 1778. He *d.* 8 Jan. 1787.

3. VERE, 1st BARON VERE OF HANWORTH, of Hanworth Palace, Middlesex, Adm. of the Blue, Lord Lieut. and Custos Rotulorum of Berks. 1760–71, M.P. for Windsor 1726–41 and for Plymouth 1741–50, Freeman of Windsor 1726, elected Mayor 1734 but did not serve, a distinguished naval officer, entered R.N. 1712–13, served in Mediterranean Capt. H.M.S. *Lyme* 1721, H.M.S. *Anglesea* 1731, and H.M.S. *Hampton Court* 1731, Commr. of the Navy 1732, a Lord of the Admiralty 1738–42, and 1744–49, Rear Adm. of the Red 1745, Vice-Adm. of the Blue 1746, Adm. 1748, ret. 1749, elevated to the Peerage as BARON

VERE OF HANWORTH, *co. Middlesex*, 28 March 1750; *b.* 14 July, 1699, *m.* 13 April 1736, Mary (*d.* 21 Jan. 1783), elder dau. and co-heir of the late Thomas Chamber, of Hanworth, by his wife, Lady Mary Berkeley, dau. of 2nd Earl of Berkeley, K.B. (*see* BERKELEY, B.), and had issue,

 1. Vere, *b.* 12 Jan. 1737, *d.* 26 Dec. 1739.

 2. Chambers *b.* 22 Feb. 1738, *educ.* Westminster, *d.* 16 July 1747.

 3. Sackville, *b.* 12 April, *bur.* 25 April 1739.

 4. AUBREY, *2nd* Baron and *5th* Duke.

 1. Elizabeth, *b,* July 1742, *bur.* 26 April 1746.

 2. Mary, *b.* 4 Dec. 1743, *m.* 2 Oct. 1762, Lord Charles Spencer, 2nd son of 3rd Duke of Marlborough, K.G., and *d.* 13 Jan 1812, leaving issue. He *d.* 16 June 1820.

His Lordship *d.* 21 Oct. 1781 and was *s.* by his only surv. son (*see page* 230),

4. Henry, of Foliejon Park, Winkfield, Berks. (which he purchased 1744), sometime of Somerset House, London, Ensign 1st Foot Guards 1717, Col. 31st Foot 1739, formerly served with 59th Foot and distinguished himself at the Siege of Gibraltar as a volunteer under the Earl of Portmore 1727, Freeman of Windsor 1741, Lieut. of Band of Gentlemen Pensioners 1728, Ranger of New Lodge Walk 1752–61, M.P. for Plymouth 1740–41 and for Thetford 1742–61; *b.* 11 Aug. 1701, *m.* 1stly, 21 April, 1729, -------- (*d.s.p.*), dau. of Governor Philips, of Stanwell, Middlesex. He *m.* 2ndly, 25 June 1739, Hon. Martha Lovelace, a Maid of Honour to QUEEN CAROLINE 1732 (*d.* 5 March 1788), dau. of 4th Lord Lovelace, and sister and heir of 6th Lord Lovelace (*see* BURKE's *Dormant and Extinct Peerages*), and *d.* 5 Jan. 1761, having by her had issue,

 1. George, *b.* 18 March 1740, *d.* an inf.

 2. Henry (Rev.), of Leckhampstead, Bucks. (to which he *s.* on his mother's death), Lord of the Manor of Leckhampstead, Rector of Greens Norton, Northants., and of St. Mary Somerset, London; *b.* 12 Aug. 1745, *educ.* Eton, and Ch.Ch. Oxford (B.A. 1767, M.A. 1769), *m.* 23 Nov. 1769, his first cousin once removed, Charlotte (*d.* 20 March, 1774), dau. of John Drummond, M.P., of Stanmore (*see* PERTH, E.), by his wife Charlotte, elder dau. of Lord William Beauclerk (*see page* 221), and *d.* 8 Nov. 1817, having had with other issue,

 (1) Henry, *bapt.* 6 Sept. 1770, *d.* an inf.

 (2) John, of Leckhampstead, Bucks., and of London, Barrister-at-law, Middle Temple, 1793, Lord of the Manor and Patron of the Living of Leckhampstead; *b.* 10 Feb. 1772, *educ.* Eton, and Ch.Ch.

Oxford (B.A. 1793, M.A. 1796), *m.* 14 Aug. 1798, Mary, eldest dau. of Thomas FitzHugh, of Plâs Power, Denbighshire, and Portland Place, London (*see* BURKE'S *L.G.*), and *d.* 8 Jan. 1840, leaving issue,

> 1*a*. Henry William, of Leckhampstead, Bucks., Lord of the Manor and Patron of the Living of Leckhampstead; *b.* 15 Nov. 1812, *educ.* Harrow, *m.* 1stly, 21 May, 1838, Lady Katherine Frances Ashburnham (*d.* 6 April, 1839), 7th dau. of 3rd Earl of Ashburnham, K.G. (*extinct*), and had issue,

> > Katherine Mary, *b.* 19 March, 1839, *m.* 1 Aug. 1864, Rev. Sir Frederick Boyd, 6th and last Bt., and *d.* 3 Aug. 1867, leaving issue, one dau. (*see* 1886 *Edn.*). He *d.* 13 Feb. 1889.

> He *m.* 2ndly, 11 Aug. 1840, Louisa (*d.s.p.* 28 Dec. 1882), 3rd dau. of Sir George Wombwell, 2nd Bt., and *d.* 8 June 1894.

> 1*a*. Charlotte Mary, *b.* 21 May 1801, *d. unm.* 7 May 1852.

> 2*a*. Catherine, *b.* 10 Sept. 1814, *d. unm.*

1. Diana, Maid of Honour to QUEEN CHARLOTTE from 1761, *b.* 24 Jan. 1741, *d. unm.* 13 Feb. 1809.

2. Henrietta, *b.* 26 Nov. 1742.

3. Mary, *b.* 25 Nov. 1743, *m.* Rev. Walter Williams, Rector of Harrow.

4. Charlotte, *b.* 24 Oct. 1746.

5. Martha, *b.* 12 Dec. 1747.

6. Anne, *b.* 5 Oct. 1749, *m.* 23 May 1794, Rev. and Hon. George Talbot, 3rd son of Hon. John Talbot, and brother of 1st Earl Talbot (*see* SHREWSBURY AND WATERFORD, E.), and *d.s.p.* 1809.

5. Sidney, P.C. (1740), J.P., of Clewer Manor, Windsor, Berks., and of Speke Hall, Lancs., Vice-Chamberlain of the Household to KING GEORGE II 1740–42, M.P. for New Windsor 1733–44, Trustee and Common Councillor of the Georgia Soc. 1739, Master of the Harriers 1738, Freeman of Windsor 1733 and Mayor 1740–1, a notorious fortune hunter who inherited the estates of Richard Topham, M.P. 1730; *b.* 27 Feb. 1703, *educ.* Eton, and Trin. Coll. Oxford (M.A. 1727, D.C.L. 1733), *m.* 9 Dec. 1736, Mary, (*d.* 20 Nov. 1766) dau. and heir of Thomas Norris, M.P., of Speke Hall, Lancs., High Sheriff of Lancs. 1696, and *d.* 23 Nov. 1744, leaving issue,

> Topham, F.R.S., of Clewer Manor, Berks. (which he sold 1766), Speke Hall, Lancs., and Great Russell Street, Bloomsbury, London, a celebrated book collector and close friend of Dr. Johnson; elected F.R.S. 1770, Freeman and Bencher of Windsor 1761, Founder member of The

Club 1764 *b*. Dec. 1739, *educ*. Eton, and Trin. Coll. Oxford, *m*. 12 March 1768, Lady Diana, the well-known artist, Lady of the Bedchamber to QUEEN CHARLOTTE 1761–68 (*d*. 1st Aug. 1808), formerly wife of 2nd Viscount Bolingbroke (*m*. diss. by Act of Parliament 10 Mar. 1768), and elder dau. of 3rd Duke of Marlborough, K.G., and *d*. 11 March 1780, leaving issue,

(1) Charles George, of St Leonards Lodge, Horsham, Sussex (which he purchased 1801), of Wigston, Galby and Frisby, Leics., and formerly of Speke Hall, Lancs. (which he sold 1797), M.P. for Richmond 1796–98; *b*. 20 Jan. 1774, *educ*. Ch.Chc. Oxford, *m*. 29 April 1799, Emily Charlotte (*d*. 22 Jan. 1832), 2nd dau. of William Ogilvie, of Ardglass Castle, co. Down, by his 2nd wife, Emilia Mary, Dowager Duchess of Leinster, 2nd dau. of 2nd Duke of Richmond and Lennox, K.G., K.B., P.C., and *d*. 25 Dec. 1845, having had issue,

1*a*. Aubrey William,[1] of Ardglass Castle, co. Down (to which he *s*. on the death of his maternal grandmother), and St Leonards Lodge, Horsham, Sussex, and Wigston, Leics., M.P. for East Surrey 1832–37, Lord of the Manor of Ardglass, Major, 99th Foot 1826; *b*. 20 Feb. 1801, *m*. 1stly, 13 Feb. 1834, Ida (*d*. 23 April, 1838), 4th dau. of Sir Charles Foster Goring, 7th Bt., and had issue,

1*b*. Aubrey de Vere, of Ardglass Castle, co. Down, and 41 Hill Street, Berkeley Square, London, J.P. co. Down, High Sheriff 1863, Lord of the Manor of Ardglass; *b*. 5 Oct. 1837, *educ*. Rugby, Cheltenham, and Trin. Coll. Camb., *m*. 1stly, 1 Dec. 1858 (*m*. diss. by div. 1895), his cousin, Evelyn Georgiana Matilda (d. 10 Jan. 1931), 3rd dau. of Henry FitzRoy, J.P., of Salcey Lawn, Northants. (*see* GRAFTON, D.), by his wife, Jane Elizabeth, 5th dau. of Charles George Beauclerk (*see page* 228), and had issue,

Sidney de Vere, *b*. 8 May, 1866, educ. Eton, and Trin. Coll. Camb. (B.A. 1887), *d. unm.* 4 July, 1903.

He *m*. 2ndly, 16 Nov. 1895, Katherine Lucy (*d*. 23 Jan. 1910), widow of Capt. J. Collier Tucker, R.N., and *d*. 9 July, 1919.

1*b*. Ida, *b*. 29 Jan. 1835, *d*. 1844.

2*b*. Diana Arabella, *b*. 1836, *d. unm.* 26 May 1855.

3*b*. Augusta, *b*. 1838, *m*. 4 Jan. 1866, Thomas Edward Howe, Barrister-at-Law, and had issue, four sons and two daus.

He *m.* 2ndly, 7 Dec. 1841, Rose Matilda (who *m.* 2ndly 20 Aug 1865, John James Johnson of London and *d.* 20 July, 1878), dau. of Joshua Robinson, of Kew, Surrey, and *d.* 1 Feb. 1854, having by her had issue,

4*b.* Louisa Katherine, of Millbeck Cottage, Keswick, Cumberland, *d. unm.* 1929.

5*b.* Isabella Julia, *m.* 19 Oct. 1867, Chevalier Surg.-Major George Albert Palatiano, M.D., of Corfu, Ionian Islands, and *d.* 13 March, 1930, leaving issue, one son and two daus. He *d.* 1910.

2*a.* Charles Robert, of St Leonards Lodge, Horsham, Sussex, and of London, Fell. of Gonville and Caius Coll. Camb. 1822–42, Barrister-at-law, Lincolns Inn, 1829; *b.* 6 Jan. 1802, *educ.* Halnaker, Sussex, and Gonville and Caius Coll. Camb. (B.A. 1823, M.A. 1827), *m.* March, 1842, Joaquina (*d.* 16 Nov. 1881), 2nd dau. of H.E. Don Jose M. de Zamora, Chief Magistrate of Cuba, and *d.* 22 Feb. 1872, having had issue,

1*b.* Sidney Joseph, *b.* 22 Dec. 1848, *d.* 7 Aug. 1851.

2*b.* Ferdinand, of Dibden, Hants., Capt. R.E., served in Afghan War 1879 (medal), and in World War I with Sussex Vol. Training Corps, formerly Major cmdg. Lakhimpur Vol. Rifles, Pres. W. India Industrial Assoc., Guardian, Trustee and Sec. to Salar Jung Minors and Estates, Hyderabad, deputy examiner of public works, accounts, Madras; *b.* 15 Jan. 1851, *m.* 9 Feb. 1872, Emily Johanna Frances (*d.* 1 Feb. 1916), yr. dau. of Col. Robert Clifford Lloyd, 68th Regt., and *d.s.p.* 3 May, 1920. Capt. Ferdinand Beauclerk had an adopted dau., Helen Mary Dorothea de Vere BEAUCLERK (dau. of Major Sydney Edwin Bellingham (*see* BELLINGHAM, Bt.)), novelist, *d. unm.* 8 July, 1969.

3*b.* Charles Sidney (Rev.), S.J., ordained a priest in the Roman Catholic Church 1888, Rector of Holywell, Flints., 1890–98, helped to restore St Winefride's Well as a Roman Catholic Shrine, also served at Boscombe, Roehampton, Malta, Clitheroe, Richmond and Accrington, a prominent advocate for the 17th Earl of Oxford's authorship of Shakespeare's works; *b.* 1 Jan. 1855, *educ.* Beaumont, and Stonyhurst, *d. unm.* 22 Dec. 1934.

4*b.* Henry Sidney (Rev.), S.J., Vicar-General to Bishop Galton and Superior of the Order in Guiana and Barbados, ordained a priest 1890, served in Foreign Missions in Jamaica, Maryland, British Guiana and Barbados; *b.* 25 Nov. 1857, *educ.* Beaumont, and Stonyhurst, *d. unm.* in Barbados, 30 Sept. 1909.

5*b*. Robert Sidney de Vere, sometime Headmaster of Kenilworth Sch., Cape Town, S. Africa, author of *Summary of English History to 1802*; *b.* 14 Dec. 1858, *educ.* Beaumont, *m.* 30 Oct. 1894, Beatrice Annie Elliott (*d.* 14 Oct. 1947), 2nd dau. of Arthur Richard Holebone, and *d.* 26 March, 1934, having had issue,

Nevill Alfred de Vere, T/2nd Lieut. 12th Bn. Essex Regt., *b.* 13 Oct. 1895, *k.* in action, 17 June, 1915.

6*b*. William Topham Sidney, of Etche Biziak, 9 Avenue des Chênes, Biarritz, France, formerly of Argentina, engineer; *b.* 3 July 1864, *educ.* Beaumont, *m.* in Madrid, 17 Dec. 1910, Lola (*d.* 1972), only surv. child of Enrique, Conde de Penalver y Marques de Arcos, in Spain, and *d.* 5 May 1950 having had issue,

1*c*. William Nicholas, *b.* 12 June, 1912, *d. unm.* 10 May, 1948.

2*c*. Henry Topham, *b.* 19 Nov. 1913, *d.* 7 March, 1929.

3*c*. ◆Rafael Charles, M.B.E. (1945), Conde de Penalver y Marques de Arcos, in Spain, late Capt. Intelligence Corps, attached S.O.E., served in World War II 1939–45, has French Croix de Guerre, with Hongkong and Shanghai Banking Corpn. 1945–70 (*31 Marryat Road, Wimbledon, S.W.19; 5 Rue C.N. Spon, Luxembourg*); *b.* 10 Aug. 1917, *educ.* Downside, and in France, *m.* at Saigon, S. Vietnam, 24 Aug. 1957, ●Noirine Mary, eldest dau. of James Bowen of Bowen's Cross, co. Cork, and has issue,

◆William Rafael, *b.* 14 Aug. 1961, *educ.* Downside

●Dolores Mary, *b.* 11 July, 1958, *educ.* St. Mary's, Woldingham.

1*c*. ●Diana Mary Ildefonsa, served in World War II in W.R.N.S. (*Etche Bizkiak, 9 Avenue des Chênes, Biarritz, France*), *b.* 1 May 1924.

1*b*. Mary, *b.* 17 April 1861, *d. unm.* 17 Oct. 1920.

3*a*. George Robert, of King's Castle, Ardglass, co. Down, Capt. 23rd Regt. Royal Welsh Fus., author of *Beauclerk's Journey to*

Morocco; b. 28 Feb. 1803, *m.* 2 June 1861, Maria Sarah (d. 18 Oct. 1923), yr. dau. of Ralph Lonsdale, and *d.* 5 Dec. 1871, having had issue,

1*b.* Amelius George de Vere, of Stanway, Essex, Lieut. 1st Vol. Bn. Suffolk Regt., served in World War I 1914–18 in France; *b.* 1 Oct. 1871, *m.* 26 Aug. 1918, ●Marguerite Olive Clair (Margot) (*Church House, Nayland, Colchester, Essex*) dau. of Louis Antoine Bertrand, of Matfield, Kent, and *d.* 26 Aug. 1939, leaving issue,

Anthony Amelius de Vere, *b.* 6 July 1920, *educ.* Bryanston, *d. unm.* 10 May 1962.

1*b.* Georgiana, *b.* 10 July 1862, *d. unm.* 10 May 1942.

2*b.* Caroline Elizabeth, *b.* 12 June 1865, *m.* 24 April, 1895, Rev. Alfred Norris Cope, M.A., sometime Vicar of Dormington with Bartestree, Herefordshire, and *d.s.p.* 8 Nov. 1952. He *d.* 4 Sept. 1936.

3*b.* Emily Kathleen, *b.* 25 Jan. 1867, *m.* 26 Dec. 1917, George Duguay, of Sandford House, Ryde, Isle of Wight, formerly of Newcastle, New Brunswick, Canada, and *d.s.p.* 16 April, 1953. He *d.* 10 May 1944.

4*b.* Ida, *b.* 7 June 1869, *m.* 30 July 1891, George Francis Berney of Croydon, Surrey, and *d.* 5 Aug. 1955, leaving issue, two sons and two daus. He *d.* 3 March 1931.

4*a.* Amelius, *b.* 1809.

5*a.* Ferdinand, served as Acting Cornet in Bengal Light Cav., *b.* 1811, *d. unm.* at Cawnpore, India, 5 Oct. 1829.

6*a.* Augustus, *b.* 1813.

1*a.* Emily Frederica, *b.* 1 March 1800, *d.* 1816 (*bur.* at Valence, France).

2*a.* Caroline Anne, *b.* 12 Jan. 1804, *m.* 20 Oct. 1829, Robert Aldridge, J.P., D.L., of New Lodge, Horsham, Sussex, only son of Capt. John Aldridge, M.P., and *d.* 11 Sept. 1869, leaving issue (*see* BURKE'S *L.G.* 1952 *Edn.*). He *d.* 26 May 1871.

3*a.* Georgiana, *b.* 1805, *m.* 10 Oct. 1826, Sir John Dean Paul, 2nd Bt., and *d.* 25 Dec. 1847, leaving issue. He *d.* 7 Sept. 1868.

4*a.* Diana Olivia, *b.* 21 June 1806, *m.* 10 April 1823, Sir Francis Fletcher-Vane, 3rd Bt., and *d.* 9 Feb. 1875, leaving issue (*see* 1934 *Edn.*). He d. 15 Feb. 1842.

5a. Jane Elizabeth, *b.* 1807, *m.* 24 July 1830, Henry FitzRoy, J.P., of Salcey Lawn, Northants., eldest son of Rev. Lord Henry FitzRoy, Preb. and Canon of Westminster, and *d.* 15 July 1892, leaving issue (*see* GRAFTON, D.). He *d.* 5 Dec. 1877.

6a. Isabella Elizabeth, *b.* 10 Oct. 1808, *m.* 12 March 1840, Adm. John William Montagu, 2nd son of Sir George Montagu, G.C.B., Adm. of the Red, and *d.* 21 July 1864, leaving issue (*see* MAN-CHESTER, D.). He *d.* 12 Dec. 1882.

7a Katherine Katinka, *b.* May 1812, *m.* 5 April 1845, Col. Sir George Ashley Maude, K.C.B., R.A., Crown Equerry to QUEEN VICTORIA, 2nd son of Rev. Hon. John Charles Maude, and *d.* 1 June 1882, leaving issue (*see* HAWARDEN, V.). He *d.* 31 May 1894.

(1) Mary, *b.* 20 Aug. 1766, *m. ca.* 1795, Count Jenison Walworth, of Heidelberg, Grand Chamberlain of the Household to the King of Württemberg at Stuttgart, eldest son of Francis Jenison, of Walworth, Co. Durham, and *d.* 1851, leaving issue, two sons and four daus. He *d.* 1824.

(2) Elizabeth, *b.* (twin) 20 Aug. 1766, *m.* 8 April 1781, her first cousin 11th Earl of Pembroke, and *d.* 25 March 1793, leaving issue. He *d.* 26 Oct. 1827.

(3) Anne.

Charlotte, *d. unm.*

6. George, of Winchfield House, Hants. (which he purchased 1767), Lt.-Gen., A.D.C. to KING GEORGE II 1745, M.P. for New Windsor from 1744, Freeman of Windsor 1744, elected Mayor 1752 & 1765 but did not serve, C.-in-C. Scotland 1758, Lord of the Manor of Winchfield, Capt. 1st Regt. of Foot 1736, Col. 19th Foot 1748, Lt.-Gov. of Gibraltar 1753, Gov. of Landguard Fort, Suffolk, 1753, Major-Gen. 1755, Lt.-Gen. 1758; *b.* 26 Dec. 1704, *m.* Margaret (*d.* 23 Oct. 1792), dau. of Thomas Bainbridge of Slaley, Northumberland, and *d.s.p.* 11 May, 1768.

7. Seymour, *b.* 24 June 1706 *d.* an inf. 1 July 1706

8. James (Rt. Rev.), D.D., Bishop of Hereford from 1746; Preb. of Windsor 1733, Canon of Windsor 1738, Chaplain in Ordinary to KING GEORGE II 1739, Deputy Clerk of the Closet 1744, *b.* 1709, *educ.* Queen's Coll. Oxford (B.A. 1730, M.A. 1733, D.D.1744), *d. unm.* 20 Oct. 1787.

9. Aubrey, entered R.N. 1723, Capt. H.M.S. *Ludlow* 1731, H.M.S. *Dolqhin* 1736, H.M.S. *Weymouth* 1740, and under Adm. Vernon as Capt.

H.M.S. *Prince Frederick* 1740; *b.* 1711, *m.* Catherine (*d.s.p.* 27 Oct. 1755), widow of Col. Francis Alexander, and dau. of Sir Henry Newton, Kt., LL.D., Envoy Extraord. to the Court of Florence and Republic of Genoa, and a Judge of the High Court of Admiralty, and was *k.* in action whilst fighting heroically at the Battle of Cartagena, 24 Feb. 1740 (*bur.* in Westminster Abbey).

1. Diana, *b.* 1697, living Sept. 1743, *d. unm.*

2. Mary, *b.* 1713, *d. unm.*

3. Anne, *b.* 1716, *d. unm.*

His Grace *d.* 11 May 1726, (*bur.* in Westminster Abbey) and was *s.* by his eldest son,

CHARLES, 2nd DUKE OF ST ALBANS, K.G., K.B., of Burford House, Windsor and Bestwood, Notts., Lord Lieut. and Custos Rotulorum of Berks. from 1727, M.P. or Bodmin 1718–22 and for New Windsor 1722–26, created K.B. 27 May 1725, carried the Queen's Crown at the Coronation of KING GEORGE II 1727, constituted Constable and Gov. of Windsor Castle and Lord Warden of Windsor Forest 1730, Lord of the Bedchamber 1738, invested K.G. 20 March 1741, elected a Freeman of Windsor 1722, High Steward of Windsor from 1726 and of Wokingham from 1740; *b.* 6 April, 1696, *educ.* Eton, and New Coll. Oxford, *m.* 13 Dec. 1722, Lucy (*d.* 12 Nov. 1752), eldest dau. and co-heir of Sir John Werden, 2nd and last Bt. of Burton and Cholmondeston both in Cheshire, Leyland, Lancs. and Holyport, Berks. (*see* BURKE'S *Extinct and Dormant Baronetcies*), and had issue,

GEORGE, *3rd* Duke.

Diana, *b.* 20 Oct. 1725, *m.* 2 Feb. 1761, Rt. Rev. and Hon. Shute Barrington, D.D., D.C.L., Bishop of Durham, 5th son of 1st Viscount Barrington, and *d.s.p.* 28 May 1766. He *d.* 25 March 1826.

His Grace *d.* 27 July 1751 (*bur.* in Westminster Abbey), and was *s.* by his only son,

GEORGE, 3rd DUKE OF ST ALBANS, of Burford House, Windsor (which he sold to KING GEORGE III 1778) and Bestwood, Notts., Lord Lieut. and Custos Rotulorum of Berks, 1751–60, and from 1771, Lord of the Bedchamber, Freeman of Windsor 1751 and High Steward from 1751, carried the Sword of State at the Installation of the Prince of Wales as K.G. 1771; a notorious roué who fled from his creditors to Brussels; *b.* 25 June, 1730, *educ.* Eton, *m.* 23 Dec. 1752, Jane (*d.* 16 Dec. 1778), dau. and heir of Sir Walter Roberts, 6th Bt., of Glassenbury Park, Kent, *and d.s.p. legit.*[2] in

Brussels, 1 Feb. 1786 (*bur.* in Westminster Abbey), when he was *s.* by his first cousin, once removed,

GEORGE, 4th DUKE OF ST ALBANS, of Bestwood, Notts., Burton and Cholmondeston, both in Cheshire, and Leigham Court, Surrey, Ensign 1775, served in American War of Independence, Capt.-Lieut. 1778, Lt.-Col. 3rd Foot Guards 1786; *b.* 5 Dec. 1758, *d. unm.* 10 Feb. 1787, and was *s.* by his first cousin once removed,

AUBREY, 5th DUKE OF ST. ALBANS, 2nd BARON VERE OF HANWORTH, of Hanworth Palace, Middlesex, and later of Bestwood, Notts., M.P. for Thetford 1761-68 and for Aldborough, Yorks, 1768–74; Hon. Freeman of Windsor 1769, and Bencher 1761, an art collector; *s.* his father as Baron Vere 1871; *b.* 3 June 1740, *educ.* Westminster, and Queen's Coll. Oxford, *m.* 4 May 1763, Lady Catherine Ponsonby (*d.* 4 Sept. 1789), dau. of 2nd Earl of Bessborough, and had issue,

1. AUBREY, *6th* Duke } *(see page 232).*
2. WILLIAM, *8th* Duke }

(see page 232).

3. Amelius, G.C.B., G.C.H., F.R.S., of Winchfield House, Hants., Adm. of the White, Principal Naval A.D.C. to KING WILLIAM IV from 1830 and to QUEEN VICTORIA, Lord of the Manor of Winchfield, entered R.N. 1782, Lieut. 1790, Capt. H.M.S. *Nemesis* 1793 and of H.M.S. *Juno,* in which he was present at the Blockade of Toulon 1794, Capt. of H.M.S. *Argo* 1795, H.M.S. *Dryad* 1796, in which he captured the French Frigate *La Proserpine,* H.M.S. *Fortunée* 1800, H.M.S. *Majestic,* H.M.S. *Saturn* 1805, and H.M.S. *Royal Oak* 1809, escorted Lord Chatham's army to Walcheren, where he assumed command of Campvere and H.M.S. *Spartiate* 1828, Col. of Marines 1810, Rear-Adm. of the Blue 1811, Rear-Adm. of the White 1812, Rear-Adm. of the Red 1814, Vice-Adm. of the White 1819, C.-in-C. Lisbon and the Portuguese Coast 1824–27, Adm. of the Blue 1830, C.-in-C. Plymouth 1836–39; created K.C.B. 1815, G.C.H. 1831 and G.C.B. 1835, elected F.R.S. 1809; *b.* 23 May 1771, *d. unm.* 10 Dec. 1846.[3]

4. Frederick (Rev.), D.D., of Winchfield House, Hants., Lord of the Manor of Winchfield, Curate of Groton, Essex, 1795–97, Vicar of Kimpton, Herts. 1797–1827, Vicar of Redbourn and of St. Michael's, St Albans, Herts. 1827–50, a celebrated cricketer, Pres. M.C.C. 1826; *b.* 8 May 1773, *educ.* Trin. Coll. Camb. (M.A. 1792, D.D. 1824), *m.* 3 July 1813, Hon. Charlotte Dillon (*d.* 26 Sept. 1866), 3rd dau. of 12th Viscount Dillon, K.P., and *d.* 22 April 1850, leaving issue,

1. Charles William, of Winchfield House, Hants. and Boulogne, France, D.L., J.P. Hants. 1844, Lord of the Manor of Winchfield, *b.* 7 May 1816, *educ.* Charterhouse, and Ch.Ch. Oxford (B.A. 1838), *m.* 15 Aug. 1844, Penelope (*d.* 15 April, 1890), dau. of Edward Hulkes, and *d.* in Boulogne, 23 May 1863, leaving issue,

    (1) Frederick Edward, of Winchfield House, Hants. (which he sold in 1908), D.L., J.P. Hants., Lord of the Manor of Winchfield, *b.* 3 July 1852, *educ.* Ch.Ch. Oxford, *d, unm.* 17 Nov. 1919.

    (2) Charles St. John, *b.* 10 Oct. 1854, *educ.* Marlborough, *d.* in Virginia, U.S.A., 12 Sept. 1921.

    (1) Caroline Elizabeth, *b.* 28 Aug. 1845, *m.* 16 April 1868, Rev. Francis William Hudson, Vicar of Great Wilbraham, Cambs., and *d.* 29 June 1915, leaving issue, two sons. He *d.* 10 June 1901.

    (2) Penelope Sarah Blanche, *b.* 25 Oct. 1846, *m.* 20 Oct. 1869, Sir St. Vincent Alexander Hammick, 3rd Bt., and *d.* March 1886, leaving issue. He *d.* 8 Nov. 1927.

    (3) Charlotte Amelia, *b.* 8 July 1848.

    (4) Frederica Jane, *b.* 17 Nov. 1850, *m.* 15 Nov. 1870, Col. John Ormsby Vandeleur, C.B., Rifle Bde., of Ballinacourty Castle, co. Limerick, and *d.* 30 June 1926, leaving issue, one son and four daus. (*see* BURKE'S *L.G. of Ireland*, VANDELEUR *of Kilrush*). He *d.* 11 June 1900.

    (5) Henrietta Mary, *b.* in Boulogne 2 Nov. 1856, *m.* 7 Aug 1877, Edward Stisted Mostyn Pryce, of Gunley, Montgomeryshire, and *d.* 28 Sept. 1932, leaving issue (*see* BURKE'S *L.G.*, 1952 *Edn*). He *d.* 14 June 1932.

2. Aubrey Frederick James, Capt. Royal Fus. (7th Foot), formerly with Scots. Fus. Guards, ret. 1847; *b.* 3 May 1817, *educ.* Charterhouse. *d. unm.* 3 Jan. 1853.

1. Caroline Henrietta Frederica, author, *b.* 19 April 1815, *m.* 12 Dec. 1851, Charles Eugène Leloup, of Brussels. He *d.* 27 April 1878.

2. Henrietta Mary, joint author with her sister of *Tales of Fashion and Reality* (1836), *b.* 1 July 1818, *m.* in Boulogne, 2 Aug. 1842, Sir Edward Rokewood Gage, 9th and last Bt. of Hengrave (*see* 1871 *Edn.*), and *d.s.p.* Jan 1887. He *d.* 3 Jan 1872.

1. Catherine Elizabeth, *m.* in Paris, 1 Sept. 1802, Rev. James Burgess, M.A., Rector of Hanworth 1805–16, and Chaplain to 6th Duke of St Albans, son of Rev. James Burgess, and *d.s.p.* in Florence, July 1803. He *d.* in Naples 27 Nov. 1827.

2. Caroline, *m.* 16 Feb. 1797, Hon. Charles Lawrence Dundas, 5th son of 1st Baron Dundas, and *d.* 23 Nov. 1838, leaving issue (*see* ZETLAND, M.). He *d.* 25 Jan. 1810.

3. Georgiana, *b.* 1776, *d.* 17 Oct. 1791.

His Grace *d.* 9 Feb. 1802, and was *s.* by his eldest son,

AUBREY, 6th DUKE OF ST ALBANS, of Hanworth, Middx., and Bestwood, Notts., M.P. for Kingston-upon-Hull 1790–96, entered Foot Guards 1781, Capt. 1783, served in America and Canada, Lt. Col. 34th Foot, *b.* 21 Aug. 1765, *m.* 1stly, 9 July 1788, Jane (Mary) (*d.* 18 Aug. 1800), dau. of John Moses, of Hull, by his wife Margaret, dau. of Sir Thomas Cave, 6th Bt., and had issue,

Mary, *m.* 6 Nov. 1811, 8th Earl of Coventry, and *d.* 11 Sept. 1845, leaving issue. He *d.* 15 May 1843.

He *m.* 2ndly, 15 Aug. 1802, Louisa Grace Manners (*d.* 19 Feb. 1816), 4th dau. of John Manners, M.P., of Hainby Hall, Lincs., and Grantham Grange, Lincs., natural son of Lord William Manners (2nd son of 2nd Duke of Rutland), by his wife Louisa, *suo jure* Countess of Dysart, and by her had issue,

AUBREY, 7th Duke

His Grace who *d.* 12 Aug. 1815, left Hanworth to his widow, and was *s.* by his only son,

AUBREY, 7th DUKE OF ST ALBANS, *b.* 7 April 1815, *d.* an inf. 19 Feb. 1816, three hours before his mother, and was *s.* by his uncle,

WILLIAM, 8th DUKE OF ST ALBANS, of Redbourne Hall and Little Grimsby Hall both in Lincs., Bathafarn, Denbigh (which he sold 1799) and later of Bestwood, Notts., entered R.N. 1782, served in East and West Indies, Lieut. 1788, Cdr. 1822 (ret.), High Sheriff of Denbigh 1803 and of Lincs. 1808, *b.* 18 Dec. 1766, *educ.* R.N.C., *m.* 1stly, 20 July 1791, Charlotte (*d.* 19 Oct. 1797), dau. and heir of Rev. Robert Carter Thelwall, of Redbourne Hall, Lincs., and Bathafarn, Denbigh, by his wife Charlotte, dau. of Sir Henry Nelthorpe, 5th Bt (*see* BURKE'S *Extinct and Dormant Baronetcies*), and had issue,

1. William Robert, *bapt.* 11 May, *bur.* 13 May, 1794.

He *m.* 2ndly 4 March 1799, Maria Janetta (*d.* 17 Jan. 1822), only dau. and heir of John Nelthorpe, of Little Grimsby Hall, Lincs., High Sheriff of Lincs. 1775, by his wife Mary, 3rd dau. of Robert Cracroft, of Hackthorn (*see* BURKE'S *L.G.*, CRACROFT-AMCOTTS *of Hackthorn*), and by her had issue,

2. WILLIAM AUBREY DE VERE, *9th* Duke (*see page* 239).

3. John Nelthorpe, *b.* 9 Dec. 1805, *bur.* 4 Aug. 1810.

4. Frederick Charles Peter, of Little Grimsby Hall, Lincs. (to which he *s.* 1825), J.P. Lincs., Capt. R.N., Lord of the Manor and Patron of the Living of Little Grimsby, entered R.N. 1823, served on Africa Station, present at battle of Navarin 1827 in H.M.S. *Asia*, A/Capt. of H.M.S. *Zebra* 1832–3, Cdr. 1834, Capt. 1856, awarded Royal Humane Soc's Silver Medal 1842 for bravery in Ireland; *heir-pres.* to Dukedom 1824–40 and 1849–65; *b.* 28 June 1808, *educ.* R.N.C., *m.* 16 Feb. 1848, Jemima Eleanora (*d.* 14 Oct. 1877), 6th dau. of James Raymond Johnstone of Alva, Clackmannanshire (*see* JOHNSTONE, Bt.), and *d.* 17 Nov. 1865, leaving issue,

1. William Nelthorpe, of Little Grimsby Hall, Lincs., D.L., J.P. (Lindsey) Lincs. 1876, Lord of the Manor and Patron of the Living of Little Grimsby, Envoy Extraord. and Min. Plen. to the Republics of Peru, Ecuador and Bolivia from 1906, entered Foreign Office 1873, A/Charge d'Affaires at Berlin 1880–90, Secretary of the Legation and Charge d'Affaires 1890–96, Consul General of Hungary 1896–8, Min. Res. & Consul Gen. in Peru & Ecuador 1898 & Bolivia 1903, author of *Rural Italy* (1888), *heir-pres.* to Dukedom 1865–70; *b.* 7 April 1849, *educ.* Eton, Cheltenham, and Trin. Coll. Camb. (B.A. 1872, LL.M. 1875, LL.D. 1888), *m.* 1stly at Berne, Switzerland, 27 April 1878, Jane Isabella (*d.* 3 Jan. 1888), 2nd dau. of Rev. James Rathborne, Vicar of West Tytherley, Hants. (*see* BURKE's *L.G. of Ireland*, RATHBORNE *of Scripplestown*), and has issue,

(1) Aubrey Nelthorpe, of Little Grimsby Hall, Lincs. (which was sold 1918 following his death), Lord of the Manor and Patron of the Living of Little Grimsby, entered N. Staffs. (Prince of Wales's) Regt. 1899, Lieut 1900, Capt. 1906, Major 1916, served in S. African war 1899–1902 (Queens Medal & 3 clasps, Kings Medal & 2 clasps) and in India from 1911; *b.* 24 March 1879, *educ.* R.M.C. Sandhurst, *m.* 21 Feb. 1911, ●Vera Eileen May (*Kennards, Amberley, Arundel, Sussex*), (who *m.* 2ndly 29 April 1919 Capt. Gerald Andrew Greig, Royal Scots Fus. (*d.* 13 Feb. 1950), son of Robert Gillespie Greig, of Glasgow), only dau. of Capt. William Holcombe Francis, sometime of Woodhurst, Shorne, Kent, late Glos. (28th) Regt., and as *heir in line* to Dukedom, *d.* at Rawalpindi whilst serving in India, 22 April 1916, leaving issue,

1*a*. ●Daphne Diana de Vere, (*Kennards, Amberley, Arundel, Sussex*), *b*. at Rawalpindi, India, 26 Dec. 1911, *m*. 19 April 1933, Comte Claude Chauvin de Précourt, Légion d'Honneur, son of Comte Charles Leschevin de Précourt, and has issue, He *d*. in Paris, 5 Sept. 1971.

    1*b*. ●François Charles Christian, Comte, late Lieut. (Cav.) French Army, (*Le Courtil, Saint-Ideuc, Paramé, 35, France*), *b*. in Hong Kong 22 Feb. 1936, *educ.* École St Martin, France, *m*. in France 5 May 1962, ●Sabine, dau. of Comte Gérard de Vautibault, of 28 Rue de Bretagne, Laval, 54, France, and has issue,

        1*c*. ●Claude Henri Aubrey, *b*. in France 29 May 1963.

        2*c*. ●Rémy François Xavier, *b*. in France 6 March 1972.

        1*c*. ●Ghislaine, *b*. in France 16 Nov. 1967.

    2*b*. Philippe Étienne, Comte, Lieut. (Res. Inf.) French Army (*27 Rue Borgnis-Desbordes, Versailles, 78, France*), *b*. in Saigon, S. Vietnam, 19 Oct. 1938, *educ.* École des Roches, France, *m*. in France, 12 July 1961, ●Marie Noëlle, dau. of René Gasquet, Légion d'Honneur, of 19 Rue Perronet, Neuilly-sur-Seine, France, and has issue,

        1*c*. ●Aude Émile, *b*. in France 28 Jan. 1962.

        2*c*. ●Laure Sabine Pierrette, *b*. in France 23 Jan. 1963.

        3*c*. ●Clarisse Agnès, *b*. in France 20 Feb. 1966.

        4*c*. Marguerite, *b*. in France 21 May 1972

    3*b*. ●Jean Yves Xavier, Comte, late Sub-Lieut. French Navy, (*Le Bouscatel, Bouchet de la Lanze, Ponteils par Génolac 30, France*), *b*. in Tientsin, China, 31 May 1943, *educ.* École des Roches, France, *m*. Feb. 1970, ●Nathalie, dau. of Dr. Dubel of France, and has issue,

    ●Pénélope, *b*. in France, 30 May 1971.

    Jean Yves de Précourt also has an adopted stepson

    ●Blaise, *b*. in France 1964.

    1*b*. ●Anne Victoria (*Kennards, Amberley, Arundel, Sussex*), *b*. in Tientsin, China, 13 Dec. 1944.

2*a*. Hermione de Vere, author and journalist, *b*. Rawalpindi, India, 30 Nov. 1915, *m*. 1 Oct. 1939, James Dewar, M.B.E., G.M., F.C.A., late F/Lt. R.A.F.V.R. (*Flat 3, 6 Hyde Park Gardens, London, W2 2LT*), only son of late James Evan Dewar of Putney, (*see* BURKE'S *L.G.*, DEWAR *formerly of Craigniven and King's Park*), and *d.* 5 Nov. 1969 leaving issue,

1*b.* a son, *b.* and *d.* 25 Oct. 1940.

2*b.* ●Peter de Vere BEAUCLERK-DEWAR, F.S.A. Scot., Lieut. R.N.R., Freeman of the City of London and Liveryman of the Worshipful Co. of Haberdashers, Kt. of Sovereign Mil. Order of Malta, Registered Genealogist, recognised by Lord Lyon King of Arms in the additional surname and arms of BEAUCLERK, and matric. arms at L.O. 26 Oct. 1965 as representor of his maternal grandfather, contributor to *Burke's Peerage* and *Burke's L.G.* and joint author (with Dr. Donald Adamson) of *The House of Nell Gwyn* (*1974*), (*Whitethorn House, Milnathort, Kinross-shire, KY13 7XU, New* (*Edin.*) *Club*), *b.* 19 Feb. 1943, *educ.* Ampleforth, *m.* 4 Feb. 1967. ●Sarah Ann Sweet Verge, elder dau. of Major Lionel John Verge Rudder, late D.C.L.I., of The Old Dairy Barn, Bibury, Glos., formerly of N.S.W., Australia, and has issue.

1*c.* ●James William Aubrey de Vere, *b.* 30 Sept. 1970

1*c.* ●Alexandra Hermione Sarah, *b.* 1 Aug. 1972

2*c.* ●Emma Diana Peta, *b.* 6 Sept. 1973.

1*b.* ●Gillian de Vere, *b.* 20 March 1944, *educ.* Beechwood, Tunbridge Wells, *m.* 24 Sept. 1964, Peter John Lawrence Silley, M.I.Mar.E., (*Park House, Eynsford, Kent, and United Hunts Club and M.C.C.*), only son of late Bernard Lawrence Silley, of Matching Green, Essex, and Mrs. Claud Alexander (*see* HAGART-ALEXANDER, *of Ballochmyle* Bt.), and has issue,

1*c.* ●Natasha Margaret, *b.* 19 Nov. 1965.

2*c.* ●Tanya Anne, *b.* 11 July 1967.

(2) Nelthorpe de Vere, *b.* 1, *d.* 2 Jan. 1888.

(1) Isabella Eleanor, *b.* 28 Sept., *d.* 9 Oct. 1881.

(2) Violet Mary, served in World War I 1914–18 (Mons Star with Ypres Bar), author, awarded James Tait Black Memorial Prize for her work *The Book of Talbot* 1933, a Poor Clare Nun (Sister Mary Seraphim) from 1950–56; *b.* in Rome, 2 Nov. 1883, *m.* 1 Feb. 1907, John Talbot Clifton, J.P., of Lytham Hall, Lancs., and Kildalton Castle, Port Ellen, Islay, Hebrides, and *d.* 20 Nov. 1961, leaving issue (*see* BURKE'S *L.G.*). He *d.* 23 March 1928.

(3) ●Florence Frederica de Vere (*Flat 9, Hatherley House, Lansdown*

Road, *Cheltenham, Glos.; V.A.D. Ladies Club*), *b.* in Rome, 8 Oct.
1885, *m.* 14 Nov. 1912, Lt.-Col. Reginald Joseph Bentinck, 7th Bn.
Northants. Regt., formerly Capt. 30th Lancers, I.A., 2nd son of
Walter Theodore Edward, Baron Bentinck, and has issue (*see*
PORTLAND, D.). He *d.* 21 May 1937.

He *m.* 2ndly, at Peking, 5 Sept. 1892, Evelyn Amy (*d.* 10 June, 1933),
elder dau. of Sir Robert Hart, 1st Bt. G.C.M.G., LL.D., of Kilmoriarty,
co. Armagh, and Peking, China, Inspector-Gen. of Chinese Imperial
Maritime Customs & Posts and *d.* at Lima, Peru, 5 March 1908,
having by her had issue,

    (4) Vera Louise, *b.* in China, 21 Sept. 1893, *m.* 28 April 1926,
George Ramsay Ackland Mills of Grey Friars, Budleigh Salterton,
Devon, son of Rev. Barton Reginald Vaughan Mills, Assist. Chaplain of the Royal Chapel of the Savoy (*see* BURKE'S *L.G.*, MILLS
of Bisterne), and *d.s.p.* 5 Jan. 1942. He *d.* 1972

    (5) Hilda de Vere, *b.* in China, 21 Jan 1895, *m.* 21 June 1933, Miles
Malcolm Acheson, B.A., B.Ed., late Chinese Maritime Customs
Service (*Stark Road, RR1 Ganges, Salt Spring Island, British Columbia,
Canada*), son of late Guy Francis Hamilton Acheson, and *d.* 16 Sept.
1964, leaving issue, two daus.

2. Frederick Amelius, Lieut. 60th Rifles, ret. 1877; *b.* 8 Oct. 1851,
educ. Charterhouse, and Cheltenham, *m.* 12 Jan. 1881, Mary Harriett
Isabella Cumberland (who m. 2ndly, 30 April 1898, Major Robert
FitzRoy Maclean Johnstone, I.A. (*see* JOHNSTONE, Bt.), and *d.*
18 Nov. 1929), eldest dau. of Rear-Adm. John Bourmaster Dickson,
C.B., and sister of 1st and last Baron Islington, and *d.* in Paris, 22 May
1887, having had issue,

    Evelyn Eleanora, *b.* 15 Feb., *d.* 12 July 1883.

5. Henry, Lieut. 87th Regt. of Foot, Royal Fus., ret. 1838; *b.* 23 June,
1812, *d. unm.* 22 Jan 1856.

6. Charles, of Lower Winchfield House, Hants., Capt. 1st Foot and
Major, Northumberland Mil.; *b.* 10 Oct. 1813, *m.* 7 Sept. 1842, Laura
Maria Theresa (*d.* 29 Sept. 1858), dau. and heir of Col. Edward Stopford,
of Nottingham, sometime British Amb. to Spain, and *d.* from injuries
received while attempting to rescue a lifeboat crew off Scarborough,
2 Nov. 1861, leaving issue,

    1. William Arthur Stopford de Vere, of Richmond, Surrey, served in
Bengal Cav. I.A.; *b.* 3 Jan. 1844, *m.* 1stly, 3 July 1869, Mary Augusta

(*d.* 20 April 1870), only dau. of Adm. Sir George Augustus Westphal, and had issue,

(1) George Montague de Vere, of Smarden, Kent, Capt. 12th Bn. K.R.R.C., formerly Lieut., Gren. Guards; *b.* 4 April, 1870, *educ.* Eton, *m.* 26 Jan. 1905, May du Bois (*d.* 4 Aug. 1942), widow of Henry Vincent Holden, and dau. of Thomas A. Meinell, and *d.* 5 April 1931, leaving issue one dau.

He *m.* 2ndly, 4 Nov. 1874, Elizabeth Susan (*d.* 25 May 1934), yr. dau. of Edward James, of Swarland Park, Northumberland, and *d.* 11 Feb. 1917, having by her had issue,

(2) Charles Edward de Vere, Lieut. K.R.R.C., served with Uganda Rifles from 1898, A.D.C. to Lord Rosmead and Lord Milner; *b.* 10 Sept. 1875, *educ.* Clifton, and R.M.C. Sandhurst, *d. unm.* in Kampala, Uganda, 14 Jan. 1900.

(1) Sybil Evelyn de Vere, *b.* 10 Dec. 1876, *m.* 15 March 1902, William Murray Thomas, of Lerryn, Cornwall, yr. son of George Housman Thomas, and *d.s.p.* 26 Dec. 1902.

(2) Diana Lily de Vere, M.B.E. (1918), *b.* 27 Dec. 1878, *m.* 4 Jan. 1912, Christian Hugh Septimus James, of Rudchester, Northumberland, 7th son of Thomas James, J.P., D.L., of Otterburn Tower, and of Rudchester, Northumberland (*see* BURKE'S *L.G.*, 1937 *Edn.*), and *d.s.p.* 30 Jan. 1954.

2. Thomas Wentworth Sydney, of Irasberg, Vermont, U.S.A., civil engineer; *b.* 21 March 1847, *educ.* Military Inst. Lexington, Kentucky, and Troy, New York, *m.* 1stly 2 Jan. 1872, Mary Frances (*d.* 17 May 1873), dau. of Hon. Ira H. Allen, and had issue,

(1) May Frances, *b.* 10 May 1973, *m.* 1stly, William C. Stetson, of Newport, Vermont, and had issue, two sons (who adopted surname of Gaynor). She *m.* 2ndly, Dr. Eben Gaynor, of Brookline, Mass., and *d.* 1935 leaving further issue, one son. He *d.* 1918-9.

He *m.* 2ndly at Ithaca, New York, 1874-5, Elizabeth Porter Yates, of Utica, New York (*d.* 13 July 1911), and *d.* in Inasberg 29 Jan. 1938, having by her had issue,

(1) William Preston, sometime of Concord, New Hampshire, surgeon; *b.* in Troy N.Y., 9 June 1875, *m.* in Irasberg 2 July 1894, Jennie Mabel Hayward, (*d.* 11 Mar. 1959) and *d.* 18 March 1921, having had issue,

Sydney Wentworth, *b.* in Irasberg 10 Oct. 1895, *educ.* Concord

Public School, Syracuse Univ., & *OTC* Plattsburg Lieut. US Army, served in World War I with 12th Aero Sqdn. 4th Army Corps, and was *k.* in action at Meuse, Argonne, France, 29 Oct. 1918.
Barbara.

●Barbara, *b.* 4 Feb. 1913 *educ.* Syracuse Univ. *m.* at San Juan, Puerto Rico 29 May 1940. ●Joseph John Betz (*2505 N.E. 7th Place, Fort Lauderdale, Florida 53304, U.S.A.*), son of George Betz and has issue,

    1*a.* ●Robert George Capt. (ret.) U.S. Army, served in Vietnam 1967–8, now with Defense Intelligence Agency, (*1334 E. Capital St, Washington-D.C., U.S.A.*) *b.* at Fort Lauderdale 23 Sept. 1942 *educ.* Florida State Univ. (B.A. 1966) *m.* at Arlington, Virginia 14 April, 1973 ●Emilie Jeanne, dau. of Lt.Col. Francis Scellato (Ret.) of Falls Church, Virginia.

    1*a.* ●Sydney Wentworth *b.* San Juan, Puerto Rico 1 Aug. 1941 *educ.* Florida State Univ. *m.* at Fort Lauderdale 19 Mar. 1971 Wendell Barnhill (*Milton, Florida U.S.A.*) son of Charles Barnhill of Fort Lauderdale, Florida.

    2*a.* ●Doreen *b.* at Fort Lauderdale 23 Sept. 1948 *educ.* Auburn Univ. Alabama, (B.A. 1970) and Univ. of Tennessee (M.A. 1972).

(2) Harry Wentworth, *b.* 19 Oct. 1879, drowned 28 July 1887.

(2) Laura Maria Theresa, *b.* 1878, *m.* 8 Oct. 1907, Dr. Percy Charles Waller Templeton, of Irasberg, Vermont, U.S.A., and *d.* 1959, leaving issue, four daus.

3. Aubrey Topham, late of Aldeburgh, Suffolk, served in R.H.A.; *b.* in Brussels, 29 Oct. 1850, *m.* 17 Sept. 1913, Gwendolen Loftus (*d.* 2 May, 1958), 4th dau. of Capt. Sir Frederic Hughes, J.P., D.L., of Barnstown House, co. Wexford (*see* BURKE'S *L.G. of Ireland*), and *d.* 14 Jan. 1933, leaving issue,

CHARLES FREDERIC AUBREY DE VERE, *13th* and present Duke (*see page* 218).

4. Herbert Augustus Corbett, *b.* 3 Jan. 1852, *d. unm.* 30 Aug. 1904.

5. George Robert Algernon, *b.* in Brussels, 15 July 1854, *educ.* Haileybury, *m.* 1stly, 13 Nov. 1873, Sarah (*d.s.p.* 15 April 1903), dau. of William Turner, of High Wycombe, Bucks. He *m.* 2ndly, 23 March 1912, Antoinette Jeanne Alice (*d.* 1 March 1926), dau. of Arni Jaquerod, of Avenue de Champel, Geneva, and *d.s.p.* at La Rochette, Chateau d'Oex, Switzerland, 29 April 1927.

1. Florence Emily Rachel, *b.* 4 July 1845, *m.* 24 April 1867, Rev. John Hart-Davies, Vicar of St. Paul's, Covent Garden, formerly Rector of Southam, Warwicks., and *d.* 3 April 1922, leaving issue, five sons and two daus.

2. Laura Maria Theresa, *b.* 3 Jan. 1849, *m.* 10 Aug. 1867, Viscount Milton, M.P., eldest son of 6th Earl Fitzwilliam, K.G., D.C.L., and *d.* 20 March 1886, leaving issue. He *d.* 17 Jan. 1877.

3. Blanche Evelyn, *b.* 1 Oct. 1855, *m.* 29 July 1903, Rev. David Evans, Vicar of St. James's Croydon, Surrey, and *d.s.p.* 30 Nov. 1951. He *d.* 20 Jan. 1906.

4. Valunga, *b.* 21 March 1857, *d. unm.* 6 Dec. 1939.

7. Amelius Wentworth, of Leiston Hall, Suffolk, J.P. Suffolk, Capt. R.N., entered R.N. 1830, served on India and Lisbon Stations, Lieut. 1841, for services at capture of Amoy and storming of Shanghai (China Medal), Cmdr. 1846, Capt. 1864, ret. 1864; *b.* 16 Aug. 1815 *educ.* R.N.C., *m.* in Bombay, 27 July 1853, Frances Maria (who *m.* 2ndly, 2 Jan. 1884, Lt.-Gen. John Walpole D'Oyly, and *d.* 9 Nov. 1910), only dau. and heir of Charles Harrison, of Bryanston Square, London, and *d.* 24 March 1879, having had issue,

1. Charles William Wentworth de Vere, Capt. 15th Hus., formerly with 2nd West India Regt., author of *A Natural Army* (1907); *b.* 8 May 1854, *educ.* Eton, and Trin. Coll. Camb. (B.A. 1877, M.A. 1880), *m.* 17 Jan. 1908, Ida Stewart (*d.* 7 Feb. 1929), widow of Albert Edward Williamson Goldsmid, M.V.O., and eldest dau. of Frederick Hendricks, and *d.s.p.* 29 Dec. 1917.

2. Amelius Francis Ward, Barrister-at-law, Lincoln's Inn, 1885, *b.* 22 March 1857, *educ.* Eton, and Trin. Coll. Camb., *d. unm.* 1 Jan. 1935.

3. William Abdy, of Tower Court, Ascot, Berks., *b.* 29 April 1859, *m.* 20 Nov. 1902, Emily Standbridge (*d.* 3 June 1917), only dau. of Thomas King, and *d.s.p.* Dec. 1912.

1. Frances Maria Janetta, *b.* 8 Sept. 1855, *m.* 19 June 1879, Major George Paynter, of Gate House, Staffs., and Eaton Grange, Leics., 3rd son of William Paynter, M.A., J.P., D.L., of Camborne House, Richmond, Surrey and *d.* 6 May 1884, leaving issue (*see* BURKE'S *L.G.*). He *d.* 18 July 1907.

2. Amelia Frances Mary Eveleigh, *b.* 29 Dec. 1860, *d.* 15 Dec. 1868.

3. Maria Elizabeth Harriet Adèle, *b.* 10 July 1863, *d.* 31 Jan. 1865.

4. Lilchen Agnes Georgiana, *d.* an inf. 23 May 1867.

8. George Augustus, Major, 6th Dragoon Guards, formerly with 10th Hus., served in Crimean War (medal) and present at Battle of Tychernaya and Siege and fall of Sebastopol (medal and clasp); *b.* 14 Dec. 1818, *educ.* Charterhouse, *d. unm.* 3 Jan 1880.

1. Maria Amelia, *b.* May, 1800, *d. unm.* 9 July 1873.

2. Charlotte, *b.* 4 April, 1802, *d. unm.* 12 Aug. 1842.

3. Caroline Janetta, *b.* 28 June 1804, *m.* 14 July 1825, 6th Earl of Essex, and *d.* 22 Aug. 1862, leaving issue. He *d.* 11 Sept. 1892.

4. Louisa Georgiana, *b.* 28 Dec. 1806, *m.* 28 Dec. 1835, Thomas Hughan, of Airds, Galloway, and *d.* 18 Feb. 1853, leaving issue. He *d.* 24 March 1879.

5. Georgiana, *b.* Sept. 1809, *m.* 10 Feb. 1829, Sir Montague John Cholmeley, 2nd Bt., and *d.* 8 Jan. 1880, leaving issue. He *d.* 18 Jan. 1874.

6. Mary Noel, *b.* 28 Dec. 1810, *m.* 15 Dec. 1837, Thomas Corbett, of Elsham Hall, Lincs., and *d.* 29 Nov. 1850, leaving issue, one dau. (*see* ASTLEY, Bt.) He *d.* 5 July 1868.

His Grace *d.* 17 July 1825, and was *s.* by his eldest son,

WILLIAM AUBREY DE VERE, 9th DUKE OF ST ALBANS, of Redbourne, Lincs., Bestwood, Notts., and Holly Lodge, Highgate, bore the sceptre with the cross at the Coronation of KING WILLIAM IV 1830; Freeman of City of Lincoln 1828, *b.* 24 March 1801, *educ.* Christ's Coll. Camb. (Hon. LL.D. 1828), *m.* 1stly, 16 June 1827, Harriot, philanthropist and formerly a celebrated actress (*d.s.p.* 6 Aug. 1837), widow and heir of Thomas Coutts, the banker, and dau. of Matthew Mellon, Lieut. Madras Inf. He *m.* 2ndly, 29 May 1839, Elizabeth Catherine (who *m.* 2ndly, 10 Nov. 1859, 10th Viscount Falkland, and *d.* 2 Dec. 1893), yst. dau. of Major-Gen. Joseph Gubbins, of Stoneham, Hants., and Kilfrush, co. Limerick, (*see* BURKE's *L.G. of Ireland* 1912 *Edn.*) and by her had issue,

1. WILLIAM AMELIUS AUBREY DE VERE, *10th* Duke

1. Diana de Vere, bridesmaid to H.R.H. Princess Alexandra (later QUEEN ALEXANDRA) 1863, *b.* 10 Dec. 1842, *m.* 18 Dec. 1872, Hon. Sir John Walter Huddleston, Q.C., M.P., of The Grange, Ascot, Berks., last Baron of the Exchequer Div. of the Supreme Court of Judicature, yst. son of T. Huddleston, R.A., and *d.s.p.* 1 April 1905. He *d.* 5 Dec. 1890.

2. Charlotte.

His Grace *d.* 27 May 1849, and was *s.* by his only son,

WILLIAM AMELIUS AUBREY DE VERE, 10th DUKE OF ST ALBANS, P.C. (15 Feb. 1869), of Bestwood Lodge, Notts. (which he built 1862–65) and Redbourne, Lincs., Lord Lieut. and Custos Rotulorum of

Notts. from 1880 and D.L. (Lincs.) from 1860, J.P. (Notts. and co. Tipperary), offered but declined K.G. 1875, Capt. of the Yeomen of the Guard 1868–74, Provincial Grand Master of Freemasons, Lincs., 1862–78 and Notts. 1877–98, hon. Col. 1st Notts. (Robin Hood) Rifle Vol. 1868, had Vol. Officer's decoration 1892, County Councillor and Alderman Notts., Memb. Royal Yacht Sqdn. 1862 and Jockey Club 1863, developed Bestwood Colliery, friend of H.R.H. THE PRINCE OF WALES, *b.* 15 April 1840, *educ.* Eton, and Trin. Coll. Camb., *m.* 1stly, 20 June 1867, Sybil Mary (*d.* 7 Sept. 1871), eldest dau. of Lt.-Gen. Hon Charles Grey, Equerry and Priv. Sec. to QUEEN VICTORIA (*see* GREY, E.), and had issue,

1. CHARLES VICTOR ALBERT AUBREY DE VERE, *11th* Duke

1. Louise de Vere (for whom H.R.H. PRINCESS LOUISE stood sponsor), *b.* 12 April 1869, *m.* 25 Oct. 1890, 1st Baron Wakehurst, and *d.* 15 Dec. 1958, leaving issue. He *d.* 30 April 1936.

2. Sybil Evelyn de Vere, *b.* 21 Aug. 1871, *m.* 4 Nov. 1899, Major William Frank Lascelles, Scots Guards, elder son of Rt. Hon. Sir Frank Cavendish Lascelles, P.C., G.C.B., G.C.M.G., G.C.V.O., and *d.* 20 Sept. 1910, leaving issue (*see* HAREWOOD, E.). He *d.* 8 March 1913.

He *m.* 2ndly, 3 Jan. 1874, Grace, who was offered but declined to be Mistress of the Robes 1886, (*d.* 18 Nov. 1926), 2nd dau. and heir of Ralph Bernal-Osborne, M.P. by his wife Catherine Isabella Bernal-Osborne, of Newtown Anner, co. Tipperary (*see* OSBORNE, Bt.), and by her had issue,

2. OSBORNE DE VERE, *12th* Duke

3. William Huddleston de Vere, *b.* 16 Aug. 1883, *educ.* Eton, *d. unm.* 25 Dec. 1954.

3. Moyra de Vere, *b.* 20 Jan. 1876, *m.* 30 July 1895, Lord Richard Frederick Cavendish, P.C., C.B., C.M.G., J.P., D.L., of Holker Hall, Cark-in-Cartmel, Lancs., yr. son of Lt.-Col. Lord Edward Cavendish, D.L., M.P., and brother of 9th Duke of Devonshire, and *d.* 7 Feb. 1942, leaving issue. He *d.* 7 Jan. 1946.

4. Katherine de Vere, *b.* 25 May 1877, *m.* 1stly, 23 Jan. 1896 (*m.* diss. by div. 1920), Henry Charles Augustus Somers Somerset, O.B.E., J.P., D.L., of The Priory, Reigate, Surrey, son of Lord Henry Richard Charles Somerset, P.C., J.P., D.L., and had issue (*see* BEAUFORT, D.). He *d.* 25 Nov. 1945. She *m.* 2ndly, 22 April 1921, Major-Gen. Hon. Sir William Lambton, K.C.B., C.M.G., C.V.O., D.S.O., Groom-in-Waiting to KING GEORGE V, 6th son of 2nd Earl of Durham, and *d* 1 Feb. 1958. He *d.s.p.* 11 Oct. 1936.

5. Alexandra de Vere, *b.* 5 July 1878, *d. unm.* 16 April 1935.

His Grace *d.* 10 May 1898, and was *s.* by his eldest son,

CHARLES VICTOR ALBERT AUBREY DE VERE, 11th DUKE OF ST ALBANS, of Bestwood Lodge, Notts., and Redbourne, Lincs. (which he sold 1917), 2nd Lieut. 1st Life Guards 1893, Capt. S. Notts. Yeo. 1898–1900, Lieut. 3rd Bn. The Royal Scots (Lothian) Regt.; *b.* 26 March 1870 (for whom QUEEN VICTORIA and H.R.H. The PRINCE OF WALES (later KING EDWARD VII) were sponsors), *educ.* Eton, *d. unm.* 19 Sept. 1934, and was *s.* by his half-brother,

OSBORNE DE VERE, 12th DUKE OF ST ALBANS, of Newtown Anner, co. Tipperary and Bestwood Lodge, Notts. (which he sold 1940), D.L., co Waterford, High Sheriff 1920, Capt. 17th Lancers 1901–2, served in S. African War 1899–1902 (medal and 6 clasps), Major S. Notts. Yeo. 1904, served in World War I 1914–19 (despatches), A.D.C. to Field Marshal Sir Douglas Haig (later 1st Earl Haig) and in World War II 1939–45 in Home Guard; *b.* 16 Oct. 1874, *educ.* Eton, *m.* 19 Aug. 1918, Lady Beatrix Frances, D.B.E. (1919), D.G.St.J. (*d.* 5 Aug. 1953), widow of 6th Marquess of Waterford, K.P., and 2nd dau. of 5th Marquess of Lansdowne, K.G., and *d.s.p.* 2 March 1964, when he was *s.* by his second cousin (*see page* 218).

NOTES

Descendants of Some Natural
Children of the Beauclerks

NOTE I

Mr. Aubrey William Beauclerk, of Ardglass Castle (*see page* 224) also had the following natural children (who bore the surname of BEAUCLERK):—

Charles (Rev.), sometime a Capt. in the Army, deacon 1860, priest 1861, Curate of Saintfield, co. Down, 1860, Perpetual Curate of Dunsverick, co. Antrim, 1861–66, and of Glencraig, co. Down, 1866–69, Vicar of St. Mary's, Belfast, 1869–75, Chaplain of Holy Trinity Church, Boulogne, from 1875; *b. ca.* 1823/4, *m.* 8 Nov. 1860, Elizabeth Maria (*d.* in Guernsey, 30 April, 1888), 4th dau. of Rev. Henry Murphy, Treasurer of Dromore, and *d.* at Boulogne, 27 Jan. 1880, having had, with other issue (five of whom *d.* in infancy),

1. Henry Wyndham, of Montreal, Canada, emigrated to Canada 1906, with Canadian Pacific Railway Co., Dir. Bank of Montreal, and Brompton Pulp and Paper Co. Ltd.; *b.* in Ireland, 14 Dec. 1869, *educ.* Merchant Taylors', *m.* 3 June 1911, Hon. Alice Josephine (*d.* 1963), eldest dau. of 1st Baron Shaughnessy, K.C.V.O., and *d.* Jan. 1937, leaving issue,

●Thomas.

●Audrey.

2. Ernest Octavius, an artist, emigrated to U.S.A., served in S. African War; *b.* 22 Feb. 1871, *educ.* Clergy Orphans' Sch. Canterbury and *d.* in S. Africa.

3. Aubrey, emigrated to U.S.A., *m.* and *d.* leaving issue, one son and one dau.

4. Herbert Charles, emigrated to S. Africa, served in Merchant Navy; *b.* 7 Sept. 1875; *educ.* Clergy Orphans' Sch. Canterbury, *m.* and *d.* leaving issue,

●Wyndham, sometime of Natal, S. Africa (1952).

1. Amy Louisa, *b.* 21 Oct. 1861, *m.* 1stly, in S. Africa, . . . Butt;

and 2ndly, Dr. Edward Bromet, of Denewood Grange, Batheaston, Bath, Somerset, and *d.s.p.* 1940.

2. Frances Maude, *b.* 30 April, 1863, *m.* Lt.-Col. William Henry Oliphant Kemmis, J.P., D.L., of Ballinacor, and Somerleaze, Selwood, Somerset, High Sheriff of co. Wicklow 1904, son of Col. William Kemmis, J.P., D.L., of Clopoke, and *d.* Feb. 1941, leaving issue (*see* BURKE'S *L.G.*,) He *d.* 18 Dec. 1939.

3. Florence Elizabeth, *b.* 1866, *m.* 1891, Richard Garrett, of Leiston, Suffolk, and *d.* 1954, leaving issue, one son and one dau.

Charlotte Jane (by Charlotte Bury), *b.* 1830, *d. unm.* Jan. 1855.

NOTE II

The 3rd Duke of St Albans (*see page* 229) had six natural children (who bore the surname of BEAUCLERK):—

1. A son, *b.* 1748, *d.* in Brussels 30 Jan. 1758.

2. George, *b.* in Paris, 20 Dec. 1755, and was *bur.* in Brussels 11 Oct. 1756.

3. A son, *b.* in Brussels Sept. 1757 and *d.* in Brussels Feb. 1758.

1. Anne-Amélie, *b.* in Brussels 5 Dec. 1756, *m.* Simon Fromont of Rue Neuve, Brussels and *d.* 3 Nov. 1826. He *d.* 20 Oct. 1823.

2. (Mariette-Victoire-) Rose, *b.* in Brussels 1 Dec. 1758, *m.* (after 1785) Huberti Offhuys, advocate of Brussels, and *d.* leaving issue,

     Anne-Amélie, *b.* in Brussels 1 Aug. 1787.

3. Marie-Agnès, *b.* in Brussels 1 Dec. 1758 (twin).

NOTE III

Adm. Lord Amelius Beauclerk (*see page* 230) had a natural son (who bore the surname of BEAUCLERK):—

Charles (Frederick Augustus de Vere) of Southampton, *b.* at Plymouth 1836, *m.* 19 March 1859, Sarah Caroline, dau. of James Paul, of Portsea, Hants., and *d.* 11 April 1882, leaving issue.

1. Amelius Aubrey de Vere, of Liverpool, Sec. and Manager of Manchester Dog Show Soc. 1896, Manager of Kennel Club Show; *b.* 1861, *educ.* Liverpool Coll., *m.* 8 March 1892, Sarah Elizabeth (*d.* 6 Sept. 1938), dau. of Thomas Newton of Liverpool, and *d.* 18 March 1910, leaving issue,

     (1) •Amelius Aubrey de Vere, J.P., served in World War I in R.N.V.R. 1914–15 and R.F.C. 1915–19, Mayor of Oswestry 1959–60

(*1 West Place, Morda Road, Oswestry, Salop*); *b.* 20 Sept. 1894, *educ.* Liverpool Coll., *m.* 26 Dec. 1923, ●Phoebe, dau. of Joseph Davies and has issue,

    ●Amelius Aubrey de Vere, J.P., served in World War II as F/O., R.A.F.V.R. (*Grenston, Croeswylan Lane, Oswestry, Salop*); *b.* 3 March 1924, *m.* 6 June 1946, ●Sydney Frances, dau. of D. C. F. Thomas of Pennymaes, Llansaintfrid, Montgomeryshire, and has issue,

        ●Alan Aubrey de Vere, *b.* 6 Feb. 1954.

        ●Eleanor Frances de Vere, *b.* 20 Feb. 1950.

    ●Marjorie Elizabeth de Vere, *b.* 5 March 1926, *m.* in Johannesburg 20 June 1964, Ellis John Zinn of Numten Lodge Roosvelt Park, Johannesburg, S. Africa. He *d.* Aug. 1966.

(2) Charles Ernest de Vere, Whittington, Salop, *b.* 12 March 1899, *m.* 3 Dec. 1923, ●Jennie Gertrude Howell (*8 Church Street, Whittington, Salop*) and died 1971 leaving issue,

    ●Jean de Vere, *b.* 24 Nov. 1924, *m.* Alec John Haywood (*Castle Stores, Whittington, Salop*), and has issue,

        ●Valerie Frances.

2. Aubrey Wentworth, sometime of Singapore, *b.* 1861, *d. unm.* 1915.
3. Frederick Wentworth, American Consular Agent at Surabaya, Dutch East Indies, assumed Dutch nationality 1896; *b.* 30 Jan. 1864, *m.* 1stly, Jane Ottolina Potter (*d.s.p.*). He *m.* 2ndly, 14 May 1903, Jacoba Jeanette Charlotta (*d.* 20 July 1961), dau. of Jan Willem Le Comte, of Surabaya, and *d.* 24 Dec. 1908 (*bur.* in Genoa), having by her had issue,

    (1) ●Charles Frederick, Colonial Admin. Service, Dist. Commr. in Tanganyika 1929–56, now Snr. Mathematics Master at Hove Coll., reverted to British Nationality 1928 (*233 Holmes Avenue, Hove, Sussex*); *b.* 23 Sept. 1904, *educ.* Brighton Coll., and Wadham Coll. Oxford (M.A.), *m.* 15 May 1930, Dorothy Charlton (*d.* 7 July 1967), dau. of John Lupton Lister, of Brighton, and has issue,

        ●Diana Charlton, *b.* 30 March, 1931, *m.* 29 Sept. 1956, John Nicholas Lewis (*Kennels Cottage, Dollarbeg, Clackmannanshire*), son of Frederick Ernest Lewis, of Bournemouth, and has issue, one son and one dau.

    (2) ●Aubrey Wentworth (*13 Melrose Road, Wimbledon, S.W.19*), *b.* 4 Sept. 1908, *educ.* Hurstpierpoint, *m.* 27 Oct. 1938 ●Joyce Muriel, dau. of Horace Langdon, of London, and has issue,

1*a*. ●Nicholas Wentworth (*4 Cairngorm Place, Farnborough, Hants*), *b*. 21 Feb. 1945, *educ*. Hurstpierpoint, *m*. 11 Sept. 1971 ●Lynda Jean, dau. of John Kirby of London.

2*a*. ●Charles Aubrey (*13 Melrose Road, Wimbledon S.W.19*), *b*. 17 Mar. 1948, *educ*. Hurstpierpoint.

1. Sarah Toft Mallory, *b*. 26 Jan. 1860
2. Blanche de Vere, *b*. 1863, *m*. Arthur George Manifold of Liverpool and *d*. 29 Nov. 1952, leaving issue, one son and three daus. He died 1908.
3. Diana de Vere, *b*. 24 Dec. 1867, *d*. June 1968.

INDEX